Additional Praise
If the Oceans Were Ink

"Power's new book takes readers on a journey through the lyrical and complex ocean of the Quran, the only book in the world put to memory by millions of people. She opens a door to the power of its prose to inspire, comfort, and ignite hearts everywhere. A must-read for anyone wishing to understand a global community's central spiritual source."

—Dalia Mogahed, director of research,
the Institute for Social Policy and Understanding,
and coauthor of *Who Speaks for Islam?*

"There are many intriguing books that trace the encounter of Westerners with Muslims from traditional backgrounds. Some of these books are love stories, others are clashes. Carla Power's *If the Oceans Were Ink* is something more radical, magical, and much more relevant: a religious encounter mediated through a gentle friendship, one that is committed to a dialogue and a search for truth. In a world characterized by so much tension and polemic, Power offers what might be our best hope for a better tomorrow: an intelligent friendship. Most enthusiastically recommended."

—Omid Safi, director, Duke Islamic Studies Center

"A former foreign correspondent for *Newsweek* raised partly in the Middle East and boasting a graduate degree in Middle Eastern studies from Oxford, Power spent a year reading the Quran with a longtime friend, Sheikh Mohammad Akram Nadwi. Their experience led them beyond stereotypes to a constructive understanding for the text's call for peace and equality. Great for book clubs." —*Library Journal*

"Lively . . . Intelligent and exceptionally informative." —*Kirkus Reviews*

✦ IF THE OCEANS WERE INK ✦

IF THE OCEANS WERE INK

An Unlikely Friendship and a Journey

to the Heart of the Quran

✦ · · · · ✦

CARLA POWER

A HOLT PAPERBACK   HENRY HOLT AND COMPANY   NEW YORK

Holt Paperbacks
Henry Holt and Company, LLC
Publishers since 1866
175 Fifth Avenue
New York, New York 10010
www.henryholt.com

A Holt Paperback® and ⓗ® are registered trademarks of
Henry Holt and Company, LLC.

Excerpt from Muhammad Iqbal's poem "On My Mother's Death"
by permission of Iqbal Academy Pakistan

Library of Congress Cataloging-in-Publication Data

Power, Carla, author.
    If the oceans were ink : an unlikely friendship and a journey to the heart of
the Qur'an / Carla Power. — 1st ed. 2015.
        pages cm
    Includes bibliographical references and index.
    ISBN 978-0-8050-9819-8 (paperback) — ISBN 978-0-8050-9824-2 (electronic
book)   1. Power, Carla.   2. Muslim converts—Biography.   3. Islam—
Appreciation.   4. Islam—Essence, genius, nature.   5. Islamophobia—Europe.
6. Islam—Public opinion.   I. Title.
    BP80.P69.P695 2015
    297.092—dc23
    [B]   2014017543

Henry Holt books are available for special promotions and
premiums. For details contact: Director, Special Markets.

First Edition 2015

Designed by Kelly S. Too

Printed in the United States of America
3   5   7   9   10   8   6   4

For Richard and Helen Power, who first showed me the world,
and for Antony, Julia, and Nic, who still do, every day.

CONTENTS

✦ IF THE OCEANS WERE INK ✦

A Map for the Journey

When I was eleven years old, I bought a tiny book containing a verse from the Quran from a stall outside a Cairo mosque. The amulet was designed to be tucked into a pocket to comfort its owner throughout the day. I was neither Muslim nor literate in Arabic; I bought it not for the words inside but for its dainty proportions. The stall's proprietress watched me bemusedly as I cooed over the matchbox-sized book. My family and I were living in Egypt at the time, and back at home I taped a bit of paper over the cover and crayoned a woman in a long blue dress, writing on top, "Jane Eyre by C. Bronte." I then placed the book in the waxy hand of my doll, which sat stiffly on a high shelf in my Cairo bedroom.

The little book outlasted the doll: I found it over a quarter century later, one sticky summer afternoon in St. Louis, wrapped in a jewelry box in my parents' house. It was a minor miracle that such a flimsy item from a market stall had endured so long. It was a major miracle that I'd found it at all, in a three-story house so crammed with exotic souvenirs that friends called it Aladdin's Cave. But somehow I did find that booklet, amid the spoils of my father's avid collecting from the Middle East and Asia: mosque lamps from Cairo, stacks of Indian brocades and embroideries, Bokhara samovars, lapis lazuli boxes, mounds of tribal jewelry, and hundreds of carpets.

Amid all this, my Quran chapter survived. By the time I found it, I knew enough to be embarrassed for having wrapped someone else's scripture in my own childish concerns. The summer I rediscovered it, during that bleak time after 9/11, shrill voices proclaimed a "clash of civilizations" between the Islamic world and the West. With suicide bombings in Kabul and Baghdad and the horrors of Abu Ghraib still fresh in my mind, my juvenile game seemed insensitive.

By then, not only had I inherited my father's immersive interest in the Islamic world, but my childhood fascination had been seasoned by studying and reporting on Muslim societies. Over the years, I'd also acquired several more Qurans. As an undergraduate, I bought a $5.99 paperback for a survey course on Islam. It sat on my bookshelf, its pages cheap and grainy, its spine barely cracked. In my twenties, when I was working at an Islamic think tank in Oxford, I received a Quran for free, courtesy of the Saudi Arabian government. Bound in blue leatherette, stamped in gilt with calligraphic script, it was one of millions of copies distributed across the globe in the 1990s as part of an official Saudi campaign. A third Quran was parrot green, with pink flowers on its cover. Inside: a pressed rose, withered jasmine blossoms, and two ticket stubs from the Cairo opera house—relics from a romantic summer studying in Egypt. On my bookshelf alone, there were three translations of the Quran, with as many symbolic meanings: one copy a textbook, another an instrument of state-sponsored propaganda, the third a repository of personal memories.

But my Qurans only hint at the book's symbolic possibilities. Since Muslims consider it the word of God, a Quran not only offers comfort and inspiration as a text, but commands reverence as an object. This power has also led to the text's politicization. Waved before a crowd, it can inspire revolutions and wars. Burned or besmirched, it triggers diplomatic incidents and deaths. Quoted or misquoted, it's been used to justify mercy, and mass murder. In an age when migration and technology have spread its message far beyond its traditional homelands, the Quran has impressive influence in Europe and America. At times, it has been the target of displays of intolerance. Dutch politicians have tried to ban it. A Florida preacher burned it, streaming the destruction over the Internet. News that American soldiers in Afghanistan had burned several copies of the Quran sparked protests and killings. And when the University of North Carolina put excerpts from it on a summer reading syllabus, right-wing groups launched lawsuits, claiming reading the Quran would interfere with students' religious freedom.

The Quran began as a series of revelations to Muhammad, a caravan trader, in the seventh century. In two decades, these words grew into a spiritual, social, and political force in the Arabian Peninsula. Today, the Quran's impact is global. Over fourteen hundred years after the Prophet Muhammad heard the first revelation, the text continues to transform geopolitics as well as personal worldviews. As the scripture of the planet's fastest-growing religion—with 1.6 billion followers, Islam is second in global popularity only to Christianity—it stands as a moral compass for hundreds of millions. Studied alongside the words and deeds of Muhammad, the Quran has been a bedrock for constitutions, leadership styles, and laws. Its words have lent legitimacy to regimes—and to resistance to them. Reading it should be a prerequisite for understanding humanity.

And yet, as I'd later discover, surprisingly few people do. Like any rich and complex text, the Quran is invoked more often than read, and read more often than its meanings are agreed upon. Hostile and casual readers have accused the Quran of being chaotic. Even pious Muslims concede that while its majesty and lyricism overwhelm, some verses confuse as much as clarify. In fact, many students of the Quran don't understand the classical Arabic they stumble through, and even top madrasas frequently overlook the book in favor of classical works on Islamic law or philosophy, texts that came into being centuries after the Quran's revelation. Many—good Muslims and curious non-Muslims alike—simply never attempt it. Even the Quran proclaims its own limitless possibilities:

Say, even if the ocean were ink
For (writing) the words of my Lord,
The ocean would be exhausted

Before the words of my Lord were exhausted,
Even if We were to add another ocean to it. (Chapter 18: Verse 109)

Revered by a population as diverse as the *umma*, or worldwide Muslim community, the Quran can refract in dazzling ways. The San Francisco civil rights lawyer may discover freedoms in the same sura, or chapter, in which a twelfth-century Cairo cleric saw strictures. A Sudanese mullah, or religious teacher, may read a command for wifely obedience; an Indonesian wife may interpret the same passage as a call for equality and compassion. The Marxist and the Wall Street banker, the despot and the democrat, the terrorist and the pluralist—each can point to a passage in support of his cause.

Sheikh Mohammad Akram Nadwi, the Islamic scholar who taught me the Quran, once told me an old Indian joke. A Hindu goes to his Muslim neighbor and asks if he could borrow a copy of the Quran. "Of course," said the Muslim. "We've got plenty! Let me go get you one from my library." A week later, the Hindu returns. "Thanks so much," he said. "Fascinating. But I wonder, could you give me a copy of the other Quran?"

"Um, you're holding it there," said the Muslim. "There's just one Quran, and you've got it."

"Yeah, I read it," replied the Hindu. "But I need a copy of the Quran that's followed by Muslims."

"The joke is right," said Akram. "All this talk about jihad and forming Islamic states, that's not what the Quran says!"

We were sipping tea in an office in Oxford, a couple of years after 9/11. I was a correspondent at *Newsweek* magazine then, and had dropped by to see him at the think tank where I first met him in the nineties and where he was still working, the Oxford Centre for Islamic Studies. We'd been talking that day, as so many millions of pairs of friends had been, of angry young men with pilot's licenses, of grizzled criminals hiding in caves, of daisy cutters and blood begetting more blood.

Crowded with desks, strewn with papers, the room where we sat resembled the headquarters of some ramshackle militia. The walls were hung with maps of South Asia, crisscrossed with arrows and studded with little red X's, from north of the Khyber Pass to down south below Bombay. On the bookshelf, spines glittered with gold-embossed lettering in Arabic and Urdu. Rows of binders labeled in English, Urdu, or Persian filled shelf after shelf.

I recognized my own handwriting on some of those binders. A decade before, I'd worked with Akram to help fill them. We'd researched together on a team of scholars—some Muslim, some Western, all male except for me—mapping the spread of Islam through South Asia. To distinguish him from all the other Mohammads who worked at the Oxford Centre for Islamic Studies, my colleagues and I called him "the Maulana" or "the Sheikh," traditional honorifics for an Islamic scholar.

And what a scholar he was. Just twenty-seven years old when we first met, he was already a rising star in the global network of traditional ulama, or Muslim religious authorities. Though he was raised in an Urdu-speaking village in the Indian state of Uttar Pradesh, the Arabic he learned at a small-town madrasa was so good that he'd begun writing grammars of the language as a teenager. He went on to the prestigious Nadwat al-Ulama, a madrasa in Lucknow, India, where he later stayed to teach and write. His earliest specialty was hadith, or the words and deeds of the Prophet Muhammad, which form the basis of Islamic laws as well as guidelines for the daily life of devout Muslims. At Oxford, he would begin the work that would gain him fame far beyond madrasa circles: a forty-volume collection of biographies of thousands of Muslim women scholars, a work that would reilluminate Islam's lost history of women as religious authorities.

That day at Oxford, the mood was bleak. More than a decade after we'd been colleagues, we were both grayer. Since 9/11, we'd watched relations between Muslims and non-Muslims fray in ways destined to remain unrepaired during our lifetimes. All the sweet optimism of our days spent researching India's Muslim scholars and mystics seemed quaint. When the Twin Towers fell, the world had cleaved in two, we were told. "You're either with us," intoned my president, George W. Bush, "or against us." In a single sentence, President Bush had dismissed the Sheikh, me, and scores of millions more. His worldview had no space for nuance or equivocation. It didn't recognize Americans who questioned the invasion of Iraq, or Muslims who deplored both the jihadis and the policies of the U.S. government.

Most of the media echoed President Bush's black-and-white vision, pounding out a steady drumbeat of declarations about two cultures, airtight and separate: "the West" and "the Islamic world." When the twain met, they assured us, trouble followed. It had been this way since the days of the Crusades and it would continue in this way until those Muslims got modernity like the rest of us. But "Islamic world" was always a flabby term. It grows increasingly useless in an era in which migration and conversion mean that Muslims now live everywhere, from Peking to Sydney to Patagonia. Equally meaningless: the statement "Muslims believe." Those pronouncements about a group that encompasses 1.6 billion people fall dramatically short in describing an *umma* that embraces people as diverse as Pathan tribals and Kansan surgeons.

But fear favors the crude stereotype, and those were fearful times. When I worked at *Newsweek*, a respected writer emailed a memo disparaging Muslim culture in terms so sweeping and vulgar that all I could think of—as I stared at his words with hot, red eyes—was anti-Semitic rhetoric out of 1930s Germany. The Sheikh heard parallel rants from his fellow Muslims. "When people say things against Americans or Jews, I tell them I've worked with both kinds of people, and that not all of them are like the ones we read about," he said.

In such a climate, our friendship felt freakish. It had always been an oddity: I'm a secular feminist, Jewish on my mother's side and Quaker on my father's; Akram is a conservative *alim*, or Muslim scholar. When we'd met, I'd been a miniskirted twenty-four-year-old, unsure of anything except her own importance. For the two years we worked together, we had found common ground in the commonplace, sipping tea, grumbling gently about our boss and sodden English winters. He was soft-spoken and gracious, quoting liberally from his beloved Persian poets, sharing homemade *biryanis*. Growing up, my family lived in a range of places in South Asia and the Middle East. In Akram, I recognized the effort it took to create familiarity in an unfamiliar place. In time, we would grow from friendly colleagues into friends.

When I visited him that day in Oxford, we sat, two bookish types, bewildered at the blood and vitriol of the battles being fought in his name and mine. Every Islam-related bit of news seemed to be bad. Every Muslim depicted in Western papers seemed to be extreme. "Nobody wants to interview Muslims like you, Sheikh," I sighed. "Pick up a Kalashnikov! Start calling for sharia law! Then you'll get some airplay!"

The conversation petered out, and our cups of tea grew tepid. The pale lemon sun had faded, giving the room an antique feeling. For some reason—perhaps the Oxford dusk, perhaps my sense of being swept aside by the zeitgeist—I suddenly remembered a World War I recruiting poster I'd once seen. A chiseled man in a three-piece suit and one of those T. S. Eliot hairdos, slicked and center-parted, was shown at home in a cushy armchair, looking glum. His blond daughter was on his knee, and his son marched toy soldiers across the floor. The caption read: "Daddy, what did YOU do in the Great War?"

Designed to spur an earlier generation of Britons onto the battlefield, the poster had precisely the opposite effect on me. It rallied me, sure. It made me worry about how my kids would look back and ask me what I'd done during these dark times, during this so-called War on Terror. It made me want to run out there, armed only with my keyboard, and attack prevailing stereotypes. I was ready to lead a charge into transcivilizational dialogue. The blithe generalizations about "the Islamic world" and "the West" were fictions, lazy catchalls employed by headline writers and zealots.

"What did *you* do in the war, Daddy?" the Sheikh repeated slowly. "That's very good, really. It is incumbent on us to work hard, in these times, to make people understand one another."

. . .

When I think back on that day in Oxford, I note that he didn't say that it was time "to take a stand." Such sentiments were for hardliners. The Sheikh's life smudged the thick black lines that Muslim extremists and American neocons wanted drawn between "the Islamic world" and "the West." Since his education had followed the classical Islamic syllabus, he'd been schooled in those great building blocks of Western civilization, Greek philosophy and ethics. Shuttling between mosque and think tank, Akram led a life in England that proved that the West and Islam weren't separate, but braided together. Unlike many Muslim religious scholars, he educated his daughters in British secular schools. What were his Oxford-born daughters if not "Western"? And also "Muslim"? And what of the Sheikh himself, who taught students at Britain's oldest university, Oxford, and also gave lessons at mosques and madrasas?

His own six daughters will never have to ask him what he did during the messy decade after 9/11. Between teaching and work at the Centre, he produced research that chipped away at the belief that Islam had never allowed women freedoms. Over those years, he uncovered a long-forgotten history of female Islamic scholarship, blotted out by centuries of cultural conservatism: a tradition of women religious authorities stretching back to the days of the Prophet. When he started, he figured that biographies of women religious scholars would make a slim volume, representing thirty or forty women. Ten years on, the work stands at forty volumes. He'd discovered nearly nine thousand women, including ones who lectured, dispensed fatwas, and traveled on horse- and camelback in pursuit of religious education. The Sheikh's work on women scholars challenges bigots of all types. The Taliban gunman who shoots a girl for going to school. The mullah who bars women from his mosque. The firebrand who claims that feminism is a Western ideology undermining the Islamic way of life. The Westerner who claims that Islam oppresses women, and always has.

Such voices rise loudest, soaring above softer ones like Akram's. Extreme messages carry furthest, without the weight of equivocation. Men spitting out sound bites denouncing the West make for arresting headlines. Conflict and cultural outliers are two great turbines of the news business, but they're particularly central to the Western media's coverage of the Islamic world. In part, this stems from the very real wars in the post-9/11 era. Yet the news stories of conflict are rarely balanced by feature stories in other sections of the media. Scanning American magazines over the years, I can't remember ever seeing a major fashion magazine cover featuring a woman wearing a hijab, or travel magazine coverage of the best hotels in Mecca for the hajj, the Muslim pilgrimage.

If Muslims rarely make it into the papers as three-dimensional human beings, there is also scant appetite in the mainstream Western media for what their scripture actually says. Never, in my seventeen years of writing magazine stories on the Islamic world, had an editor asked me to write about, or even cite, the Quran, and how Muslims understand it.

This gap was particularly glaring in my case, as someone who had been exposed to Muslim cultures nearly all my life. I had lived in Tehran, Kabul, Delhi, and Cairo growing up, and I had studied Islamic societies in college and graduate school. And yet what most interested my professors and editors was not faith, but the politics that grew from it. I had churned out papers on the split between Islam's Sunnis and Shias, on Egyptian Islamists, on Moroccan marabouts, but never on the central text that united them all: the Quran. Writing for *Newsweek* and, later, *Time* magazine, I wrote on mosque design and yuppie Muslims, headscarves and punk bands, Islamic hedge funds and halal energy drinks. I also wrote stories on violent leaders who made the news: jihadis, bin Laden, the Taliban, Pakistani extremists. I wrote on their political views, but never, really, on the piety they claimed inspired them all. And I certainly never reported on the Quran.

To be fair, Islam is so all-encompassing that one can easily swerve from its spiritual aspects. Its foundations, the famous five pillars, are mostly centered on actions rather than beliefs: reciting the *shahada*, the statement that "There is no god but God, and Muhammad is His Prophet"; performing the five daily prayers; giving to charity; fasting during the holy month of Ramadan; and going on hajj. With guidelines on everything from dressing to eating to trading, Islam is woven through the world itself rather than confined to church on Sundays.

Still, it's telling that the few times I did turn my attention to the Quran, I merely dipped into it. I studied a few suras for an undergraduate seminar. I read the verses scholars cite on topical issues, like women's dress codes and wife beating. I shivered at the muscular beauty of its poetry. At times, I wondered about what a deeper appreciation could bring to one's existence. Reading *Madrasah Life*, Akram's first-person account of a day at his seminary in Lucknow, I was struck by his description of his early-morning ritual—a dawn recitation from the Quran, before he attended congregational prayers at the mosque. A favorite chapter was "al-Zumar," or "The Crowds," which had a verse on God's forgiveness that would inevitably make him cry:

> Say: O My slaves who have transgressed against their own souls
> Do not despair of God's mercy. Surely God forgives all sins.
> Surely He is Oft-Forgiving, Most Merciful.

"On reciting it," Akram wrote, "I experience such joy that I keep reciting it over and over again."

As a nonbeliever, I knew I couldn't replicate Akram's ecstasy. As an English speaker without classical Arabic, I knew I'd lose the poetry of the original words. But a bit like the nun who, while drifting off to sleep, allows herself a few seconds of wondering about sex, I found that Akram's description suggested the limitations of my own cozy secularism. It rankled that I could be missing one of the most powerful experiences on offer. I'd read of Muslims who believed the Quran could stop earthquakes. The mother of a friend recited it to keep calm while being robbed at gunpoint in her own home. In mosques in Lahore and Cairo, I'd watched grown men weep at the sound of its words.

To date, my appreciation of Muslim civilizations had merely involved observation, as when admiring the medallions on a Turkoman carpet or the sweep of calligraphy around a Mughal arch. It was polite and restrained. Weary of being a well-behaved visitor in the realm of the believers, I wanted to try a year of immersing myself in Akram's worldview, and the most obvious way to do that was to read the Quran with him. As a journalist, I'd spent years framing Muslims as people who did things—built revolutions, founded political parties, fought, migrated, lobbied. I craved a better understanding of the faith driving these actions. I'd reported on how Muslim identity shapes a woman's dress or a man's career path, a village economy or a city skyline. Now I wanted to explore the beliefs behind that identity and to see how closely they matched my own.

To go beyond writing about Muslims as headlines, I knew I needed to engage in an extended conversation, exploring the issues that made the news but stretching far beyond them into how the Quran shaped a Muslim's worldview. I wanted to go to the book at the source of the faith and to begin to understand how it guided one learned believer's life. I hoped to understand the Quran's impact not just on culture and politics, but on an individual as well.

Several years after our Great War conversation, I approached the Sheikh and proposed a project that would eventually became this book. I wanted to immerse myself in his teachings, attending his lectures on the Quran and other Islamic issues and having occasional one-on-one lessons over the course of a year. Rather than attempting a comprehensive investigation of the entire Quran, which would be the work of a lifetime, not a year, the lessons would be a springboard for discussing all manner of topics. Some would be taken from the standard playbook of Western obsessions with Islam: I was curious about Akram's views on women's rights, polygamy, and sharia law. I was eager to hear his reading of the so-called "Verse of the Sword," which bin Laden used to justify his jihad. But I also wanted our conversations to range into areas seldom touched by stories in the media. I wanted to know more about what the Sheikh saw as the Quran's most important themes, and how they'd shaped his life. Which verses and which hadiths (words and deeds of the Prophet) had guided him, as migrant, husband, and father? I hoped to hear his thoughts on marriage and child rearing, and on Judaism and Christianity. I wanted to learn more about the Quran, but I also wanted to work as a sort of cultural cartographer, charting where our worldviews overlapped and where they clashed. I wanted to map out what divided us, and what united us.

To my surprise, he readily agreed. He said yes, not just to the lessons, but to what would be unprecedented intrusions for so private a man. In the course of the year, he endured scores of interviews and numerous visits to his Oxford home. When I asked to shadow him through a typical day, from the gym to the mosque, he let me. He allowed me to accompany him back to India, where we visited his old madrasa and ancestral village. He encouraged me to interview his family and students. Never did he try to limit who I talked to, the questions I asked, or what I wrote.

Why would he consent to such a regime? It helped that I'd written about him before, and that we'd known each other for twenty years. But ultimately, he agreed to my project for much the same reason that I wanted to do it. "There's so much misunderstanding about Islam and Muslims," he said. "People only hear the words of the extremists. The ulama, their voices are never heard."

"But why study with him?" asked a Muslim friend. "Why this particular sheikh?"

She had nothing against Akram per se; she didn't know his work. Still, she knew that there are hundreds of English-speaking sheikhs in Britain and America, and that many of them are willing to teach women. Some would doubtless take on a non-Muslim like me. Choosing an Islamic scholar is inevitably complicated, since Sunni Islam famously lacks a clergy and a central organizing structure. With no archbishop's office or local diocese to steer one toward a particular scholar or imam, anyone seeking Islamic knowledge can study with anybody who will teach them. So her question was a good one: Why choose Akram? Why not an Islamic progressive, one whose worldview lies closer to my own? Why not write on Amina Wadud, the African-American scholar who produced the first feminist reading of the Quran? Or Hamza Yusuf, the Berkeley-based cleric with a Los

Angeles madrasa, who can riff on Homer and Florence Nightingale as easily as on fourteenth-century Sufis?

I chose Akram for many reasons, chief among them being the fact that his outlook is so different from my own. Western journalistic coverage of Islam occupies a cramped space, focusing either on violent extremists or hidebound fundamentalists. Occasionally, we Western readers get exposed to what are dubbed "moderates"—shorthand for Muslims whose beliefs make no intrusion on politics or public spaces. The horizon isn't exactly broad: we're invited to peer either into the abyss—or a hall of reflecting mirrors. If I wanted to see where my own worldview intersected with and diverged from an Islamic one, then it made sense to read the Quran with someone who had trained in a traditional madrasa, outside the West.

Akram's years in an Indian madrasa anchored him far more securely in the Islamic tradition than the radicals, many of whom learned their Islam on weekends or at teach-ins. As a working *alim*, consulted by ordinary Muslims in Britain about practical issues from marriage to mortgages, he has a vantage many academics at Western universities simply don't share. "Akram is really different," observed David Damrel, a former colleague from the Oxford Centre for Islamic Studies, now a professor of comparative religion at the University of South Carolina Upstate. "There are some scholars who engage with local communities, but rarely with people outside of them. There are others who teach at Western-style universities. Akram has done both. As an imam in Oxford, he didn't simply engage with Western-style academics. He was also on the front lines, at the mosque."

Educated in India and Saudi Arabia, fluent in Urdu, Hindu, Persian, Arabic, and English, Akram has an outlook built from layered identities. During his youth, the culture of the village of Jamdahan mixed with his madrasa training, which began locally, then in Jaunpur, and then finally at Nadwat al-Ulama in Lucknow, India. After twenty years in Britain, and seasons spent studying in Damascus and Medina, the Sheikh has a cultural scope that spans continents. Even by the standards of an educational tradition in which bright village boys can go far, the Sheikh's near-seamless transition from a village

prodigy to a global scholar is a stunning example of Muslim cosmopolitanism. Rare is the working *alim* who has taught Oxford undergraduates. "Offhand, I can't think of anybody who has made such a
dramatic leap," said Damrel. "I can't think of anyone who has done it
so gracefully, and done it with eyes wide open."

Nowhere, it seemed, did the Sheikh feel out of place. He was at
home in both the West and in India, since for him, his true home lay
somewhere else altogether. "This tiny earth, it's not your place," he
once told me. "You have to sit here for a very short period—sixty or
seventy years. It's a testing place, then you come back to your real
place."

If I admired the grace with which Akram navigated the world, it
was partly because my own journeys through it had been somewhat
meandering. My cosmopolitanism, spread broader and thinner than
the Sheikh's, was born of a childhood being towed around the world
by a restless father. A man who yearned for minaret-studded skylines
lit by scimitar moons should never have taught Wills and Trusts at
law school in St. Louis. Summers were spent in Europe, and every few
years my parents would take leave from their universities to teach
farther east, taking my brother and me to live in Iran, Afghanistan,
India, and Egypt.

My father flattened the earth for us, making its exploration a sort
of spiritual quest. During these years abroad, my brother and I discovered "home" was less a single place than wherever we happened to
be. I was a well-trained little nomad, comfortable most places as long
as I had my parents, a Laura Ingalls Wilder paperback, and the occasional playmate. My earliest lessons in cultural difference were crude,
but they were a start: in Qom, the Iranian city of seminaries and
scholars, every female, even five-year-olds like me, wore a chador, the
black cloak worn by Iranian women. In Afghanistan, you never went
sleeveless, never photographed someone without permission, and
never refused a cup of chai. When I could, I tried to understand the
cultural differences between Islamic societies and my own, but I also
loved seeing their similarities. Initially, this desire sprang from trying
to make foreign places home. The compare and contrast routine

helped knit together an existence split between the Midwest, the Middle East, and Asia. As I grew older, this exercise became academic and professional: I studied the interplay between Western and Islamic cultures in college and graduate school, and later wrote on it as a journalist. After 9/11, the topic gained a political urgency, with fear and anger convincing both Muslims and non-Muslims that "They" hated "Us." To study with Akram was not just to cultivate a deeper understanding of Islam. It was to test the boundaries of my own faith: a zealous belief in the virtues of trying to understand what's really foreign, and what just looks that way.

Our experiment in cross-cultural conversation started in a café, just off Oxford's main shopping street. With its sumptuous display of triple-decker cream cakes and cutesy name, the Nosebag, it seemed a strange place to hold a Quran lesson. In earlier centuries, the Nosebag might have been the sort of coffeehouse where more sober Oxford undergraduates repaired for table-pounding debates over Locke and Sophocles. The Sheikh and I sat at a dark wooden table under a low ceiling, gazing out leaded windows onto a gray winter drizzle. Britain starts its Christmas preparations the minute the first leaf falls, so though it was early November, a choral version of "O Come All Ye Faithful" piped from a speaker. Two American grad students gossiped about their professors. Gray-haired ladies in cashmere rustled their shopping bags, talking softly of their Christmas finds.

We'd agreed to meet at the Nosebag because it was convenient, just around the corner from the Sheikh's office. I put my copy of the Quran on the table between us and tried to ignore my inner twinge of embarrassment. It felt unseemly, somehow, holding an earnest discussion of a holy book out in the open, where others could hear us. Briefly, I had a half-formed thought of setting up a cardboard sign on the table: "This Conversation for Research Purposes Only."

The Sheikh saw nothing odd in studying the Quran over midmorning tea in Oxford's shopping district. My own sense of religion may be confined to houses of worship, but Islam takes a broader view.

"The whole world," the Prophet Muhammad once observed, "is a mosque." At airports during hajj, or pilgrimage season, I've seen the pious prostrating outside duty-free shops and next to boarding gates. Muslim cabdrivers pray behind the taxi office at New York's LaGuardia Airport. I once saw a turbaned Afghan standing on the empty storefront display platform of a St. Louis grocery. Eyes closed, palms curved heavenward, he was praying, connecting with the Infinite over Grand Boulevard's lunchtime traffic.

Akram and I embarked on our study of the scripture through a decidedly more mundane activity: eating cheese scones and sipping strong mugs of English Breakfast tea. The Sheikh looked nothing like the Western stereotype of a Muslim scholar that day. In his herringbone tweed, khakis, and black lace-ups, he just resembled an affable professor. His beard is shot through with gray, but his face retains a younger man's smooth and open quality. He has eyes the shade and sheen of polished teak. Though I'd known the Sheikh for twenty years, I felt nervous.

"Sheikh," I opened hesitantly, "I've never actually read the Quran." I waited for the gravity of my confession to sink in. Admitting as much at this stage in my career felt shameful, akin to a literature professor revealing she'd skipped Homer and Hamlet.

"Most Muslims haven't read it either," Akram said brightly, buttering his scone. "And even if they have, they don't understand it. The Quran is alien to them. Usually, they'll just go to the books of law. Or if they're interested in piety or purifying the heart, they'll read Ghazali"—a philosopher—"or Sufis like Rumi."

Akram's calm unnerved me. I knew, of course, that many graduates of the Muslim world's lesser seminaries hadn't really read Islam's scriptures. The boys in village madrasas, rocking back and forth, lisping lines from the Quran in classical Arabic, a language they didn't understand, might have been literally reading, but not much more. The suicide bombers and jihadist foot soldiers who had been promised a reward of seventy-two virgins in paradise were duped. Nowhere does the Quran mention such rewards for murder. Yet I assumed the graduates of the great Islamic institutions, like Cairo's venerable Al-

Azhar, or the Sheikh's own alma mater, Nadwat al-Ulama in Lucknow, would know the Quran intimately, if not by heart.

"Even people who go to good madrasas don't necessarily know it as well as they should," said Akram, briskly brushing scone crumbs off his khakis. "In fact, the Quran is often the weakest part of the madrasa curriculum."

I leaned forward, assuming I'd misheard. His voice is as soft as it was when he was a young *alim*, and despite his two decades in England, his accent still bears the strong stamp of provincial India.

"Really?" I stammered. "But it's . . . I mean, it's the Quran! It's obviously the basics of what religious scholars are studying?"

"It's not. Far more effort and class time is given to the texts of jurisprudence or hadith." The branches of Islamic knowledge that came after the Prophet's death, like law and philosophy, had only made the Muslim world's injustices and divisions grow, he continued. They'd moved mankind further from the source. The message of the Quran and the sunna, the example of the Prophet Muhammad, had been buried by a mountain of academic debate. In the centuries after Muhammad, scholars erected an elaborate system of *fiqh*, or jurisprudence, a man-made legal scaffolding based on interpretations of the Quran and hadith. Developed after the death of the prophet in AD 632, these four schools of law differ on issues from the proper prayer postures to whether or not believers may eat lobster. The medieval religious scholars who developed *fiqh* were frequently far more conservative than the Quran, and often much more punitive than the Prophet Muhammad. "Read the books of Islamic law, and you'll see they are much harsher on women," said Akram. "You know when they get really against women? When all the scholars start studying philosophy." The misogyny running through *fiqh*, said the Sheikh, was a matter not merely of scholars' medieval mores, but of the influence of the Greek philosophers on them. Aristotle, a man who held that the subjugation of women was both "natural" and a "social necessity," influenced key Muslim thinkers who shaped medieval *fiqh*, argued Akram. Before Aristotle became a core text, and before the medieval scholars enshrined their views on gender roles in Islamic law, men and women were accorded far more equal freedoms in Islam, he explained. He sketched peaks and troughs in the air, as if plotting the rise and fall of sexism through history.

"God Rest Ye Merry, Gentlemen" was reaching its crescendo above us. "So why do people get obsessed with following the schools of law?" I asked. "Why not just go back to the Quran?"

A wide, bright smile. "People can be lazy." Consulting scholars and obeying their rules was safer and easier, said the Sheikh. "You don't need to read, or question, or think. You've got other people thinking for you. If you become open, it's a challenge." He glanced at his watch, checking to see how much time remained before the noon prayer. "You see, Carla, what's happened, really, is that we in the Muslim world have destroyed the whole balance. We've become obsessed with these tiny details, these laws. What does the Quran keep repeating? Purity of the heart. That's what's important! Why has cutting off a thief's hand—something it mentions once!—become of such importance to some people?"

As a scholar, he was incredulous; as a journalist, I wasn't. Gore and absolutes always grab people's attention faster than poetry and nuance.

Akram smiled conspiratorially. "People are really very shocked when I tell them that the four schools of law aren't really that important," he said. "If people would just read the Quran, most of these differences would finish."

I wasn't convinced. More people were reading it, but it still created controversy. Men still used the Quran to legitimize their actions when they beat their wives. Bin Laden had used the Quran to declare war on all those he deemed infidels.

There's reading the Quran properly and reading it sloppily, the Sheikh continued. All too often, people read it selectively, taking phrases out of context. "People just use it for whatever point they want to make," he shrugged. "They come to it with their own ideas and look for verses that confirm what they want to hear."

The Quran was not a shopping list for the good life, said Akram. Pious Muslims like him, and eager students like me, need to stand back for a panoramic view of the text. The careful reader couldn't be distracted from its overarching messages and interlinking themes. Its very design was miraculous, one of the infinite signs of God's grace.

"A book as miracle," I nodded.

"Ah! Now is it a book?" he slapped his thigh gleefully. "That's the first question you need to ask! Is it a book, or not?" He leaned forward, warming to the question. Was not the man-made concept of a book, with a beginning, middle, and end, too puny a word to describe something as infinite as the Quran?

"After all," he continued, "it doesn't read in the order it was revealed. The first revelation Muhammad received doesn't come until very late, until sura 96."

This was not good news. I was prepared for subtlety, but like a Broadway producer, I'd hoped for a tune I could hum.

The Quran may not unfold chronologically, but its ordering was deliberate, sent down from God, explained Akram.

"Why do you think the order was changed?"

"Since God was specific, there must be a reason." He sat back, satisfied. Many things were open for discussion, but not divine strategy. It was a lurch, this switchback route from ambiguity to certainty and back again.

"So, in this sense, it's a book, right?"

"Yes. The Quran keeps calling itself a book. It's a book sent down to the Prophet, and it revealed to the people what they needed, when they needed it." But being no ordinary book, he continued, the Quran didn't always make sense as other books did. "You'll be in a verse about the law of divorce," he says, tracing a line on the table, like a football coach planning a play. "Then suddenly there will be a bit about prayer, and then go back to divorce." He sat back. "How is one supposed to make sense of that?"

I had no clue, and in that, I certainly wasn't alone. Among the most stridently confused readers of the Quran was Thomas Carlyle. The Victorian writer was a great admirer of the Prophet Muhammad and of Islam itself, but found its Holy Book "as toilsome reading as I ever undertook . . . a wearisome, confused jumble."

But it wasn't a jumble, insisted Akram. "You will see, and be amazed, how it fits together. If you move the verses around, you'll be surprised to find that they don't work out of order."

I was beginning to see why many Muslims focus on concrete rules rather than the Quran's subtleties. Wrangling over mundane problems like veils and pork derivatives was far easier than wading through thickets of Quranic verse. How comparatively simple, to debate whether M&Ms are halal (permissible) or *haram* (banned). Few mortals could rise to the challenge of appreciating a divine design. I felt overwhelmed, and it must have shown, because the Sheikh smiled. "Look, the Quran is difficult. To read it in the original, you need to know classical Arabic, which very few people want to take the trouble to learn."

I certainly wasn't going to. I remembered well the old grad student wheeze about learning Arabic—that it's just the first twenty years that are tough. I patted my translation, sitting right next to the teapot, and I made to open it, eager to get started, but the Sheikh went on. "To really understand it, you'll need to know a lot," he said. "To understand the stories of the Prophets in it, you need to know your Bible stories."

I gulped. My knowledge of the Bible was cobbled together from Renaissance paintings and reading *Paradise Lost* in sophomore English.

To understand the text, you need to understand the context, the Sheikh continued. To make sense of the rules it sets down, you need to understand Arab society during the age it was revealed: "So if you don't know the customs and traditions of the Prophet Muhammad's time, you can't make sense of it."

My background in seventh-century Arabia was rudimentary, and my Arabic nonexistent.

The Sheikh beamed as he reached for his coat. "And of course, if you're lazy, you can't make sense of it."

I was frequently lazy. I thought of Carlyle, a Victorian, a Scotsman, and a philosopher—in short, a man emphatically not of lazy stock—who nonetheless warned, "Nothing but a sense of duty could carry any European through the Quran."

. . .

As any child's primer on world religions will tell you, Islam began as a desert faith. My time studying with the Sheikh felt a lot like desert travel. The sun can dazzle, and the air's clearness can compress the appearance of distances. A far-off dune can look near; the horizon can loom, then recede in a blink. A strong wind can cover paths and footprints with sand. Such was the experience of studying with the Sheikh. The Quranic landscape was neither dry nor parched, but to a Western secularist like myself, unschooled in scriptures of any faith, it often lacked landmarks. I found myself setting mental boundaries, then having to reset them, again and again.

We made an odd little caravan, the Sheikh and I, a pious believer and a skeptical secularist. Yet surprisingly often, I'd pad up to a topic I'd assumed would be divisive, and we found ourselves agreeing. Some issue that mullahs or politicians had fulminated about for years would be revealed as utterly trivial. Then, just as suddenly, I'd trip across a phrase that seemed perfectly innocuous, only to discover craggy complexities lurking beneath it. I'd find myself staring across canyons of incomprehension. It could be quite dizzying.

But disorientation is a good teacher. Reexamining beliefs—most importantly, your own—lies at the heart of the Western secular tradition. Disorientation is also a sign of the power of God, and a theme of some of the Quran's most ravishing passages.

The Sheikh was never truly disoriented. He had his *qibla*—his direction—and that direction was God. Having embarked on a journey of sorts, we could only move forward, together.

THE ORIGINS

The Quran in Twenty-Five Words

A few days before my lesson on the Quran's first sura, I went to a Sunday lunch party in North London. At the table, I met a man—I'll call him Hans—with crisp graying hair, brushed apple-green tweeds, and a languid Continental accent. Born in Vienna and educated at Cambridge, Hans had pronounced on subjects from primary school pedagogy to F. Scott Fitzgerald's prose before he'd even finished the first glass of Prosecco. After he told me about the book he'd published, on a literary journal in wartime Paris, he learned I was a journalist and asked what I was writing about. When I told him, he looked as though he'd just swallowed the backbone of his sea bream.

"The Quran," he spluttered. "But, why?"

An awkward pause. On hearing this daring dismissiveness from so refined a man, I felt as flummoxed as he seemed. A year or so earlier, a British Muslim politician had charged that Islamophobia "passed the dinner-party test" and was now, disgracefully enough, an acceptable form of discrimination in polite society. I'd hoped she'd been exaggerating, since I hadn't come across it in my tiny, tolerant circle until now. I swallowed my fish and ran through the reasons. They seemed so self-evident that I restrained myself from reciting them in the singsong tones I use to chide my children to brush up to the gum line: A lifelong personal interest in Islamic societies. A worldwide population of 1.6 billion Muslims and counting, a number that was ever-growing, Islam being the planet's fastest-growing faith. Post-9/11 wars. A crucial new issue in European parliaments and American elections. The text's power, its poetry. I felt vaguely silly as I rattled off the list. Until a minute ago, I'd assumed that the sort of person who rereads *Tender Is the Night* and writes on twentieth-century intellectual history would deem reading the Quran a worthy pursuit. I finished my monologue, triumphantly forked some kale into my mouth, swallowed, and parried. "Why? What do you think about Islam?"

"They're living in the medieval ages," Hans said breezily. "They need to get up to speed with the rest of the world."

I'd heard this dozens of times before—from London taxi drivers, on Midwestern talk radio, and even from cultivated types like Hans. Had it not been for the din of kids bickering over whether to watch *Peter Pan* or *Snow White*, perhaps I would have retorted that fundamentalists can't be dismissed as medieval. That they don't exist outside modernity but are very much a part of it, with their use of technology, their sophisticated global networking, and their keen sensitivity to media cycles. Had I not been on my second Prosecco, and conscious of other guests waiting for us to tie up the strands of our conversation, I might have told Hans what various scholars have posited: that the anti-Western, antisecular rhetoric of Muslim fundamentalists is a response to the fraying social fabric in fast-changing, increasingly polarized societies. That for new migrants to big cities or foreign countries, the mosque provides shelter from loneliness. That for people unmoored from home or family, a prescriptive faith provides an anchor. I didn't launch those arguments, deciding that they were a shade heavy for a Sunday afternoon, what with our hosts taking advantage of the rare winter sunshine and opening the sliding doors onto their deck. I took an easier tack. "Well, of course, you're probably just going by what you read in the papers," I nodded. "Believe me, I know, as a journalist: Who makes the best stories, who gives the best quotes? The extremists, the crazies. So who do we tend to hear from? The people who shout the loudest."

"But where are the moderates?" he asked. "Why aren't they speaking up?"

"Well, they're there—they just don't make the headlines," I answered. "Quietism doesn't make for news. Sometimes they're writing op-eds, or working with interfaith groups or NGOs. But you're not going to hear about them, since they're not blowing things up or blowing off steam."

"But are there any Muslim moderates, really?" he asked. "I mean, real moderates?"

"Of course there are!" I said. "You've got millions and millions of Muslims who view their faith in much the same way that most Christians or Jews or Buddhists do—as a private matter. And if you're looking for Muslims trying to square their faith with universal human rights, you've got mini reformation movements going on: women and gays and minorities going back to the Quran and reading it for themselves, not letting the local mullah tell them what to think. You've got lots of scholars, and lots of ordinary Muslims, trying to take back their religion from the radicals who've styled themselves as leaders without any training in Islamic law or tradition. There are Sufis, reacting against the strictness of the mullahs . . ."

"But what about Saudi Arabia?" he pursued, pushing his chair back from the table with the air of a wrestler limbering up before a match. "What about the Taliban? What they do to women . . . In Saudi Arabia, women can't drive. Under the Taliban, they couldn't go anywhere without covering up . . ." The other guests, sensing a low hum of tension, began to gather their plates and ferry them to the sink.

"They aren't practicing Islam," I replied, perhaps a tad too smugly. "That's local or tribal custom made into national law. Yes, those laws and restrictions are terrible, but they're not Islamic. All you have to do to find out that it's got universal values—ones very much like yours and mine—is go back to the sources."

Our hosts had returned to the table bearing chocolate cake, so we came to an uneasy truce in the interests of gluttony and good cheer. Together we stepped, a bit shakily, onto the safer conversational turf of the dangers of Iranian nukes and the virtues of Neapolitan pizzas.

I knew I hadn't swayed him, but I had complete confidence that the sources, as read by Akram, would reveal a just and humane faith. I left the party troubled by Hans's prejudice, but charged with righteousness, and braced by my own certainty.

I carried this clean, bright feeling to Oxford with me a few days later, where it only grew on seeing Akram again. As we walked up the steep stairs to the Nosebag, he talked about how he'd spent the day before in Leicester, meeting with women and Muslim community leaders to talk about allowing women to pray in mosques. During the Prophet's era, women prayed freely in mosques along with men, but in time, many cultures began restricting their presence. Over the centuries, the scholars' consensus that women didn't have to go to mosques to pray if they couldn't get away from home and the kids morphed into a cultural norm that said they shouldn't. In many parts of the Muslim world, women stopped going to the mosque—or were prevented from doing so.

Pointing to Islamic history, Akram challenged this. "The women were so happy, really," he said, allowing himself a nanosecond of quiet triumph. "Not everyone was convinced, but it was a start." Since news of his work on women scholars began to spread, Akram had been called out on scores of such diplomatic missions. The man who began his career as an expert on hadith has become a celebrated defender of Muslim women's rights within a traditional Islamic framework.

In Leicester, he'd told the mosque authorities about his work assembling the names of historical women who didn't just pray in mosques, but debated and lectured in them, teaching male students as well as female ones. I hoped that he also told them, as he had me, of the tenth-century Baghdad-born jurist who roved around on lecture tours, teaching women in Syria and Egypt; and of Umm al-Darda, a prominent seventh-century jurist from Damascus. Akram found that as a young woman, she used to sit with male scholars in the mosques, discussing theology. "I've tried to worship Allah in every way," she wrote, "but I've never found a better one than sitting around debating other scholars."

That quote alone made me want to adopt Umm al-Darda as an unofficial patron saint for this project: I loved the image of her sitting in the mosque with men, secure in her knowledge that debate was a holy thing. Akram's research suggested she was very much her own woman. An orphan, she'd go to mosque without covering her head, and for a time she could be found praying in the men's rows rather than the women's. In her classes in Damascus and Jerusalem, she counted men, women, and even a caliph—a Muslim leader—among her students.

When we reached the café cashier, there was a gentle tussle over who would buy the tea. The bored blonde behind the register watched our friendly match of "allow mes" and "no, reallys" and "next time, it's mines." As elaborate as calligraphy, as old as our acquaintance, the ritual was particularly reassuring today, after my jarring conversation on Sunday. Hans's knowledge of Islam was shaped by the news of fundamentalists and extremists. Their certainty and anger came from a brittle interpretation of Islam, not from *adab*—the suppler, subtler concept of a humane and educated manner. The Prophet Muhammad once declared that *adab* nearly "equals two-thirds of religion." The Sheikh's own *adab* went beyond graciousness. I suspect it also had something to do with the quiet of certainty. He enjoyed the profound peace of a man who observed his duty as a Muslim: being a "slave of God." Over the course of the year, I would watch, not a little envious, as I saw how this enslavement brought him considerable calm.

Reverence for the Quran doesn't always confer calm. Earlier in the year, the news had been full of riots and protests, after American soldiers at the Bagram Air Force Base outside Kabul had been discovered burning Qurans with trash. The books had been confiscated from prisoners on suspicion that they were being used to pass on extremist messages. President Barack Obama apologized, but that hadn't prevented a furor, and the deaths of thirty Afghans and six American soldiers. This tragedy was one of several following rumors—some true, some false—of the Quran's destruction by American troops in the tense post-9/11 world. *Adab*, like truth, is a casualty of war.

The reading for the day was short but powerful: "Al-Fatiha," or "The Opening," the Quran's first sura. It's been called Umm al-Quran— the Mother of the Quran—since the key themes of the Quran are packed into its twenty-five Arabic words. Some non-Muslims have likened it to the Lord's Prayer, but it is more than that, so tightly knotted are its words into the fabric of Muslim life. Pious Muslims recite it seventeen times a day: twice during dawn prayers, three times while praying at sunset, and four times apiece in the three other prayers. "Al-Fatiha" can greet good news, seal a contract, or smooth bazaar negotiations. Some Muslims carve it on tombstones; others say its words while undressing to protect them from the prying eyes of jinn, or spirits. One hadith holds that the chapter is "a source of healing for every ailment except death," which is perhaps why its words make for a popular amulet, rolled up, encased in gold or silver, and worn around the neck. It hangs on the wall in Muslim homes across the world, protecting the inhabitants from harm. Once, the verse saved a woman I know during a robbery. She calmed a pair of thieves holding her at gunpoint in her bedroom by pointing to the words of Al-Fatiha, framed and hanging on the wall. She swore on it that she wouldn't scream if they left quietly. At the sound of her words—and the sight of the Quran's—one man slowly lowered the gun he had held to her head. They left soon afterward, leaving her unharmed.

I opened my Quran to the first verse and began reading:

In the Name of God, the Benevolent, the Merciful,
Praise is Proper to God, Lord of the Universe,
The Beneficent, the Merciful.
Ruler of the Day of Requital,
It is You we serve, to You we turn for help.
Show us the straight path,
The path of those You have favored;

Not of those who are objects of anger, nor of those who wander
astray. (1:1–7)

"It is You we serve." With this phrase—which in some translations
is "Thee alone we worship"—the old polytheism of the Arab tribes of
the Arabian Peninsula was to be replaced with one God, uniting individuals from a collection of tribes into a community of faith. For the
pagan Arabs of Mecca and Medina, the Quran brought not merely a
new faith, but a reimagined social order. No longer were you just a
member of your tribe or family, but of something much larger: a community of people called Muslims, united by worshipping a single
Supreme Being. No longer would there be the scrum to worship hundreds of minor gods and goddesses, as Mecca's pagans had done until
Islam arrived. In its place, there was utter submission to the all-
powerful Creator.

But this statement didn't simply declare monotheism. The line
proved even more radical. In four short words lay the concept of the
dignity of the individual, bestowed on him by his creator. "When it
says 'Thee alone we worship,' it means people aren't allowed to worship any angel, any man of money, or any man of power," explained
Akram. "A Muslim submits only to God."

There. Right there lay the justification for everything from the
Arab Spring revolts to the Islamic women's movement. With breath-
taking linguistic economy, sitting just inside the first verse of the Quran,
lay the words that punctured tyranny. They were gentle weaponry
against husbands who ruled over their wives, or presidents who tor-
tured their people. In a God-centered universe, no person had the right
to rule over another person, since all were equal before their creator.
It gave people an inherent dignity vis-à-vis their fellow humans. Such
a satisfying sura. I wondered what Hans would make of it.

Akram pointed out that the line "to You we turn for help" is an
indication of Islam's central tenet of submission. "It shows mankind
asking how to worship," he noted. "It is saying, 'We are helpless people.
We need more of your favor. We need to know how to worship You.'"

Here again was the surrender that Islam—derived from the same

Arabic root word as "peace," but literally meaning "submission"—demands of a Muslim. "When you see the word 'worship,' or *ibada* in Arabic, this is the sort of extreme humiliation that is only allowed in the case of God," observed Akram. "That's why we have to bow in prayer. Before him, we require an extreme humbleness." While Christianity and Judaism drew their names from people, the word "Islam" refers to a relationship rather than a single figure—that between every believer and God.

Up to now, the lesson had been going well. Akram's reading of "Al-Fatiha" described a just and expansive worldview. The verse's emphasis on the individual's direct association with God, unbrokered by clerical middlemen, was reassuringly democratic. The concept of extreme humility before God felt familiar, and admirable. It was only in the last three lines that I felt any disquiet:

> Show us the straight path,
> The path of those You have favored;
> Not of those who are objects of anger, nor of those who wander
>   astray.

"The Quran wants you to walk in the path of God," the Sheikh explained. "The path of God is the straight path."

"And who are those whom He's favored?" I asked, assuming it would be pretty much anyone who stuck to the straight path. It was rather more specific than that. "God has bestowed His favor on four types of people," said Akram.

I sat up straight, ever the eager student, fingers hovering above the laptop keyboard. "Prophets," I transcribed.

"*Siddiqeen*. These are people who aren't prophets, but whose true nature is so powerful that it puts them on the straight path, like Maryam—the Bible's Mary, who followed God's instructions, with a pure and clean heart."

Oh. Then: "Martyrs."

Next?

"Other righteous people."

I hoped it was a catchall category.

His elaboration—"Those whom God has favored" —was a rather narrower demographic than I'd been hoping for. Wondering how broad the definition of "righteous" was, I found a clue in the next line: "Not [the path] of those who are objects of anger, nor of those who wonder astray."

"And what kinds of people are they?" I asked, fully expecting to hear a list roughly similar to that in the Judeo-Christian tradition, beginning with *A* for adulterers and ending with *U* for usurers.

The list was far shorter than I expected. "Well, some people have said that 'those who are objects of Thine anger' refers to the Jews," said Akram, whose calm suddenly grew unnerving. "God became angry with the Jews after they rejected Jesus Christ. God's favor can be taken away from you at any time."

"Jews" struck like a pebble. It is a hard, small, unyielding word. It always seems to jam the conversation in a way that the adjective "Jewish" doesn't. I thought of that famous line from the British director Jonathan Miller. "I'm not a Jew," Miller said. "Just Jew*ish*. Not the whole hog, you know."

The Sheikh continued. "God does not favor people who have gone astray. Some people think this part means Christians, who went to extremes by confusing their prophet Jesus with the divine. The Quran wants Muslims to remember that Jesus is only a man."

"But aren't the Jewish people and the Christians 'Ahl-e-Kitab'?" I asked, plaintive now. "People of the Book?"

Islam's famous respect for Ahl-e-Kitab, literally the People of the Book, as the followers of the two other great monotheisms are known, was invariably invoked at interfaith events.

"Yes, they are," said the Sheikh. "We respect the Jewish people and the Christian ones."

The Sheikh did not believe that the last line of "Al-Fatiha" referred to Jews and Christians specifically, but to any Muslim who veered off piety's path.

. . .

The lesson ended shortly after that. I rode back to London, queasy from hours on a stuffy bus and rattled by hearing Akram recount the potentially hostile reading of that final line. Like Hans's casual denunciations of Islam at lunch, it suggested that prejudice lurked in unlikely places. It disturbed me. Not as a Jew, but as a humanist. Maybe studying the Quran with Akram was too risky, like getting your parents to teach you how to drive. In unpacking the Quran's first sura, we'd strayed from the carefully pruned list of topics we'd stuck to for twenty years. We'd veered off our own straight path and onto the hard shoulder of the road. So much of my enthusiasm for Islamic society had been born of the pleasure of finding similarities with my own outlooks. I'd reveled in finding shared values under superficial differences. So much of the pleasure of Akram's friendship was the sheer surprise of connecting with someone whose outlook diverged so spectacularly from my own. And yet here, in our first lesson, I was already hearing things I didn't want to hear.

Such disturbances were necessary, of course. To study with Akram was, among other things, to test the limits of my own tolerance. To date, my pluralist outlook had been a laissez-faire business, more a cosmopolitan habit than a true challenge to my beliefs. It meant tacos at lunch, the mantra "Om" before yoga class, and Chinese herbs during hay fever season. Over the years, I had embraced diversity twice daily at least, on those morning commutes spent sitting on New York subways surfing on the sea of languages, or on London buses scanning the horizon of heads, some in hijabs, others bald or dreadlocked.

This first lesson with Akram hinted that my engagment with other worldviews had been more about pageantry than pluralism. I knew some old-fashioned Republicans, but none who had stuck with the GOP after George W. Bush's presidency. I had lots of Jewish friends, but most were cultural Jews; none were Orthodox. Any Catholics I knew had lapsed long ago. Nobody in my social circle denied a woman's right to choose an abortion. I might identify as someone who celebrated diversity, but in reality, my worldview was pretty cramped.

The bus lurched into London and let me out at my stop, sadder and less certain than when I'd boarded it that morning. Standing on the pavement, I hiked my backpack on my shoulder and glumly wondered what Hans would say.

The next day, with grim determination, I made straight for Bloomsbury. When I was a graduate student, I used to shake off Oxford's straight-backed sobriety by going to work in the library of the far hipper School of Oriental and Asian Studies at the University of London. Just studying there felt liberating. The students had piercings and hijabs; the halls were plastered with posters for world peace and against racism. Even the bright, clean-lined library felt less constrained by history. I made straight for the stacks devoted to *tafsirs*—commentaries on the Quran—and pulled down a stack of them. I wanted to regain the tight, bright certitude I'd felt before.

I sat with my tower of *tafsirs*, finger-scanning index columns for "Al-Fatiha" and for "Quran—attitudes to Jews and Christians." I found some comfort in an introductory text by Fazlur Rahman, a great twentieth-century Muslim reformist. In *Major Themes of the Quran*, he cites a verse from the second sura: "Those who believe [Muslims], the Jews, the Christians and the Sabaeans—whosoever believe in God and the Last Day and do good deeds, they shall have their reward from their Lord, shall have nothing to fear, nor shall they come to grief." Ultimately, concludes Rahman, these words have an "obvious meaning," which is simply that those "from any section of mankind—who believe in God and the Last Day and do good deeds are saved."

There. It was ultimately about belief in God, and being good. A flood of relief. That I could do. I regained my faith in Islam as being a force for harmony between faiths.

✦ 2 ✦

An American in the East

For my father, taking his family to live for years overseas was a salve
for both his chronic discontent with American society and his clinical depression. He was a law professor in Missouri, but he felt far
more fulfilled in foreign places, all the more so if they had the "grapes,
melons, and olive trees" he deemed necessary for civilization. And so
my childhood was split between suburban St. Louis and cities across
the Muslim world. Admittedly, the list of foreign postings—Tehran,
Delhi, Kabul, and Cairo—looked pretty suspicious. My mom's family
assumed my dad was a CIA operative cunningly disguised as an eccentric professor. He wasn't with the Agency: he moved us abroad less for
professional reasons than aesthetic and emotional ones.

The closest thing my family had to a belief system was a firm faith
in the restorative power of travel, so I was raised ignoring religious
texts. The daughter of a lapsed Quaker father and a Jewish mother
whose faith lay in bagels and dim memories of the dreidel song, I
never read a scripture growing up. Ours was a secular household,
whose churches were art galleries and parks and whose default setting was doubt. My parents, both professors, didn't care much for
faith. It might have been useful for our forefathers, who schlepped in
the shtetl or struggled on homesteads in the Great Plains, but it wasn't
for my parents, with their advanced degrees and their Miles Davis

LPs. Transcendence, they believed, was found in Titian paintings or sunsets, not in holy books or holy men. My only religious training was the odd Sunday we made it to the Ethical Society, the humanist congregation where we drew pictures of children of many lands and sang songs about the gift of simplicity.

When my mother's Judaism did surface, it was as a culture, not a faith, and even then it was explained as something she'd had in her childhood, like saddle shoes or braces. If she remembered, we might hide the matzo on Passover, or light the menorah on Hanukah. Occasionally she'd surprise us with some dimly remembered Yiddish from her Lithuanian grandmother: dismissing *Love Story* as "schlock," and declaring me a "vilde chaya"—wild child—when I roughhoused with my brother. And yet I did feel Jewish, vaguely, though it meant little more than a distinctive strain of urban cosmopolitanism, comprised of coffee-dark irony and a subscription to the *New Yorker*. The only relic of my father's Quaker heritage was a fierce belief in thrift. That, and stories of great-aunts who used to "thee" and "thou" one another, and the vague sense that going to a Quaker meeting might be nice, sometime. "I would love to believe," my father would say, spreading his arms wide, as though waiting for some deity to arrive in his embrace. None ever did.

In the empty space where faith might have resided, my father stuffed travel and artifacts brought back from it. At home in St. Louis, we lived amid flaking gilt Buddhas, Indian miniatures, and piles of oriental carpets—barricades my father built to blot out Missouri. For him, St. Louis was a city of curt nods to neighbors, of gas pumped in surly silence, of long walks hunched against the winter cold. But with a family to support, he had settled for a job teaching law there. It was bearable, he found, as long as he could travel in Europe in the summers, and every couple of years take a fellowship or unpaid leave to live overseas.

It was in Iran, in the early seventies, that he had first found a potent antidepressant in Islamic culture. The slower rhythm of the days, punctuated by cups of tea and calls to prayer, soothed him. Bazaar culture, where meandering conversations cushioned the cut-and-thrust

of commerce, struck him as more human, and more humane, than
the mall. For once he felt at home. Squatting against a wall at an
Isfahani mosque, or debating the merits of a Turkoman saddlebag in
the bazaar, he was no longer the wallflower at the Law Review mixer.
For a man who never joined anything but his immediate family, Western Asia offered him a sense of belonging. Even as a kid, I saw the
transformative effect that crossing cultures had on him: it went
beyond a value to become a survival strategy.

My own first apprehension of Islamic societies was purely sensual,
a matter of surface textures. A mosque's turquoise dome against a
brown-sugar desert. The dusty, meaty smell of wool carpets laid out
in the sun. The efficient grace with which Iranian women gripped the
edges of their chador—the head-to-toe Iranian veil—in their teeth,
freeing their hands for babies or shopping bags.

As a child trying to make the foreignness around her familiar, I
made crude attempts at cross-cultural understanding. At five, my
favorite game was "Iranian Ladies"—an American kid in Tehran's version of House—which I played wrapped in my child-sized chador. Six
years later, living in Kabul, I daydreamed of a stall, somewhere deep in
the bazaar, that might have sold Bubble Yum, Bonne Bell Lip Smackers,
and Levi's jeans, the items my eleven-year-old self most yearned for
from the United States. All my mental maps of the region were drawn
on a small, highly personalized scale. The Khyber Pass was the road
American teens took to the State Department orthodontist in Islam-
abad. Peshawar had a Chinese restaurant with delicious dumplings,
and a gold bazaar where they let you try on tiaras sparkling with real
rubies and emeralds.

Living in Kabul, I wasn't the only one with a myopic vision of the
region: during the 1970s, if Westerners gave Afghanistan any thought
at all, it was as an exotic playground for thrill seekers and eccentrics.
Hippies came in search of a finer grade of hash than Delhi's or Goa's.
Oxbridge classicists scoured the countryside for antiquities left by
Alexander the Great. My father arrived looking for Kashgai rugs, sweet
Bokhara melons, and the longest possible distance between himself
and the faculty lounge at the St. Louis University School of Law.

Despite his love for both Iran and Afghanistan, my father had an outlook on Islamic culture that was more orientalist than immersive, more an aesthetic appreciation than an acknowledgment of a living tradition. In his letters home, the faith appears only as the source of sumptuous mosques and shrines, peacock blue tiles, and prayer rugs. We hovered on the outskirts of society, oblivious to the formative events unfolding in the Middle East even as we lived there. From our balcony in Tehran we watched the Muharram processions, in which men flagellate themselves, sometimes with whips or chains, singing "Yo, Hussein," mourning the death of the Prophet's grandson at the Battle of Karbala. My parents had no idea that such energy, harnessed to hatred of the Shah's regime, would be strong enough to tow a revolution. Nor did they foresee that Islam would be a potent tool for Afghan fighters against the Soviet army. Or that it provided a framework for Egyptian discontent with its dictators.

Until 1979, Islam had been shriveling back into the private sphere, or so went Western conventional wisdom at the time. The future of the Middle East belonged to secular modernizers like the Shah or Saddam Hussein, sound men who'd buy our tanks and planes, who'd build roads and dams and, if not democracy, at least security. On New Year's Eve 1977, President Jimmy Carter had toasted the Shah, calling Iran "an island of stability" in a rough region. The future was Western, and secular. Islam was a pastime for village women, or wizened elders crouched in mosque courtyards.

It was only later that we began to realize how blinkered that vision had been. In the winter of 1979, the news carried pictures of grim women marching the streets of Tehran in black chadors. Scragglybearded men shouted "Yankee, go home." The same winter brought other images, equally shocking: the Shah and his wife, the Empress Farah, swathed in furs, on the tarmac at Tehran airport, leaving Iran for a "vacation" in Egypt, never to return. Two weeks later, an Air France jet brought home a hatchet-faced Ayatollah Khomeini, to an ecstatic welcome.

When we'd lived in Tehran, the Shah had seemed like a secular god, with his Peacock Throne and an impossibly beautiful empress, whose coronation crown had been bigger than any I had seen in my fairy-tale books. To me, the Shah felt all-powerful and all-seeing, with his cold, dark eyes staring out from portraits on the wall of every shop and bank. But then so had President Sadat when we'd lived in Egypt in 1979, the year he signed his peace treaty with Israel. Two years later, I was poring over images in *Time* magazine of a bullet-riddled reviewing stand and a president assassinated by a member of Islamic Jihad.

Even then, I felt vaguely ashamed that we'd been so clueless: our distance from the societies on which we'd perched seemed suspiciously close to a moral failing.

"How could you not have known?" I demanded, with all the self-righteousness of adolescence. We were back in St. Louis, and my parents and I were watching footage of the Iran hostage crisis on the six o'clock news. Onscreen, American diplomats, bound and blindfolded, were being paraded through the grounds of the American embassy, a place that I'd loved because the restaurant had Heinz ketchup and sugar packets on the tables.

I stared at my parents accusingly. "All this was going on, and we were there, and never knew?"

"Well, we did know something was rotten, below the surface," my mother replied gently. "All that building, and cash, and signage. But you had the feeling it was all just one block deep, and behind the beautiful façade, everything was terrible."

Back when we lived in Iran, there were rumors that the head of SAVAK, the Shah's secret police, was a student in my father's criminal justice class. The Shah's shadow even loomed over my mother's Shakespeare course. As a portrait of a weakened tyrant, *King Lear* proved a particularly tricky play to teach. Try as my mother might, she couldn't make her Iranian students understand why Cordelia wouldn't give her father Lear the flattery he demanded. Obedient subjects of the Shah, "King of Kings, Light of the Aryans," heirs to centuries of courtly obeisance, her class remained perplexed. Or perhaps, conscious of the rumors of on-campus SAVAK stooges, simply pretended to be.

While the Shah's dictatorship shaped the lives of ordinary Iranians, most of the West remained starstruck with his regime. The year we lived there, he threw what the Ayatollah Khomeini dubbed the "Devil's Festival," a party celebrating twenty-five-hundred years of the Persian monarchy. Party planners built walls hiding whole neighborhoods, lest the foreign dignitaries have to look on them. A florist flown in from Versailles coaxed a rose garden from a scorpion-infested desert at Persepolis. In air-conditioned tents, world leaders drank 1945 Château Lafite-Rothschild and ate roast peacock. The guests were dressed in clothes that could have been conjured in the fevered dreams of a five-year-old: even Haile Selassie's dog wore a diamond-studded collar.

For years before the Persepolis celebrations, both secular and religious critics of the regime had been preaching against this cult of Western-imported surfaces. Many were exiled, imprisoned, or hassled by SAVAK, but their words reverberated from exiles abroad and were circulated in banned pamphlets. In 1962, the Iranian writer Jalal Al-e-Ahmad clandestinely published *Gharbzadegi*, or *Plagued by the West*, an attack on the Iranian elite's obsession with aping the West. "A West-stricken man . . . is like a dust particle floating in space, or a straw floating on water," wrote Al-e-Ahmad. "He has severed his ties with the essence of society, culture, and custom."

Studying the history of the region only increased my sense that we'd been oblivious to the societies we had lived in. As individuals, we were hardly Ugly Americans. And yet, for all my parents' Farsi lessons and fascination with Iranian mosques and carpets, I realized we'd been part of what amounted to an American invasion of Iran in the 1970s. Though culturally sensitive, my mother and father were still members of the fifty-thousand-strong force of Americans brought to consult on pipelines and penal codes or to sell refrigerators or missiles—and to drive Iran along the road to Westernization.

Because we were American, the laws of the land couldn't touch us. I witnessed our inviolability one cold winter night when my family had arrived in Shiraz on a sightseeing trip. As my parents unloaded the bags from the taxi, they told me to watch out for my two-year-old brother. I didn't, at least not closely enough, and he waddled into the street, to be knocked down by a truck. He was fine, if stunned, but the incident drew a crowd, and a couple of policemen. My parents assured the officials that the fault lay not with the truck driver but with them, for thoughtlessly leaving a toddler in a five-year-old's charge. Still, the driver was hauled off to prison, for the simple reason that we were Americans. The Shah had signed an accord with Washington, known by Americans as the Status of Forces Treaty (SOFA) and by Iranians as the Capitulation Treaty, which gave Americans immunity on Iranian soil. My father spent the rest of the night at the police station, pleading for the driver to be released.

I thought no more of the incident until some two decades later, when my Farsi professor at Oxford had us translate one of the Ayatollah Khomeini's sermons. Dating from 1964, just after SOFA, it was the speech that would get the Ayatollah banished from Iran until the fall of the Shah. "If someone runs over a dog belonging to an American, he will be prosecuted," Khomeini noted. "But if an American cook runs over the Shah, the head of state, no one will have the right to interfere with him."

Other readings added troubling new dimensions to my memories. In college, like millions of other students in the 1980s, I became enamored of the works of the literary and cultural critic Edward Said. For centuries, he wrote, the Western vision of the East had been a fantasy—one that had more to do with Western fears and imperialism than it did with the societies themselves. In Said's view, Western depictions of Eastern cultures were pageantry, an extension of the very real political and economic subjugation of Asian and African peoples by European colonial powers. Studying the British Raj in India, I recognized my parents in rough outline in the descriptions of the sahibs who came to lay down Westminster's laws in Bengal, or the memsahibs who recreated Wiltshire gardens in the Punjab. With his grant from Washington to help codify Afghan constitutional law, my father wasn't part of a formal empire. Still, his presence in Kabul, along with that of many other Americans, hinted at the desultory Great Game played in Afghanistan between the Soviets and the Americans. Before the Russians finally invaded in 1979, it played out in tit-for-tat development projects. The Soviets built Kabul's airport; the Americans provided its communications and electronics. The Soviets hollowed out the Hindu Kush to make the Salang Pass; the Americans dug a dam in Helmand.

To be an American kid in Kabul was to be doubly childlike: high compound walls and Westerner-only clubs and commissaries preserved an imperial detachment from Afghan society. In many ways, my life in Kabul was more American than it was in St. Louis. We watched *Star Wars* on a Betamax, played tennis, and lived in a white two-story house with a dog and a yard. "Just like a Southern Californian split-level," my mother wrote, "if you squint hard enough!"

Like most British sahibs of the Raj, we had limited relationships with the locals. We were fond of our servants, and we exchanged pleasantries with the Supreme Court justices and ministry officials who occasionally came to dinner. But memories of my time in the region are curiously devoid of real friendships, or even extended conversation, with Afghans. With his good Farsi and his weekends spent with rug merchants, my father was, of the four of us, the closest to Afghan culture. Later, he would say that his years in Kabul were the happiest in his life.

In a way, his generation was the last to indulge in the orientalist fantasy of a distant, self-contained Islamic world. In the 1960s and 1970s, Westerners could just about convince themselves that Islam lay in lands far, far away, just as they had done since 1095, when the Crusaders rode off to wrest Jerusalem from the Saracens. Up until 1979, one could go to the East to find one's personal bliss in a hash bar or a Sufi lodge, or to forge a career building dams or roads or penal systems. Back then, before the Iranian Revolution, before the wars in Afghanistan, the Middle East and Central Asia remained in their place.

Today, the space between the United States and Afghanistan has shrunk to nothing at all: mothers in Milwaukee fret about foot patrols in Helmand. Kandahar is a household word, and Kabul a routine PR stop for presidents and generals. Migration, as well as war, has smudged the lines between the Muslim and non-Muslim worlds. There were

Muslims living in the West during my father's day, of course, just as they had for hundreds of years. But it wasn't until the 1960s and 1970s, when migrants from former European colonies began settling in the West and raising children, that there was a sense that Islam would remain a permanent presence there. In the eighties and nineties, the immigrants were joined by refugees from dictatorships and wars. To Paris and Peoria, Berlin and Los Angeles came Iranians on the wrong side of their revolution; Iraqis persecuted by Saddam Hussein; Libyans hoping to outrun Muammar Ghaddafi's secret services; and Algerians, Afghans, Somalians, and Sudanese fleeing civil wars. They raised children, built mosques, started lobbying and voting in their new countries. They bridged the distance between those two seemingly distinct spaces, "the Islamic world" and "the West."

For Edward Said and the postcolonial critics inspired by him, the West saw the Islamic world as static, peopled by types rather than living, breathing people. The epigraph to his seminal work, *Orientalism*, was a quote from Karl Marx: "They cannot represent themselves; they must be represented." Working as a journalist, there were moments when I saw this premise at work. In a story meeting, discussing how we should cover a horrific bombing in Israel, I suggested that we might want to get a Palestinian reaction as well as an Israeli one. "I think we know what they're thinking," snapped an editor. My first month at *Newsweek*, in 1995, I was sent to write a story on tensions between Christians and Muslims in inner-city Philadelphia. When I got there, I found peaceful coexistence, and reported accordingly. But right before we went to press, I found myself pleading with an editor not to run the headline screaming above the piece: "Jihad in the City." To his credit, the headline was changed.

Again and again, the categories we had used to describe Muslim groups collapsed on close scrutiny. The term "Taliban" has become synonymous with puritanical anti-Western fighters. But on a reporting trip to the Taliban's Kabul, I heard the foreign minister's press secretary rhapsodize, in excellent Italian, about the gardens of Rome, from his days studying archeology there. Another high-ranking Talib mused on the glories of Las Vegas: "An amazing place," he said. "But I lost ten dollars in the machines of Caesars Palace." The young Talib named Jang who was assigned to *Newsweek*'s photographer Nina and me as a guide was no terrifying zealot, but a terrified young boy, one who, we surmised, had never before spoken to women outside his family. He would chew on the ends of his turban cloth and blush if we laughed. "Dear sister," Jang would say, giggling. "I have never been with journalists before." Even our questions about mountains and street names seemed to embarrass him: once he even buried his head in his hands. "If you really want to scare him, you could touch him," suggested a middle-aged Afghan man. We never had the courage, and remained obligingly timid with him during our visit. In private, we called him "our Talib."

Knowing that stereotypes often crumbled when examined up close, I wrote feature stories on Islam, ones I hoped would serve as counterpoints to the Muslims who made the news pages. I covered innovative mosque designs, Islamic entrepreneurs, and hip Bay Area Muslims. Such pieces were well-meaning but superficial. I made snapshots of Muslim lives rather than considered portraits of them. The subtext was that these Muslims were just like Westerners, and my stories reminded me of those pages in the supermarket tabloids showing celebrities doing ordinary things, like carrying squirming toddlers or sipping lattes. Muslims buy stocks and shares, just like regular folks! They network! Work out! Guzzle energy drinks, so long as they're halal! These pieces were a break from the news parade of jihadis and burqaed women, but they still shuttled between the worn poles of Same and Different. They still took Western culture as the North Star, the guiding light around which every other culture must arrange itself. These articles were less about Islamic culture on its own terms than about the West and its obsessions.

To read the Quran was to shoulder a legacy, but also to shuck it off. What my father had begun—this need to connect with the foreign by pacing up and down Asia—I would continue. Except that my exploration would be conducted through a scripture, and a friendship. His journeys were taken in a world where exoticism still—only just— existed. Mine was to be an expedition for a connected, globalized world, a world in which the geographic distance between the Muslim world and the West was disappearing, where increasingly "Muslim" and "Western" were not diametrically opposed, but overlapped.

3

A Muslim in the West

When I tell people that I am studying with a Muslim scholar, the first thing non-Muslims usually want to know is what kind of Muslim scholar. "A moderate?" they'll ask. "Or a fundamentalist?" Or sometimes, "Is he liberal or conservative?" The terms vary; the subtext doesn't: Is he "one of us"? Or "one of them"? This is the language we are left with, after the trauma of recent decades. It's now too easy to slot people into the neat grooves worn by the media and the "clash of civilizations" crowd.

But how to characterize the Sheikh? Hours in the library with a stack of books on modern Islamic movements didn't help. Does his work on women scholars make him progressive? Do his calls to return to the Quran and traditions of the Prophet make him a reformist, or a neotraditionalist? Do his literal readings of the Quran on the flames of hell and the lush gardens of paradise make him a Salafi or a Wahhabi?

The more I studied with the Sheikh, the less helpful I found all the available labels, both Western and Muslim. What is the Sheikh, anyway? A traditionally trained scholar who scandalizes conservatives and disappoints progressives. And sometimes just the reverse. A champion of women's rights who accepts that Islam allows polygamy. A defender of individual conscience, but not Western-style individualism.

A champion of creative thought, so long as it's based on proper Islamic scholarship and classical sources. Think for yourselves, he counsels students, but don't change Islam's God-given Truth. "The Message," he cautions, "is the Message." He is traditional, yet is frequently criticized by others claiming to be traditional. He is a proponent of fundamentals who draws fire from fundamentalists. Every time I thought I'd found a term to describe him, the opposite also seemed to apply. To try to categorize the Sheikh was to flail.

As it turned out, flailing was entirely appropriate. I discovered this, to my relief, when I visited Tim Winter, a professor of Islamic studies at Cambridge University. Trying to fit Islamic thinkers into Western categories was a nonstarter, he told me. "Islam doesn't have a spectrum," said Winter, who also goes under his Muslim name, Abdal Hakim Murad. "There are Muslims who come from very literalist traditions who are massively pro-women. There are others who are very mystical, but also very political. Any combination is possible. The danger is always when you try to impose the idea that Christianity is the default religion."

I left Winter's office vowing to try to avoid rigid categories. I'd flail on.

Even Akram's fellow Muslims seemed to have a difficult time pinning him into the available categories. "He's very conservative, isn't he?" said an activist, after meeting him to discuss his work on Islamic scholars. No, indeed, he's very liberal, said the outraged Muslims who thought that his work on women meant he was championing unrestricted mixing between men and women.

When Akram first arrived at the Oxford Centre for Islamic Studies in 1991, the Centre's director "wanted to know my mind," he recalled. The director was a suave administrator with well-cut suits and a keen interest in fundraising, and so he administered what was, back then, the litmus test for Muslims. What, the director asked Akram, should be done about *The Satanic Verses*?

At the time, the Salman Rushdie controversy still roiled in mosques and the media. The Ayatollah Khomeini's fatwa, calling for the death of the novelist whose book he said insulted Islam, remained a very real threat to Rushdie. The novel dares to raise questions of the Quran's authenticity as the word of God, and it contains scenes depicting a brothel with whores who take the names of the Prophet Muhammad's wives. Muslims around the world saw the book as a slur on the Prophet Muhammad, his family, and the Quran.

The wounds were especially raw in Britain. The British Muslim community draws overwhelmingly from South Asia, a region where sensitivities about both the Quran and the Prophet Muhammad are particularly keenly felt. While Arabs can claim the Prophet Muhammad as a fellow Arab, and Arabic as a shared language of the Quran, subcontinental Muslims cannot, so defending the honor of the Prophet and the Quran can become a precious cultural totem. First- and second-generation South Asian Muslims were pained that Rushdie, a fellow Indian Muslim migrant, would turn on the most dearly held aspects of their Islamic culture to spin a bit of fiction. The Rushdie affair galvanized British Muslims as no issue had before, bringing bearded men in *shalwar kameezes* and karakul hats into Britain's streets and consciousness. They burned books, shook placards, hoisted ugly effigies of Rushdie wearing horns. The controversy was not just a lightning rod for the general discontents of a young and tender migrant community. It was also a blunt sorting tool for those who would seek to sort the world into "moderates" and "radicals"; into "us" and "them."

So it was hardly surprising that the Centre's director wondered what the young scholar, fresh out of madrasa, thought Muslims should do about Rushdie's work.

"Ignore it," replied the Sheikh.

In the fevered climate of 1991, suggesting a do-nothing strategy meant condemning oneself to a cultural no-man's-land. Camps had been established. Deep trenches had been dug, dividing the protectors of free speech and "Western" values from the defenders of the faith. "At that time, everyone thought we should protest," said Akram.

To suggest ignoring both the novel and the fatwa? How, exactly, would that work? What cultural team did this young madrasa grad play for?

Islam's, it turned out. Protesting, the Sheikh reasoned, would only hurt Muslims. The *Satanic Verses* firestorm didn't injure God or the Prophet, neither of whom needed defending. But it did great damage to the world's view of Islam. "When we did march and protest, no single person changed their mind about Islam," he said. Had British Muslims used the controversy to correct misconceptions and reach out to the wider British community, it might have done them some good, said the Sheikh. But burning books and complaining were a waste of time.

Besides, as a scholar, he didn't think much of the Ayatollah's fatwa. "It was a useless fatwa, of no benefit to Muslims," recalled the Sheikh. "It was more of a political fatwa than a real one. After the war with Iraq, Khomeini was not very liked in Muslim countries. This was just Khomeini trying to get back respect in the hearts of the Muslims."

When Akram recounted his unwillingness to engage in the *Satanic Verses* controversy, I was reminded of Cordelia, King Lear's daughter, who refused to produce a public display of love for her father. While her sisters proclaimed their devotion to Lear in loud and tinny voices, Cordelia merely said: "Nothing." Like Lear's youngest, Akram refused to join in the passion play of politicized emotion. He wouldn't play the part of the insecure migrant torn between cultures. He wouldn't agree to being one of those Muslim mummers featured on the news, vengeful and furious. As postcolonial storms raged in India and Britain, he sat watching. To those looking for a good show, a spectacular clash of civilizations, he said nothing.

Cordelia may have been the still and sane voice of morality in *Lear*, but boy, did she suffer for it. She was exiled, jailed, and by the end of the play, dead. Akram's independence had made him a target for criticism, too. In a post titled "Dr. Akram Nadwi's disastrous mistake!" one blogger ranted that Akram was "the epitome of the word controversy" and that he "seeks to undermine the sunnah by demeaning the practices of Islam." For a time, there was a blog called "Akram Nadwi's Strange Views," whose posts included discussions of the

Sheikh's attitudes on topics ranging from "Segregation" to "Wearing Pig Hide/Leather."

In one online chat room, I found someone calling him a Salafi, a proponent of the rigid, puritanical Islam now associated with fundamentalists and zealots who condemn anyone who deviates from their strict moral codes. (After the Arab Spring, a *New York Times* headline read "Don't Fear All Islamists, Fear Salafis.")

Somewhat nervously, I called to ask why people might be calling him a Salafi.

"Simply because I say we should come back to the Quran and the sunna of the Prophet," he replied mildly. "Salafis say this, too."

I nodded, thinking that I'd heard exactly the same back-to-basics call from Islamic feminists and progressives. Then again, I had also heard this repeated by jihadis, reformists, modernists, neotraditionalists, queer Muslims, dictators, democrats, and Marxist-Socialists. Regardless of the labels they choose or have chosen for them, Muslims agree on one thing, at least in theory: the primacy of the Quran and the hadith. "Anybody who claims legitimacy in an Islamic context ultimately has to root their discourse in the founding narrative," Tim Winter had reminded me. "It's the same with Christianity."

The Salafi label still intrigued me, though.

"So, uh, are you a Salafi?" I persisted.

"No," he answered. "I'm not this, I'm not that. I'm just Muslim."

In such a politically riven environment, he explained, it was hard to convince people that one is truly independent. "In the beginning, when I started lecturing, people thought 'everyone belongs to a group,'" he said. "Now, most people realize that I don't belong to one."

It was true that he'd shared platforms with a motley assortment of fellow Muslims, from psychiatrists and conservative Deobandis to Sufi mystics and female professors. Appearing onstage with women speakers had even landed him in trouble with various firebrands who suggested that the shared platform violated the tradition of keeping the sexes separate. No woman, they claimed, should address an assembly of men.

Most unnerving for some of his fellow Muslims have been the

times the Sheikh has pointed out practices that have nothing to do with Islam, but with habit or cultural tradition. When the Sheikh first came to Oxford and began giving sermons at his local mosque, he shocked the congregation with his views on prayer caps. Was it necessary, one man asked him, for men to wear prayer caps when they prayed? No, responded Akram. It was simply a South Asian custom, not an Islamic requirement at all. The congregation was nonplussed. To pray bareheaded? But their fathers had prayed in caps, and theirs before them! Outrageous.

Another controversial fatwa: the Sheikh's declaration that women could cut their hair short. Consternation. Did this endorsement of hair cutting mean the Sheikh was preaching Westernized thinking? Had he been swayed by fashion into forsaking Islamic doctrine? As it turned out, he had based his fatwa on a hadith that reported that after the Prophet died, his wives all cut their hair short. If short hair was good enough for the Prophet's widows, he reasoned, it was certainly permissible for the Muslims of today. "Some people think women shouldn't cut their hair short, because that is what Western women do," the Sheikh said. "They think I am a liberal. But really, I am just going back to the sunna of the Prophet."

For a time after the prayer cap controversy, the invitations to speak at mosques dried up, leaving the Sheikh without a place to teach. So he began giving lessons from his living room, starting at 6:30 in the morning. In time, usually accompanied by his daughter Hala, he began filling seminar rooms, and later mosques and auditoriums. Sometimes, the suspicions that he was a "liberal" meant that mosque officials would ask him to muffle his message. When he first went public with his work on women scholars, various men begged him not to publish. They didn't doubt his scholarship; they knew the sources he based his research on were authentic. But it would make them look bad, particularly in the eyes of the West. Sometimes when the Sheikh visited a mosque to deliver a speech, the mullah asked that he not mention some fatwa or other lest it upset the congregation. One mullah in the north of England asked the Sheikh not to mention his fatwa on the *niqab*, the veil that leaves just a slit for the eyes. In that mosque, most of the women wore it, he explained. Akram's opinion that *niqabs* are optional, not obligatory, might create a stir. Ever the polite guest, Akram complied.

If the Quran served as the spiritual and philosophical foundations for the Sheikh, the Prophet's life was a model for how he put them into daily practice. "Islam is not an idea," he told me one day via Skype. "It is a history."

A mere three sips into the first coffee of the morning, I was confused, and said so.

"Well, in other religions, such as Christianity, they emphasize abstract ideas, like closeness to God, and being a good neighbor, and loving one another."

"So aren't you concerned with these values, too, as a good Muslim?"

"Yes, of course, but we don't want spirituality to come through these big ideas. Christians are not so concerned about what Jesus did. They're not concerned with the details of the way he led his life. Our spirituality comes through doing the five prayers, as the Prophet Muhammad did. Or through giving charity, just as the Prophet did. We want the closeness to God through this history." Without the particulars of this history, Islam wouldn't be so very different from any other faith, the Sheikh observed.

Or even, I hazarded, from my own secular set of values.

"Yes, right! Because at the end of the day, every religion and creed calls for justice. Everybody knows you need to be nice to people. To give people justice and their rights, to do charity. You don't need Islam for this! Doesn't the United Nations have the same concerns? These ideas you can make from your own home!"

Islam anchored these universal human values in the history of the Prophet Muhammad. "This morality is not abstract," said Akram. "They are connected to the details of a history, the life of the Prophet Muhammad." Loyalty to that history—to the Prophet's sunna, or words and deeds—is what makes Muslims different from all the other humans striving to be good. Preserving the Prophet's sunna in everything one did, from brushing one's teeth to building a system of government, thus became a sacred act. "Islam has been revealed to the Prophet Muhammad, and he taught it to his Companions, and now it is a duty for us to transmit it to the next generation exactly as he transmitted it to them."

The caffeine had hit my bloodstream, and my deep-seated skepticism about there being a single history—of absolutely anything— spilled over.

"But surely, Sheikh, that history depends on who tells it? You of all people should know that. The history of women scholars, before you went back and found them, had been pretty much erased—probably because Islamic history had always been told by men."

"Yes, of course, you have to verify this history. You have to weigh it up, look at different reports. You have to look at the sources, and examine if there is any way to prefer one over the other one."

Then he had to hang up. He was sorry, but some visitors had come to see him. They'd come all the way from Boston, in America, and he didn't want to turn them away. There had been a bombing at a marathon, by two men claiming to act in the name of Islam. There was advice to be dispensed on how to respond.

By the standards of any era, the Prophet Muhammad's life was extraordinary. Born in AD 570 in Mecca, he was orphaned young in a society where family and clan were a person's only sources of protection. Penniless and parentless, he was raised by his grandfather and later by his uncle, growing into a striking man, with dark, intense eyes and long hair that he wore in two braids. As a young man, he worked as a simple shepherd in a town built on trade. His natural gravitas soon drew the attention of Khadija, a widow who was one of the wealthiest Meccan traders. She had heard of the bright young man known around Mecca as al-Sadiq al-Amin, the Trustworthy. She entrusted him to take a caravan to Syria, and later, despite being fifteen years his senior, married him.

One day when Muhammad was alone in a mountain cave near

Mecca, his habitual spot for spiritual contemplation, he suddenly heard a pronouncement by the Angel Gabriel: "Read!" Bewildered, the forty-year-old Muhammad asked what it was that he should read. "Read!" pressed the angel, embracing and squeezing the terrified man so tightly that he thought he would die. Muhammad protested that he was not a reader. After a second and third heart-stopping embrace, Muhammad stopped resisting and began to speak the words that crowded into his head:

> Read, in the name of your Lord, who created:
> created man of clotted blood.
> Read, for your Lord is most generous,
> the one who taught the use of the pen,
> taught man what he did not know. (96:1–5)

Terrified at the words tumbling out of his mouth, Muhammad assumed he was possessed by a jinn—an evil spirit. He rushed out of the cave and began climbing the jagged mountain, preparing to hurl himself off it in despair. On the precipice, he heard the voice of the angel again. "Oh, Muhammad," Gabriel said. "You are the Messenger of God."

After that first encounter, Muhammad would continue to receive revelations for the next twenty-three years, until his death in AD 632. The 6,236 verses of what would eventually become the Quran are by turns lush and harsh, poetic and prescriptive, intimate and majestic. Some verses came down unbidden, catching the Prophet while he was eating dinner or having his hair washed. Others arrived in response to a particular issue Muhammad or his community faced. Sometimes Gabriel would arrive at a public gathering, or appear while Muhammad was strolling in the desert. At times, a ringing bell announced the advent of the verses. Some messages descended in pictures, others in dreams.

None came to Muhammad easily. At times, he would burst into sweat from the strain. "Never once," he said, "did I receive a revelation without thinking that my soul had been torn away from me." After a verse descended, he would recite it aloud to his Companions,

the earliest Muslim converts. Some would memorize it, and the men
Muhammad had designated as scribes would set it down, preserving
the verses on palm leaves, scraps of wood or parchment, or the shoulder bones of camels.

Aside from his few Companions, the rest of Mecca wasn't nearly
so receptive. He was a madman, it was whispered in the souk. One of
those poets-for-hire or soothsayers who plied their trade on the caravan routes. He was pelted with garbage, with dirt. A sheep uterus. No
matter. He kept preaching.

The message he brought made him powerful enemies. Islam's concept of a single, all-powerful deity challenged Arabia's polytheists—
and Mecca's economy. Much of the town's wealth derived from the
hajj, the region's annual pilgrimage to the Kaaba, or the black granite
cube housing idols of the various gods worshipped by tribes. The idea
of a single omnipotent God overthrew the traditions of tribal gods—
and the 360 statues of them kept in the Kaaba.

Muhammad's social egalitarianism challenged prevailing social
hierarchies. Mecca's power brokers weren't keen on a man preaching
that all people are "as the teeth on a comb." Much like the first followers of Jesus, Muhammad's earliest Companions were often drawn
from the poor or disenfranchised sectors of society. To a tribal culture, Islam brought a radical new concept: a community based not
on family or clan, but on faith. No longer could wealth or bloodlines
protect you. Just piety.

The new faith introduced other forms of equality as well. Islam
didn't tolerate the Arab custom of burying girls at birth. Women were
no longer to be regarded as chattel, but as human beings with rights to
inherit property and to dispose of their own wealth as they saw fit. The
rich should give to the poor. All races were equal under God.

For twelve years after his first visit from the Angel Gabriel,
Muhammad stayed and preached in Mecca. But as opposition from
the town's powerful ruling Quraysh tribe grew, and as his Companions faced increasing persecution, the Prophet recognized that they
needed to emigrate, and he began dispatching them to Yathrib, 210
miles away.

In AD 622, on news that the Quraysh were plotting his murder, Muhammad himself joined the other Muslims in what was to become Medina, or "the City," short for "City of the Prophet." The move, known as the Hijra, or "migration," was so pivotal as to mark the start of the Muslim calendar. In Medina, Muhammad and his Companions were to build Islam's first mosque: a courtyard with a roof of palm fronds supported by trunks, surrounded by huts for Muhammad's family. It was there that his role as a spiritual leader expanded to include a political role as well. He became the de facto leader of a multifaith community, drawing up the Constitution of Medina, which outlined the rights and responsibilities of Medina's inhabitants, whether Muslim, pagan, or Jewish. It was a pact of mutual nonaggression, recognizing people's distinct affiliations yet guaranteeing justice for all. "To the Jew who follows us belongs help and equality. He shall not be wronged, nor shall his enemies be aided. The peace of the believers is indivisible." All disputes were to be settled by Muhammad. All clans would be allied to defend Medina from outsiders.

The years in Medina were marked by military clashes with the Meccans. Nine battles and eight years later, Muhammad rode into Mecca in triumph, without bloodshed. The Prophet's first act: to enter the Kaaba and smash the Arab idols in it with his staff. His final years were spent teaching and consolidating Islam as Arabia's preeminent religious and political force. In 632, not long before his death, he performed his final hajj, during which he addressed 144,000 pilgrims from a mountain outside of Mecca. A few months after his speech, he died.

Much like the Quran itself, Muhammad's life is so rich that one can find pretty much whatever one wants in it. People have ascribed any number of roles to the Prophet, revealing rather more about themselves than Muhammad: politician, diplomat, warrior, devoted family man, polygamist, human rights advocate, revolutionary. The Marxist Islamist Ali Shariati, preaching against the Shah's regime just before Iran's revolution, found a fellow traveler in Muhammad. Jihadists stress his wars; humanists stress his mercy when he won them. Those working for social justice cite his charity toward the poor; his generosity frequently left his own family hungry. Islamic feminists invoke him as a gender revolutionary, Islamist statesmen as a democrat and author of the world's first constitution.

Non-Muslims have handpicked from the Prophet's life to bolster their own polemics. The Enlightenment philosopher Voltaire used Muhammad in his arguments against clerical power and superstition, writing a play called *Mahomet, or Fanaticism*. The nineteenth-century writer Thomas Carlyle considered him a hero. Others were less complimentary, their slurs against the Muslim prophet tending to fall into one of three camps: clerical, sexual, or military. From the eighth century onward, Christian writers, defensive about this young upstart faith, denounced Muhammad as an impostor, a liar, a Christian heretic, or a magician, intent on undermining the Church. Sex provided another preoccupation of hostile Western orientalists, starting with the medieval Christians. Learning of the Prophet's polygamy, they vigorously applied themselves to attributing all sorts of perversions to the Muslim prophet. Medieval Europe's obsession with Muhammad as a warrior grew during the Crusades, providing useful propaganda for societies embarking on holy wars to wrest Jerusalem from the clutches of the Saracens. The image of a faith built on military conquest endured long after Jerusalem fell: in 1744, George Sale, who produced the first English translation of the Quran, would write that "Mohammadanism was no other than a human invention, [which] owes its progress and establishment almost entirely to the sword." Today's image of Islam as a faith of terrorists fits neatly into the tradition of Crusader tales.

In truth, the nine battles Muhammad fought were mere skirmishes. In the Prophet's great victory against his enemies in Mecca, the Muslims lost fourteen men, and Meccan casualties numbered just seventy. In the Prophet's great defeat, only sixty-five Muslims died. Centuries of polemic, however, mean the Western obsession with the Islamic sword continues to this day. Aided and abetted by the actions of jihadis, the old images endure. Media headlines and online computer games invoke "the Sword of Islam." Cartoonists have drawn Muhammad brandishing scimitars, and with a ticking time bomb for a turban.

The Prophet Muhammad became a target for polemicists almost from the moment he began receiving his revelations. For a revolutionary, that was just part of the job. "Prophets," the Sheikh once observed, "must be prepared to be hated, as they love to be loved." But in Muhammad's case in particular, all this mythmaking stood in stark contrast to the details of his life, set down with reverent obsessiveness in classical Islamic sources. In the history of the world, no major prophet has had his life recorded so closely as the Prophet Muhammad. After the Prophet's death, his Companions—a lovely term, more democratic than "Disciples" and friendlier than "Followers"—recorded every detail of his words and deeds that they could remember. These details were assembled into collections of hadith, which gathered together are seen as Muhammad's sunna, or practice. Hadith collections contain information on everything, including the way the Prophet used to eat, make love, wash, and praise his Lord. For a snapshot of hadith's wide horizon, I opened one of Akram's books on jurisprudence. Here's a chunk from the index of hadiths, picked at random:

> The Prophet once prayed a funeral salah and then went to the grave
> of the deceased and threw three handfuls of soil from near the
> deceased's head
>
> The Prophet ordered that masjids built in the houses must be
> cleaned and perfumed
>
> The Prophet ordered the martyrs of the Battle of Uhud to be
> buried in their bloodstained clothes
>
> The Prophet ordered the mu'adhdhin [the callers to prayer] to say:
> "Pray in your places," on a cold, raining night

Here, in four random moments from the Prophet's life, lie the roots of Islamic law on burial, mosque maintenance, and the leeway to pray at home instead of the mosque in stormy weather. "The Quran is guidance, it's not laws," Akram once told me. "It gives you the direction.

Like if you want to go from here to London, it's basically south. The Prophet comes and gives the main roads to make it easier." Muhammad's wife Aisha called him "the Quran walking." For Muslims, his life mapped out Quranic values on a human scale.

In daily life, the Sheikh would try to follow the Prophet's example in scores of ways. Whenever he walked into the kitchen, he placed his right foot first, as the Prophet used to. He would eat breakfast with his right hand, just like the Prophet, and comb the right side of his hair first. Before using the toilet, he would utter the Prophet's customary prayer: "Oh, Allah! I seek refuge with you from all evil and evildoers." There was a prayer, too, on leaving the toilet, just as there was one on leaving the house. His observance of the Prophet's sunna spread beyond mere habit and into manners. He didn't ever want to keep his guests waiting, because the Prophet never did. Since the Prophet always used to go to the mosque after returning from a journey, so as not to take his family by surprise, the Sheikh made sure to phone his own family to tell them he was coming home.

Following the way of the Prophet, Akram once counseled, "makes life so much easier." Take social gatherings, he ventured. Suppose you're serving guests some water. Do you start with the more important guests? The elders or the kids? Easy, he responded: start from the right, since that's what the Prophet did.

As a youth, Akram had begun a lifelong effort to emulate the Prophet, not just in habits and manners, but in character. Because the Prophet had counseled his Companions "to do things gently and softly," Akram tried to do the same. "When I was young, I made an effort to control my anger," he said. It worked. "Now, to become angry is an effort with me!"

The Muslim men who make the headlines tend to focus on the Prophet as a political leader. Not the Sheikh. For him, Muhammad was primarily a teacher about the fires of hell and how to avoid them. "The Prophet is not calling people to get power, or to establish an Islamic government," he said. "He's teaching them one thing: to fol-

low the plan of their Creator and to save people from the fire of hell."
Unsurprisingly, for a man who often gives eight-hour seminars,
Akram was keenly attuned to Muhammad as someone who would
try, over and over, to explain his message. "He never forced people to
believe anything," Akram told me. "Anybody who forces people to
change their beliefs, they are not a teacher. Learning should come
from understanding properly, not from being forced."

Once, I asked Akram what it was he most admired about the
Prophet. He thought for a moment, and then said quietly, "That he
knew his limits." He knew his limits as a husband, not presuming to
dictate to his wives how to behave. He also knew his limits on what
lay in other people's hearts. A well-known anecdote tells how, during
a battle against a non-Muslim tribe, a Companion killed a man who—
just as the blade fell—had pronounced the *shahada*, "There is no God
but God, and Muhammad is His Prophet." The Companion thought
the deathbed conversion was insincere, but the Prophet Muhammad
refused to presume. "Did you split open his heart?" he demanded of
the Companion. Only God truly knew what lay inside it.

Akram showed a similar reluctance to pass judgment. David
Damrel, who shared an office with him at the Centre, recalled the phone
ringing one day with a frantic parent on the line seeking advice from
the Sheikh. Their unmarried daughter had revealed she was pregnant.
What should they do? Sex outside marriage was denounced as a major
sin in the Quran. "Akram's answer surprised me,'" said Damrel. "He
told them, 'This poor woman has already sinned, so there will be consequences in the afterlife.'" But on earth, in this life, a parent's role was
to ease her way. "He told them to help and support her," recalled Damrel,
"and not to judge her in this world."

Hearing this anecdote, I suddenly glimpsed the narrowness of my
own vision of broad-mindedness. In my creed, sex, drugs, rock and
roll, and any number of other explorations were fine, so long as nobody
got hurt. Such tolerance derived from the assumption that this life is
all we have, and that every individual has freedom. Akram's tolerance
came from a belief in just the opposite: in a God-centered universe,
nobody has freedom, and nobody has the right to judge others. That is

God's job. The Quran is not merely a guide, but a means to broaden the mind. "Don't look at this tiny world," he suggested. "Things are much bigger than you can imagine. There's a past beyond your past, and a future beyond your future."

Akram's awareness of his own limits guided his life. Given his status in the British Muslim community, it would have been easy to overstep them. At the mosque and his lectures, Akram was asked to pronounce on issues from paradise to hair dye. Before I watched him at work, I assumed that a sheikh served fellow Muslims much as local Irish or Italian priests once served their flocks: as moral guides who occasionally crossed over into pronouncing on social or political affairs. Sometimes, the Sheikh did serve as a sort of father confessor. But only God, not one's fellow humans, could pass judgment. An *alim*'s role was to make life easier for people, not harder: "If a person is going to repent, that's enough, really."

But the engaged Islamic scholar does far more than the parish priest. In Akram's case, it was as though an Ivy League professor moonlit as an advice columnist while serving as an attorney. In his spare time, he wrote scores of books on Islamic theology, Arabic grammar textbooks, biographies of great men, memoirs, philosophy, and even literary criticism.

He'd stop writing in the evenings, when visitors often rang his doorbell or his cell phone seeking advice. Young newlyweds, worried that mortgages violated Islamic bans on interest-bearing loans. Bereaved families observing burial rites. Businessmen, drawing up their wills, asking for guidelines on inheritance law. Fractious couples demanding divorces. (He found his work as marriage counselor particularly satisfying, said his daughter Sumaiya: "He's generally very happy when he's managed to get two people together again.")

Such work drew on his natural kindness, and his cultivated *sabr*—patience. There was the woman who kept phoning—sometimes every ten minutes or so—worried she was not a good Muslim. The very fact that she was concerned, he told her gently, proved she was. He listened to lonely widows and divorcées desperate for husbands for companionship and sex. On occasion, he even made house calls, as when a spooked homeowner asked him to check that his house didn't have jinns (supernatural creatures). "Just call me," he chuckled. "The jinn will run away!"

Much to my frustration, as a journalist trying to create a portrait of him, the Sheikh was a studiously reserved man. In this, he was consciously following in the steps of the Prophet Muhammad. He was also sidestepping the conventions of the confession culture promoted in pretty much every corner of Western civilization, from the couches of Upper West Side psychoanalysts to the pages of Proust. For Akram, serving up one's loves, hates, predilections, and memories in public was alien, if not downright vulgar. "When Muhammad began preaching in seventh-century Arabia, he did not call people to his religion by talking about himself, or about his childhood traumas!" he once exclaimed. Indeed, despite the exhaustive cataloguing of the Prophet's words and deeds, there's scant information on his inner life, in the modern sense of the term. "We sense very little of his own thoughts or inner turmoil," writes the historian Jonathan A. C. Brown. "Even when his infant son Ibrahim dies and the Prophet sheds tears, his Companions react with surprise. He has to explain to them that he also grieves at such a loss."

Akram, too, had lost a son, a baby who'd died back in India. "It was the one time I'd seen the Sheikh sort of tear up," recalled Damrel. "But still, even so, his focus was on the afterlife." Once, years after the death, I marshaled the courage to ask him about it. I received the briefest of responses. Characteristically, the Sheikh talked not about grief, but about God: "He sends us these issues," he said, "to test us." To the student who raised his hand and asked how to deal with tragedies like a child dying, the Sheikh advised him to follow the Prophet's sunna. "If your son dies, you can weep, but you cannot make noise." When his child Ibrahim died, the Prophet wept, but the tears were silent, and he cautioned Muslims against ripping their clothes or wailing loudly, as the pagan Arabs did.

Most Muslims feel love for the Prophet, but Akram's vast knowledge of hadith tied him to Muhammad particularly tightly. Akram was bound to Muhammad by a heavy set of intellectual chains. For this is what a hadith is: a chain of narration linking people through knowledge of the Prophet Muhammad, down through the generations. The *isnad*, or chain of hadith, is a sort of holy game of telephone stretching across the centuries from the Prophet to the present. Akram has scores of these chains coiled in his memory. His strongest *isnad*—since it is the shortest, with the fewest links connecting him to Imam Bukhari, the great ninth-century compiler of hadith—has just fourteen people in it. At one of our meetings—which happened to be in a kebab house in Oxford, where a CD player blared an Iranian singer warbling of lost love—he recited the chain of names:

My teacher Muhammad b. Abd al-Razzaq al-Khatib informed me,
and Abu al-Nasr al-Khatib informed him,
and Abdullah al-Talli al-Shami informed him,
and Abd al-Ghani al-Nabulusi informed him,
and Najm al-Din Muhammad al-Ghazzi informed him
and Badr al-Din Muhammad al-Ghazzi informed him,
and Abu al-Fath Muhammad b. Abi al-Hasan al-Iskandari informed
    him,
and Aisha bint Ibn Abd al-Hadi informed him,
and Abu al-Abbas Ahmad b. Abi Talib al-Hajjar informed her,
and Abu Abdillah al-Husayn b. al-Mubarak al-Zabidi informed him,
and Abu al-Waqt 'Abd al-Awwal b. Isa al-Harawi al-Sijzi informed him,
and Abu al-Hasan Abd al-Rahman b. Muhammad b. al-Muzaffar al-
    Dawudi informed him,
and Abu Muhammad Abdullah b. Hammuyah al-Sarakhsi informed
    him,
and Abu Abdillah Muhammad b. Yusuf b. Matar al-Firabri informed
    him,
who was informed by Imam Muhammad b. Ismail al-Bukhari.

Once, he dazzled a group of students by reciting a chain of narrators all the way back to the Prophet. Sometimes, out to dinner with important donors to the Centre for Islamic Studies, he'd oblige the director by reciting a chain or two for them. Invariably, they'd beg for more. "People become so amazed, really," he said. "Nobody does this anymore."

Proof of Akram's reach lies in his collection of *ijazas*, diplomas issued by an Islamic scholar or Sufi sheikh. If a sheikh gives you his *ijaza* in a book or subject, you are certified to teach it to someone else. If you've got one, you're in an *isnad* linking you to your teacher, and then to your teacher's teacher, all the way back to the book's original author. More generally, it has come to mean an endorsement, a sort of letter of recommendation. Akram's *ijaza* collection now stands at over five hundred, a number that grows every year. Once, when I went on vacation in Syria, Akram asked me whether I could pick up an *ijaza* from the city's head mufti, or sharia law expert, much as a baseball fan would ask a friend to score a Yankees cap from Manhattan. I duly went to the mufti's office in Damascus and presented him with a letter of introduction from Akram. I sipped tea in his study as he wrote out the *ijaza* and then asked me to take a photo of him behind his desk. "It was lucky you got it for me," Akram noted when we were reminiscing about it. "He died soon afterward."

Whenever I travel to South Asia or the Middle East, I try to remember to ask him whether he needs an *ijaza*. "I don't need one from Delhi," he said, on a recent venture. "But Jaipur . . . let me see if there's anyone there . . ."

The Prophet Muhammad was often far more flexible than the legal scholars who followed him and developed *fiqh*, the Sheikh assured me.

"For example, if someone has [sexual] relations in the daytime during Ramadan, then in Islamic law, you have to free a slave," Akram explained. "If you don't have a slave to free, then you have to fast continuously. If you can't do that, then you have to feed sixty people."

I nodded. The law itself wasn't familiar, but the severity and specificity of the punishment for transgression chimed with the popular image of a stern sharia law.

"So a gentleman came to the Prophet during the month of Ramadan, and he said to him, 'I must destroy myself, I must kill myself.'

When the Prophet asked why, the man explained," said Akram: "'I came home, and my wife had nice jewelry on, nice ornaments, and I couldn't control myself. I had relations with her. And now I don't know what to do.' So the Prophet said, 'Okay, do you have a slave to free?'"

The man didn't own a slave.

"So the Prophet said, 'Well, then you must fast continuously.' And the man says, 'Well, in just one day fasting, this happened! What would happen if I were to fast continuously?' So the Prophet says, 'Well, then you have to feed sixty people.'"

The man didn't have food for sixty people.

"So the Prophet said, 'Okay, stay here,'" continued Akram. "Luckily, somebody had brought the charity of a gift, enough to feed sixty people. So the Prophet came back and said, 'Here, give to the people.' And the man said, 'In the whole of Medina, there's no house poorer than my house. Nobody is worse off than me.'"

Here the Sheikh cracked into a wide smile, slapped his thigh, and shook with laughter.

"And so the Prophet said, 'Okay, so go and eat.'"

As so often happened when he spoke of the Prophet, the Sheikh's description was vivid and intimate, as though Muhammad were an esteemed living relative, not a man dead fourteen hundred years.

The problem, continued the Sheikh, when he'd stopped chuckling, is that law had hardened into a career. Being a mufti, or legal expert, kept you from going back to the essence of the faith. Like any prestigious profession with its own benchmarks for excellence, work as a mufti is hobbled by convention or precedent. The Sheikh was determined to avoid the stifling effect of the so-called four schools of thought—Maliki, Hanbali, Shafi, and Hanafi, each named after the jurist who founded it. These legal structures, which range from the relatively broad-minded Hanafi school, which dominates in South Asia, to the stricter Hanbali school, common to Arabia—have frequently encouraged divisions in the Muslim community and distracted people with niggling differences of opinion. Too often, *fiqh* simply required one to agree or disagree with earlier scholars, he held, not explore other possibilities. "Once you have a system, you have to think inside it. That's true in medicine, like where drug companies don't want people to look into homeopathy. And it's true in Islam, where the expansion of *fiqh* is preventing people from going back to the Quran and the sunna of the Prophet."

I had a sudden, bizarre image of Akram in a Bay Area coffee shop, with beads, long hair, and a Berkeley PhD. If you closed your eyes and just listened to him railing against the systems, he would fit right in.

There was a kind of machismo associated with laws that hadith didn't possess. "Lots of Muslims think *fiqh* makes you strong," he said, making fists and curving his arms like a circus strongman. "But all these rules lead to extremism, while the Quran, and the Prophet's sunna, want to teach people to be moderate."

He paused. "The more I read it, and the more I think about it, I am increasingly convinced that the only way is to come back to the Quran, and to the hadith." His brow unfurrowed slightly. Differences of opinion on such matters were understandable, he said. Rules laid out clearly in the Quran and sunna must be followed, but as for the raft of issues where jurists disagree, one was free to make one's own choice. "There are so many differences among the Muslim community," he concluded, "and still we survive."

Indeed, it's arguable that the differences within the *umma* have helped Islam to thrive. The simplicity of its basic tenets meant it spread from Arabia to Asia within decades of its birth. Islam's suppleness is one reason the faith is flourishing everywhere from rural Africa to Brooklyn brownstones. But this flexibility has come with a price, for it means that practices not associated with the faith are often bolted onto it, welded into what's considered "Islamic." When I asked Akram about why practices like female genital mutilation are so widespread in Islamic communities in Africa, he observed that Islam allowed local customs so long as they didn't contravene it. "Of course, if these practices hurt people, that's another matter," he added.

Akram had grown up steeped both in his village culture and in his faith. At times, I envied him. He had never been to the movies, and had never had a Hindu friend. But over the course of our yearlong journey, I began to suspect that he was rather more cosmopolitan than I ever would be. His *taqwa*, or God-fearingness, and profound knowledge of his Indian Muslim heritage weren't necessarily blinkers, but anchors. My own identity, both cultural and religious, was a patchwork. When he fretted over how Islam had become mere identity for many Muslims, a matter of clannishness and fashion rather than piety, I recognized myself, only more so. It's just that my identity hinged not on purity or unity, but on its mongrel qualities. As a secular cosmopolitan, I had roots everywhere and nowhere: a Midwesterner with Middle Eastern experience, now married to a British husband, raising kids with Anglo-American outlooks.

As his reputation in Britain has grown, Akram has attracted many ardent students, men and women who get up on weekends to catch 6:00 a.m. trains, or who gather in carpools in gray British dawns to drive the length of the island to hear him talk. In the early years, when students came in ones and twos, he taught from his living room in Oxford, often starting right after dawn prayers. By the time I began studying with him, he could fill an auditorium. On weekends, his Magnificent Journey lectures, a series on the Quran held in Cambridge, were not just eight-hour lectures, but family outings. Mothers dandled babies. Weather permitting, boys played cricket outside. Three pounds bought you a *biryani* or baguette at lunchtime, and there were always tables set up with cookies and tea, one at the ladies' entrance, and the other at the men's. (I'd blithely ignored the distinction at the first lecture. Having seen Akram's brother Muzzammil waiting in line for tea, I had bounced up to him to talk. I'd reached the front of the tea line and was just reaching out for a cup when a smiling man pointed out the line across the hall. "That's for the Sisters," he said.)

These students of the Sheikh's, who referred to one another as "Sisters" and "Brothers," possessed a marked sweetness and seriousness of purpose. There was the young optometrist who'd told her boss in no uncertain terms that she wouldn't be at work on Magnificent Journey

Saturdays. Another woman, Samina, who drove hours from Hertford-shire, regularly dispensed M&M's among the Sisters to help them keep up their strength. Before prayer times, when the lecture hall's bath-room was crowded with women doing *wudu*, or ritual ablutions, the atmosphere had a purposeful conviviality, as women crowded to wash their feet and faces in the institutional sinks. I applied lipstick as they did *wudu*, and I phoned home to check in during prayers, but my fellow students didn't seem to mind that there was a non-Muslim in the class. Quite the contrary: they were curious about the book I was writing, and eager to share their thoughts on the Sheikh.

One Saturday, I met three sisters, none of whom wanted to give their names, but all of whom wanted to explain why Akram's Islamic lectures were so different from any others they'd attended. While many of the ulama refused to take questions from the audience, the Sheikh welcomed them. "His message is a lot more positive, and a lot more spiritual, than the sort of things we grew up on," said one. A petite woman in her thirties, she'd not had time to attend Islamic lectures since her kids were born. Back in the 1990s, she'd found the vibe on the Muslim lecture circuit to be far angrier than the Sheikh's. "There was all this negativity, as though people were trying to push an ideology," she said. "There was this whole judgmental tone. Lots of paranoia. It was 'them' and 'us.' They told us we shouldn't integrate. They'd talk about the jihad and the *kafir*"—the nonbelievers.

The bunker mentality was alienating, and she knew it was a dis-tortion, but back then, "I was very new to it all, so I didn't have the confidence to speak up." Her children would, she hoped. She had just managed to persuade her husband, a cricket fan, to forgo his Saturday games so that the whole family could attend the Sheikh's seminars.

The crowd the Sheikh attracted tended to be a lot like the three sisters: young, well-educated, British-born, and yearning for freedom from the cultural baggage their parents or grandparents brought from the Old Country. His students wanted to learn about Islam based on texts, rather than the customs of the Punjab or Gujarat. They were keen to separate "culture" from the sharia itself. "Culture" was what I kept hearing whenever anyone referred to any practice that had crept in over time and ossified to religious law. Female genital mutilation; caps for prayer; purdah, or the traditional seclusion of women from public view—I'd heard all those things dismissed as "culture, not Islam."

I met two of Akram's star students for tea and cakes one day. Arzoo Ahmed and Mehrunisha Suleman, or Mehrun for short, were both in their twenties; they began attending his classes on weekends in 2005 and never left. Their expertise had soon reached the level where they would be taking madrasa-level exams, which the Sheikh said would make them *alima*, or women scholars, themselves.

Both women were gifted students in secular curriculums as well. Mehrun held a physiology degree from Cambridge, a master's in global health sciences from Oxford, and was pursuing a PhD in the ethics of clinical research. Arzoo had earned two Oxford degrees: one in physics, and a second in medieval Arabic thought. They shared a flat in Oxford, as well as an infectious warmth and articulate confidence. When I met them for tea and cakes in the Ashmolean Museum, they bubbled with an earnest excitement about the Sheikh. "He's a gem," pronounced Arzoo. When I mentioned I had first met him in 1991, her bright eyes widened, and a grin lit her pretty, round face. "You're so lucky!" she sighed. "How amazing!"

The Sheikh's teaching style had evolved over the years they had been studying with him. During his earlier classes, in London, he'd teach very much in the old-school madrasa mode: he'd read the hadith aloud in Arabic and explain a few terms. In a class on *fiqh*, he'd go over the juristic work of the scholars in great detail, explaining the reasoning behind the scholars' fatwas.

"They were quite entertaining, those classes," mused Arzoo. "With the boys asking hilarious questions," added Mehrun.

There were many wacky questions on the issue of *wudu*, or ritual ablution before prayers. "Like, 'When you're in water, in the sea, and it's prayer time, how do you do *wudu*?'" offered Mehrun, shaking her head slowly, smiling. "'Like, 'Do you have to get out and jump in again to do the ablutions?' It was hilarious."

"But he'd never say, 'What a stupid question,'" ventured Arzoo.

The "What if?" crowd gradually stopped coming as the lessons got longer. But after two years, the tenor of the classes changed. The Sheikh walked into the class the first day after summer break and said, "We're not going to focus on reading the book, we're not even going to focus on finishing the chapter," recalled Arzoo. "I'm going to go through this book, and explain why the hadith is written the way it is, why the hadith are put in a particular order."

The new approach allowed the students to scrutinize their tradition afresh. "You can't find this kind of discussion anywhere," said Arzoo. "Not in a textbook, not in a madrasa."

"We were just blown away," added Mehrun. "That he thought he could trust us to reach that level of knowledge." When they tackled Bukhari, one of the six great books of hadith, the Sheikh diverged from simply studying the words and deeds of the Prophet, said Mehrun, and pressed the class to discover the intricate construction of the work itself. The questions he posed about the texts—Why was this scholar included? Why was that hadith excluded?—reminded me of my undergraduate literature classes in deconstruction.

The Sheikh was teaching differently not only from his earlier classes, but from his own training. He threw out all the methods he'd been taught at Nadwah, and instead pressed for fresh thinking. "He keeps emphasizing, 'I want to teach the tools of learning, so that you can learn to think for yourselves, and actually come up with these new findings for yourselves," said Arzoo. "He said, 'I can't teach you everything, but I can teach you how to think, and if I know that you are at the stage where you can reason through your arguments, and use the sources correctly, then you will have to go away and discover for yourself all the things that I haven't taught you."

Islam's critics frequently argue that the faith stifles thinking. Such critiques grew particularly loud during the *Satanic Verses* controversy, after the Ayatollah Khomeini's fatwa against Salman Rushdie. The British writer Fay Weldon wrote that the Quran, in contrast to the Bible, offers "food for no thought. It is not a poem on which a society can be safely or sensibly based. It forbids change, interpretation, self-knowledge, even art, for fear of treading on Allah's creative toes."

And yet the Prophet Muhammad was careful to tell his Companions that blind faith, without thought or action, wasn't enough. In a famous anecdote, Muhammad came across a Bedouin walking away from his camel, having neglected to tie it up. When he asked the man why he didn't secure the beast, the man said, "I put my trust in Allah." Muhammad's response was pithy: "Tie your camel first, then put your trust in Allah."

To follow blindly, the Sheikh told his students again and again, went against Islam's spirit. Muslims had to think for themselves even as they submitted to one truth, to one eternal message. He encouraged his students to think differently from him—as long as they tethered their arguments to the classical sources. At times, he shocked some of the less flexible scholars by suggesting that Muslims should bypass Islam's four schools of law and go straight back to the Quran and the Prophet's sunna, or example. He had even supplemented his exhaustive knowledge of the Islamic sources by a broad, if eclectic selection of Western books, from nineteenth-century British orientalists to Nietzsche and Sartre.

But then, Akram's own life was a deft shuttle between tradition and exploration. Though he'd grown up in an Indo-Islamic culture, he'd made his name teaching British Muslims. While he was raised in a house with strict gender segregation, he produced historical research that undermined that very tradition. Only when I followed him back to India, to his ancestral village and his alma mater, did I start to see how his faith had anchored him even while propelling him out into the world.

4

Road Trip to the Indian Madrasa

If the Sheikh believed that a return to original sources was central to understanding Islam, I hoped that a return to his origins would help me understand the Sheikh. To see how a village boy from Uttar Pradesh had grown into an Oxford *alim*, I shadowed the Sheikh when he returned to his ancestral village and his beloved Lucknow. When I'd asked whether I could come along on his trip, he agreed, as long as I could cope with what he termed "Eastern toilets" and would deliver a speech at the madrasa he had built in his hometown of Jamdahan.

I made my way to India, landing a few days after Akram's arrival. The day before my trip from Lucknow to his village, Akram reminded me at least three times not to miss the 8:45 a.m. Doon Express, en route from Dehradun. There was one train that day that stopped at Lucknow before heading near the village of Jamdahan, and the Doon Express was it. To miss the train would be to miss the Sheikh's first trip back to his childhood home from England for four years. To miss it would mean skipping the chance to meet his parents and to see the fields where his grandparents had farmed barley and sugar cane, just as their ancestors had under the British, and before them, under the Mughals.

So I made sure to catch the Doon Express, and the seven hours on it passed quickly, not least because I had the sheer pleasure of saying that I was on the train from Dehradun—a sentence redolent of Rudyard Kipling, or a Bing Crosby–Bob Hope road movie. Curled up on the bottom bunk of a sleeper car, I watched Uttar Pradesh through a window so dirty that the green fields looked grainy and sepia-tinted, like a nineteenth-century daguerreotype. Halfway through the trip, I forced myself upright and onto my iPad: I had a speech to write. When I'd asked Akram what the topic should be, he'd been unhelpfully vague: "Just say how happy you are to be there."

Indian trains are ferociously social places, so I wrote slowly. The porter wanted to chat: he was a fan of Manchester United, or at least of saying the phrase "Manchester United." The partridge-plump matron in the opposite bunk admired my bracelet, clicking photos on her phone to show her jeweler. Every stop brought a parade of men with tin trays, offering chai and fried snacks.

The trip had a poetic symmetry to it. A day's travel across a stretch of the subcontinent to see a sheikh was just the sort of journey Akram and I had been researching when we first met. In Oxford, our days were spent following the intellectual and geographical paths of South Asian scholars. We'd hunch over histories and biographical dictionaries, sketching links between men and towns, between scholars and mosques, between mosques and madrasas. Islam arrived in South Asia in the early seventh century, brought by an army of Arabians under the command of a seventeen-year-old general, Muhammad bin Qasim. Later, it spread through trade, traveling scholars, and Sufi mystics. For the two years I worked on the team with the Sheikh, my job was to scan nineteenth-century British records of South Asia for mentions of any sheikh or saint, mosque or Sufi shrine. Months plowing through page after brittle, yellowed page of the *Archaeological Surveys of British India* proved that the Oxbridge men sent to rule the subcontinent were nothing if not thorough. Duty, a Victorian zeal for classification, and sometimes genuine enthusiasm for India meant that these colonial officers missed nothing. They detailed every caste and subcaste of Indians, noted even the dinkiest Punjabi hamlet and the farthest-flung Himalayan hill town. Soon, the walls of the Atlas

Room hung with maps covered in spidery webs of connections. They traced the travels of sheikhs' disciples who had fanned out across the region, building madrasas and mosques of their own. On the maps, red arrows swooped across the Indian Ocean, showing how Arab traders had sailed over to buy spices and silks, bringing the new faith with them. They showed the routes of Indian scholars who went west to study with the great sheikhs of Baghdad, Cairo, and Damascus, and who went north to Samarkand and Bukhara. Many would eventually circle back to their hometowns, setting up madrasas to teach local youths what they'd learned in the big city.

With the money he earned in Oxford, Akram would continue that tradition, building two madrasas in his village, one for boys and one for girls. The Sheikh had been the first person in Jamdahan's history to make it to Lucknow's prestigious Nadwat al-Ulama, and he wanted to prepare local boys to follow him there. In six years, his madrasa had sent twelve students to Nadwah, impressive for a remote village of thirty-five hundred. The pass rate helped put Jamdahan on the map. "When I first went to Lucknow, I used to have to tell people I was from Jaunpur"—the nearest city, he told me. "Now, I can say I'm from Jamdahan."

I juddered along toward Jamdahan, munching on a soggy *samosa* from the lady who liked my bracelet. I wondered what to say in my speech, beyond the obvious theme about the importance of mutual cultural understanding. It felt a trifle presumptuous, lecturing Indians on blending cultures and tolerating disparate faiths. The South Asian zealots who call for an India ruled by "Hindu" values, or for a "pure" Islam, ignore the subcontinent's long history of cultural mix. Central Asians, Arabs, Portuguese, French, Dutch, and British—all came to trade and rule, and India managed to find room enough for all of their cultural influences. During its more confident periods, South Asian Islam was expansive and open, absorbing influences from both West and East. Centuries of living alongside Hindus had fostered a Muslim culture of saints and shrines, flowering alongside orthodox madrasas. The Muslim emperor Akbar had even designed a syncretic faith of his own, the Din-i-Ilahi, which aimed to braid together the best elements of South Asia's various religions. Even Urdu, the language of South Asian Muslims, is a blend of Arabic, Hindi, and Persian. One reason the Sheikh was so comfortable with the world, I suspected, was that the world had always come to India.

I was met at the station by a smiling band of male Jamdahanis led by Akram's brother, Muzzammil. Fifteen years younger than his brother, Muzzammil was Bollywood handsome. His teeth were bright, and the white of his loose, long shirt dazzled—which may be why he wore oversized aviator shades. With Muzzammil was Shahnawaz Alam, the head of Akram's madrasa, whose high cheekbones suggested Central Asian ancestry and whose red-hennaed beard marked him as a hajji—a veteran of a Meccan pilgrimage.

We piled into a car borrowed specially for the occasion and putted out of town down narrow roads scuffed with dust. On either side of the road lay rich farmland, and we passed emerald rice paddies, mustard fields, and houses of scar-pink brick. Muzzammil wheeled around from the front seat to talk. Like his older brother, he lived in Britain, teaching at a madrasa in Slough. His British-born teenage students were capable enough, he said, but not as respectful as Indians would be. "They call me 'freshy,'" he said ruefully. "Because of my accent."

We arrived at the madrasa, a tidy white compound with turquoise trim. Inside was a two-story building with a series of classrooms. It was sparsely decorated, but a courtyard by the mosque, shaded by neem trees, softened the effect. On the main road, a huddle of students gathered around the madrasa "canteen," a shack of palm leaves and bamboo selling sweets and fried snacks. Their living conditions are minimal, Muzzammil told me. There are no dorms, so students sleep on the classroom floors at night.

The Sheikh had included the standard classes on Arabic, the Quran, and Islamic jurisprudence, as well as classes on the English language, in a departure from the classic madrasa curriculum. Despite the spartan conditions, the madrasa had an impressive record: sixty-five *hafizes*—Muslims who have memorized the Quran in its entirety.

"All this, in eight years!" I said to Shahnawaz. "You must not sleep much!"

"If I slept," he grinned wolfishly, "would I have nine children?"

He ushered me into a classroom, furnished with Quran stands to keep the holy book from touching the floor, and five clocks, each showing a time for that day's prayers. (Prayer times, linked to the sun's position in the sky, change daily.) A ceiling fan scythed the thick air, running on a generator specially brought in for my visit. The Sheikh arrived, looking uncharacteristically harried, trailed by the entire madrasa faculty. A half dozen or so young men, they smiled shyly, bobbed their heads, and sat on the floor facing me. A student arrived with a tray laden with dates, cookies, and a can of Red Bull. Shahnawaz presented me with an elaborately wrapped gift from the madrasa trustees—a biography of the Prophet Muhammad—with a card addressed to "Honourable Ms. Carla Power, the Well-Known American Journalist." I should rest, Muzzammil urged. I've been traveling for nine hours, it's hot, and I'm to deliver my speech right after evening prayers.

Red Bull and gifts were not the greetings most Americans would expect from a madrasa. After 9/11, Westerners learned the word "madrasa" as a place where dull-eyed boys rock back and forth, rote-learning the Quran. Madrasas were cast as jihad factories where the great Muslim unwashed were taught to hate the West. Like many others who'd reported on extremism from Pakistan over the past couple of decades, I'd visited the infamous Madrasa Haqqania, alma mater of numerous jihadis and Taliban leaders. In the late 1990s, professors at Haqqania, run by the media-savvy, flame-haired cleric-politician Sami-ul-Haq, obligingly spat out quotes about the need for armed jihad in Afghanistan, the venal dealings of Western powers, and the righteousness of Osama bin Laden's struggle.

But many madrasas undermine the stereotypes. An ad for English classes hung in the Lucknow bazaar, promising "Attractive Offers for Madrasa Students" and illustrated with a picture of a flapping American flag. The Sheikh had once arranged for me to visit a West Yorkshire madrasa, in the heart of Brontë country, all gray slate walls and windswept moors. The atmosphere recalled a Muslim version of the muscular Christian upbringing that I imagined the Brontë sisters probably enjoyed in their father's parsonage. Veiled girls in long cloaks strode in pairs across sodden hills and giggled softly in dorms as neat and white as unbroken eggs.

Not all madrasas are built on rote learning and rigid certainty. In New Mexico I had observed a class at an Islamic center built of buttermilk adobe. A California-born sheikh, Hamza Yusuf, guided the class through a text by an eighth-century Egyptian scholar, showing the students its calls for tolerance and pluralism: "We say, ultimately, 'God knows best,' where decisive knowledge about a matter is not clear to us."

Over tacos at a nearby cantina, Yusuf, a former surfer with a neat goatee, bemoaned the decline of the traditional madrasa system. Much of the rot occurred under European colonial rule, when Islamic seminaries were deemed relics from a premodern age, holding back progress and the spread of Christian values. With the dilapidation of traditional madrasa learning came the erosion of *adab*, or intellectual etiquette. By the late twentieth century, measured moderation was all too often drowned out by the shrill certainty of radicals. Yusuf had worked hard to counteract such voices—both Muslim and non-Muslim. Invited to the White House after the attacks on the World Trade Center, he brought President George W. Bush a Quran bristling with Post-it notes.

After late-afternoon prayers, Muzzammil escorted me to the courtyard and motioned me to sit in a line of straight-backed chairs facing the audience. A goat wandered the yard, nosing at the bougainvillea. I smiled gamely at the crowd of youths clicking my picture on their mobile phones. I was not allowed to reciprocate, much as I wanted to: Akram had nervously asked me to refrain. So I sat, hands folded in lap, and watched the audience fill the rows of red plastic chairs. Farmers trooped in from the fields in white dhotis and turbans. Shirtsleeved shopkeepers sat stiffly. The Sheikh greeted the local grandees, who as honored guests were allowed to join me on the dais, facing the audience: The mayor of Jamdahan. A doctor. Akram's uncle, who once had been an assistant to a high court judge in Bombay. The audience filled every last seat, to the Sheikh's great satisfaction. "The last time the madrasa did a program, very few people came," he whispered. "This time, they keep asking when it is going to start."

I was incongruous at the madrasa but was beginning to enjoy it. I like being the odd one out, having learned long ago the profoundly relaxing properties of being spectacularly out of place. Whether you're the new kid in the fifth grade, or the only woman to have delivered a speech at Jamdahan's madrasa, little is expected of you, and most lapses are forgiven. Like my father before me, I feel most at home when I'm away from it, freed from the expectations of my own culture. My father knew the principle of outsiderdom well. Indeed, a lifetime of being the odd man out helped draw him to the Muslim world. In St. Louis, he was the shy, slight figure, alone beside the punchbowl at parties. In a University of Tehran seminar, or meeting Kabul's legal establishment, his foreignness camouflaged his eccentricities. In St. Louis, his persona made him eccentric. In Asia, it was only his culture that rendered him a curiosity.

Being a curiosity, of course, was the only way I was allowed inside the madrasa. In a courtyard full of men, I was the only grown woman. "It's not considered proper for Jamdahan's women to appear at public meetings," Muzzammil explained. As so often happens, local customs overshadow Islamic teachings. The disparities between Islam's teachings and real-life practice gape most widely when it comes to women. The Prophet's wives rode camelback, but that doesn't prevent the Saudis from banning women from driving cars. Both the Quran and Muhammad stressed the importance of education, but Afghan and Pakistani reactionaries blow up girls' schools in the name of Islamic "tradition." In many Muslim cultures, tradition holds that women pray not in mosques, but at home. Despite having produced a world expert on gender roles in early Islam, the village of Jamdahan was no exception. Local mores meant that the only female at my talk was the Sheikh's ten-year-old niece, who took a back-row seat, next to her cousins. And yet the Sheikh himself had written about how the Prophet explicitly encouraged women's presence in the mosque—and welcomed their children and nursing babies with them. When he'd hear a baby cry during prayers, he'd shorten the prayer session out of consideration for its mother. (Even not having a *jilbab*—a loose overgarment—was no excuse, records one hadith. If you can't find your own, Muhammad counseled, borrow one from someone.)

As the courtyard filled up, I began to see what a delicate diplomatic negotiation Akram had embarked upon simply by having me speak. My presence here might offend the sensibilities of more conservative madrasa sheikhs, or upset purdah, the tradition of screening women from public view. I tugged my hijab down more tightly. "Everyone," the Sheikh had said quietly, earlier that afternoon, "is waiting for you to make a mistake."

I was grateful that he trusted me not to make one. Welcoming me, an American woman, traveling alone without her husband, made his madrasa a target for slurs. There might be gossip that the place was "liberal"—shorthand, in the minds of some conservatives, for an erosion of proper Islamic values. In particular, the Sheikh worried about detractors from a rival madrasa nearby, which followed the Deobandi tradition, stricter than his own. Concern about the Deobandis had prevented Akram from calling local papers to send reporters to cover my speech. "You know," he explained, "people gossip." (As it turned out, a reporter showed up anyway, interviewed me, and stuck me in the local paper, using a photo pulled from the Internet.)

The madrasa had other critics, too. Akram had built the place on public land, carped a couple of villagers. One citizen had even tried to take him to court, in an effort to get the madrasa moved. A few ultraconservatives had grumbled about his building a madrasa for girls. Some villagers had even started a whispering campaign, saying that Shahnawaz should be dismissed as director of the boys' madrasa. "I don't know exactly why," hazarded the Sheikh. "Maybe because they were jealous, or something." In any case, Akram resisted. "They say 'Remove him,' but if we do, they'll just want to do the same with the next head," he shrugged.

A young student with a wispy beard began the afternoon's program, reciting from the Quran in a soulful voice. More than a chant but less than a song, it quieted the audience. A second teenager declaimed a very, very long poem he had composed in praise of the Prophet—a classic warm-up for madrasa events. Then I took the microphone and delivered my speech, pausing and passing the microphone to the Sheikh after every paragraph so that he could translate it into Urdu.

We're living in dangerous times, I told the assembly, full of mutual misapprehensions between Muslims and non-Muslims. The United States, like India, could be an open and confident country. But fear of the Other can render societies rigid. A loss of confidence can stop cultures from mixing and flexing when confronted with fresh currents. As India's Muslims had experienced with the rise of Hindu fundamentalism, or with the tensions with Pakistan, setting oneself against an Other was a cheap and easy way of getting heard, or getting votes, or getting a following.

The Sheikh was making a stand against such thinking simply by letting me study with him. "The more we talk, the more I see how many ideals we share," I told the audience. "Like him, I want peace and security, good education for my kids, and a just society." But Americans are often ignorant of how much they share with Muslims. "The best weapon against mutual hostility and ignorance of Islam," I said, "is occasions like this."

The next words sounded as if they were penned by a not very promising State Department underling: "Cultural dialogue is the world's most powerful weapon against extremism of any kind," I pontificated. "Genuine engagement between people holding different points of view is the best hope for making this increasingly polarized planet work." Having put the tenets of my creed before them, I indulged myself with a memory of my youngest, Nic. She was two the day I had to visit a local London madrasa for a magazine story. The babysitter had canceled, so I took her along, though she was fractious as any toddler at dinnertime. The madrasa was a basement room below a North London corner grocery. I clambered down the steep stairs, Nic clumping grumpily after me, to find a roomful of children, each with a Quran, working through their suras, murmuring in Arabic. The sound of recitations soothed her. Together we sat cross-legged on the grubby carpet, focused on the children who were focused on their Qurans. Just minutes before, Nic had been headed for a tantrum. Somehow, the sounds of the Quran being recited unknotted her mood, and mine.

Hoping the closing anecdote hadn't been too It's a Small World, I looked out at the crowd. "In the spirit of cultural exchange, I'd like to open the floor to questions." I smiled in my best Town Hall Meeting manner.

The first one came from a bespectacled journalist. "Is the American media controlled by Jewish people?" he asked.

I gulped. He was looking at one, I was tempted to say. Besides, I never know what people mean when they say "the media," any more than I do when they say "Muslims." I knew Akram was nervous enough about my speech; saying that my mother was Jewish wouldn't help matters. So I wimped out, sidestepping the issue with an anodyne comment on the dangers of generalization and America as a melting pot.

The political questions kept coming, polite but pointed. "Why is the United States so unswerving in its support for Israel?" demanded a wiry young man.

I spoke of history, of the Holocaust, and of a powerful lobby.

"What is the reason that American politicians always seem to act against Muslim interests?" asked Akram's courtly, mustachioed uncle.

I reminded him of the war in Bosnia, in which we'd championed Muslims against Christian Serbs, but I had to concede that yes, it often seemed that political Islam scared the American public.

His question reminded me of a mirrored question from the West— the plaintive litany after 9/11: "Why Do They Hate Us?" I had helped report the famous *Newsweek* story that attempted to answer the question. I had watched President Bush on television assuring America that we were attacked because "they hate our freedoms." But the very question was misguided: everywhere I went in the Muslim world, our freedoms weren't hated, but envied. The bitterness was not aimed at Americans, or our democratic values, as Bush claimed. It was at our

callous misuse of power, our continued willingness to prop up dictatorships in countries like Egypt and Saudi Arabia that denied their
people the very democracy we purported to want to spread. It wasn't
"us" they hated, but our policies.

The Jamdahanis' questions, I realized, were far more to the point
than platitudes about shared values. For village men who'd never met
an American before, the intersection between Islam and the West was
shaped by geopolitics, not tales of toddlers being touched by the
Quran. It dawned on me that the anecdote about Nic made no sense
to a madrasa crowd. For the truly devout, it would hardly be surprising that my child was moved by divine words. Only a secularist would
be impressed that the Quran could soothe a crabby child. For the
faithful, it was obvious she would be.

Stars started to gleam in a darkening sky, as if on a low-set dimmer
switch. Akram and Muzzammil bundled me into a bicycle rickshaw
with my baggage, and the rickshaw driver pulled me over the pits and
ruts of Jamdahan's unpaved alleys. A boy ran beside us, holding up a
bike light to show the way to Akram's home.

We arrived at a two-story house with an atmosphere as intensely
feminine as the madrasa's had been masculine. Akram was nowhere
to be seen, for reasons I would later discover. A tiny, smiling mob of
women and children surrounded me. A girl grabbed my hand and led
me inside, and I yielded to the warm bossiness of Jamdahani hospitality. In the inner courtyard, Muzzammil introduced me to his and
Akram's three sisters, their clothes a riot of russets, purples, and saffron
yellows. Muzzammil's wife, Azeema, was plump and pretty, with a
complexion the color of honey. As I was introduced to the family,
only one figure remained silent and seated: Akram's mother, who
nodded brusquely and followed my movements with a rheumy,
unblinking gaze. I later learned that she was about seventy years old,
but she looked around forty, her glowing skin preserved by a life spent
indoors in the *zenankhaneh*—the women's part of the house. Her
lower lip was russet, stained from years of chewing *paan*, the betel nut

and tobacco mixture often wadded up in a leaf. She prepared *paan*
several times during my time there. In a ritual nearly as frequent as
prayer, she would lean over, plastic bangles clacking, and bring out
the *paan* box from below the charpoy, the traditional twine and wood
bed. She'd open the box, with its cunning little compartments of
leaves, herbs, and red *paan*, massage them into a paste, and fold it into
a neat package wrapped in a leaf.

Akram's mother never seemed to speak, but even though she was
silent, she loomed. I went to the guest room to put my bags down
before dinner and to pull off my headscarf, assuming it was fine to be
bareheaded in the *zenankhaneh*. I assumed wrong. Wordlessly, without a smile, Akram's mother pointed at her head. I put the *dupatta*
back on. "People here love tradition," Muzzammil told me. "And
they're willing to endure some discomfort and inconvenience to
preserve it."

Dinner was for one. The sisters led me to a table full of mutton,
curries, and salads and motioned me to sit. Then they stood around
me in a sympathetic huddle and watched me eat. Two of them whirled
fans above my head. Midway through my first plate, Azeema gestured
at my hands: I was eating with my left one, traditionally reserved for
cleaning oneself after the toilet. I switched clumsily, and made a foray
at conversation. "You must be so proud of Akram," I said, between
mouthfuls. "What do you think about him becoming a world-famous
alim? Could you have predicted it?"

My heartiness felt too loud, too bald. I sounded as if I were announc-
ing the Super Bowl.

Titters from the younger women; silence from their mother.

Muzzammil looked embarrassed. "We live in a village," he explained.
"We think about bread, and nothing more."

Later, back in Oxford, I asked the Sheikh's eldest daughter how he
was viewed by his Jamdahan family. "They don't know much about
him," she said. "They know he's educated, he lives in the West, and
that he's on TV."

• • •

The house was built for purdah, with women carefully screened from the alleyway outside. The men slept out front, the women in the back. I wondered where married couples went for privacy but couldn't summon the courage to ask. The women's bedrooms were windowless, and the outside world was reduced to a rectangle of sky hung high above the central courtyard. Muzzammil's red motorcycle was propped in the corner, hinting at the promise of open roads. The household's command center consisted of three charpoys, wooden beds pushed together to form a giant platform, and it was filled with Akram's family. I watched the charpoy island multitask as a couch, a salon for the ladies who drop by to pay social calls, a nursery, and even as a kitchen counter, with one sister squatting atop it, deftly slicing ladyfingers with a small scythe.

Just before dawn prayers, Muzzammil's wife, Azeema, motioned me to follow her to the roof, the only space where women could move freely outside without their *niqabs*. Even after a single night in purdah, standing on a rooftop in full view of the village felt slightly daring, like the first foray onto the beach in a new bikini. Next door, a neighbor sat cross-legged, bent over her Quran stand. It was the only time I saw anybody alone in Jamdahan.

Dawn prayers, the Prophet said, are witnessed by both the angels of the night and the angels of the day. It was easy to imagine otherworldly creatures listening to the woman's soft recitations. The morning mist was burning off, and the neem trees and palms came into focus, as though a giant camera lens was slowly turning. A peacock strutted in a nearby field. Dragonflies darted. As a boy, Akram had played *kabbadi*, the Indian running game, in these fields. Evenings, after school, he'd walk the family buffalo to the riverbank, where he'd play with other boys waiting for their buffalos to finish watering.

Three centuries ago, under the Mughals, the Sheikh's ancestors had owned most of the land around Jamdahan, until the British came and pushed through land reforms. ("When people in the village speak of the British, they say they were good," he said, with a smile. "Except for my family!") The Sheikh's grandfather farmed these fields himself, growing wheat, barley, and sugar cane. He couldn't read or write himself, but he knew swaths of the Quran by heart and made sure that his son, Akram's father, memorized it in its entirety and so earned the title of *hafiz*. As a young man, Akram's father started work in a nearby textile factory, where he taught himself not merely to operate the machines, but to fix them. When Akram was a young boy, his father had amassed enough capital to move to Bombay and open a clothing shop. Glimpsing the world outside convinced him that his sons would need more formal education than he had received. For a devout rural family with dwindling land ownership, sending sons to madrasa allowed them to hold on to tradition while preparing for a changing rural economy.

Besides, Akram in particular was proving to be a nimble student. At five, he'd begun his education at the one-room madrasa down the alleyway, across from the white mosque with the mint-green tiles. Sitting on a floor mat, he mastered his alphabet—the *qaida*, or base—a word that would, in time, gain dangerous new connotations. At six, he'd started committing the Quran to memory, but after finishing two of its thirty sections, he decided that memorization was boring. By the time he was eight, he'd outstripped the local madrasa's curriculum. So his grandfather packed a bag with the Quran and a Persian primer and walked him down the main road to a larger madrasa, two miles away.

There, he began studying Persian, a subject he loved so much that he'd be the first to school in the mornings and the last to leave at night. On Fridays, the day off, he would cry. "Once, my father even beat me, he was so annoyed that I always wanted to be at school," recalled Akram.

At night, he'd drag his charpoy out into the alleyway and curl up with a kerosene lamp and his copy of Saadi's *Gulistan*, a celebrated eleventh-century collection of stories and verse. The neighborhood boys would join him on the charpoy, and he'd read aloud to them. For a year or so, Jamdahan's villagers, inspired by Akram's virtuosity, began sending their own sons to the same madrasa. The Jamdahani boys formed a gang of sorts, sitting together at lunch and skirmishing with boys from other villages. Within a year, most had dropped out, going back to work in the fields. But Akram remained, riding his bicycle for miles through the countryside to hear lectures at mosques. "Every time I heard there was a pious person speaking at a mosque, I'd go," he recalled. By the time he was fifteen, he'd written his first manuscript, a book on Arabic grammar.

In the afternoons, Akram would sit by his grandfather's charpoy and read the Quran to him. He was reading it aloud at the moment the old man died. Akram looked up to see that his grandfather had stopped breathing in the middle of a sura. He scarcely paused. "My father said 'Keep reading,' and I did." He repeated "Ya Sin," the sura recited after a death, forty times.

Akram's brother Muzzammil and two of his sisters have memorized the Quran and become *hafizes*. At Akram's urging, all his younger sisters studied in a women's madrasa in Azamgarh. All the adults in the household read from the Quran at least once a day, and several times on Fridays. "If you read the Quran, it doesn't matter if you understand it or not," Muzzammil assured me. "Just by reading it, you get a reward."

I instinctively scoffed at this, this reading-that's-not. Until I thought back to the rooftop reciter I'd heard that morning. I hadn't understood the words, but hearing them had brought me an uncanny sense of peace.

Throughout my visit at his house, Akram was nowhere to be seen. Except for Muzzammil and his father, the household was populated entirely by women and children. When I toured the house to see every sister's separate kitchen, each with her own pots and wood-burning stove, I caught a glimpse of a gray and gentle presence that turned out to be Akram's father. We exchanged the briefest of glances, then both looked away. For a man of his generation, to have a woman, unrelated and without a hijab, wander onto his sleeping veranda must have been highly improper.

Later, back in Oxford, Akram explained that he had stayed away from his family's home because he was observing purdah. In the village, purdah's dictates took precedence over family togetherness. "I don't like to mix with the wives of my brothers," explained Akram. "Had my wife been there, it would have been different. Besides, there were so many women from the village who had come to see you. It wouldn't have been good." My presence had created a crush of women and girls from the whole village, curious about what an American woman might look like. "All those women who came to see you," he marveled. "It was like a wedding, when they come to see the bride."

In part, Akram stayed away out of consideration for his sisters. "I wanted to give them their freedom: they wouldn't have been so free, the wives of my brothers, in front of me. With me there, they can't laugh loudly, they can't talk freely. Inside the house, women are free, and men are not."

Something like regret moved across his face. For a second, I saw how purdah could be double-sided, reducing freedom for men as well as women. Curtains can cut out light and air for people on either side of them. They don't block everyone's view of the world equally, of course: purdah's restrictions are drawn most tightly around women. Akram's sisters and mother would never go outside without covering their faces with a *niqab*, the Islamic covering that leaves just a slit for the eyes. Nor could they venture out to the markets in nearby Khetasarai without a male escort. The Sheikh didn't believe in restricting women's movement like this, but the rest of the village did.

The Sheikh's eldest daughter, Husna, was just nine when the family left Jamdahan, but even as a kid, the rules of purdah applied. By seven, she was no longer allowed to play freely outside. "We could go down the street to the shop if it was an emergency," she later recalled. Since everyone else kept their daughters indoors, venturing outside made you an automatic target for catcalls and comments.

Husna's years in Jamdahan had left her with a reserve and an accent that her Britain-raised sisters lacked. When she explained to me the strictures surrounding purdah observed in the Jamdahan ancestral home, I finally understood why I barely saw the Sheikh during my visit there. The household's purdah was so strict, Husna recalled, that sisters and brothers barely spoke to one another: "My older auntie would speak to my dad, but the rest of the sisters wouldn't, or not much. They were shy."

Husna, too, described herself as shy, and even years later, married and living in Oxford near her parents, she continued the purdah conventions she learned in India. "I don't speak to men, or if I do, I keep it to a minimum," she said matter-of-factly. "I don't speak with my sister Sumaiya's husband—there's no need to talk, really. Even now, I hardly speak to my dad."

"Sorry?" I gasped. "Really?"

"Yes. Like, if it's raining, and I have to go home, I ask my mom to tell him that I need to go," she said. "She'll ask him to drive me, rather than me."

Jamdahan, I was once again reminded, was a place for women and old men. With nearly all its fathers and husbands off working in the Gulf or beyond, and observing purdah on their visits home, its men and women lived largely separate lives. In the West, we worry about families fracturing under the strains of divorce, work pressures, or generational differences. Sulky teens or workaholic spouses create their own divisions. But there are other ways to split up families.

In the Sheikh's house in Oxford, purdah is practiced, but less strictly than in Jamdahan. When the Sheikh has male visitors, they'll often repair to one room, and his wife or daughter will close the door of the sitting room, to preserve a sense of separateness. But there's far more freedom here than in India, particularly for the younger generation. Akram's second-eldest daughter, Sumaiya, rolled her eyes skyward when she recalled a hesitant non-Muslim asking her whether she knew how to drive a car. "I could drive before my husband did!" she chortled.

When Sumaiya wanted to wear a *niqab*, Akram was shocked, but he figured it was her choice. "Islam wants women to cover everything with loose clothing when they leave the house," said Akram. "But this covering of the face—this *niqab*—developed later on, after the Prophet's day."

"But why don't you tell your family in Jamdahan that?"

"To someone who has grown up in the village, they think it is totally Islamic. They can't separate what is tradition from what is Islamic. They only thing people in Jamdahan know about the *niqab* is that the Hindus don't wear them, and Muslims do." Like many village customs, "they are traditions not done from religious knowledge, but to build their identity as a group."

"But Akram, you're an authority!" I chided. Even the oldest men in the village deferred to him on religious matters. In a rare break with Jamdahani hierarchies, it was he, not his elders, who led prayers in the mosque, out of respect for his religious learning. "You're a world-famous scholar," I wheedled. "Why not tell them they don't have to wear *niqab*, so long as they're modest? What about telling them about your stuff on women scholars? About all those women who rode alone on camelback to get to classes in the first few centuries of Islam? That woman in medieval Samarkand who issued fatwas? Or that other scholar, who lectured male students, standing at the Prophet's grave?"

"Nobody would listen," he said. "People would say, 'Oh, he's gone to Nadwah,' or 'Since he's gone to Britain.' I can say it in Lucknow. I can say it in Oxford. I can't say it in the village. If you're going to change people's minds, you can't start from the village."

Changing tradition, like putting in electricity or running water, needed the right infrastructure. The *niqab*'s popularity derived in part from the widespread harassment of Indian women, said the Sheikh. "At the moment, you can't imagine how much disrespect there is for women in India," he said. At the time, his fourth daughter, Maryam, had just started her undergraduate degree, studying Arabic at the University of London. "In Britain, if Maryam travels to London, there's no problem," he said. "But in Jamdahan, you really cannot imagine a girl going out without her face covered." Since everyone wore it, you made yourself a target if you didn't.

The way to change people's mindsets, says Akram, was education. To this end, he's built a madrasa for Jamdahan's girls, set in the rice paddies just beyond the old brick kiln outside town, and put his brother-in-law Abu Bakr in charge of it. As so often happens in girls' madrasas, the standard of teaching, he conceded, was not high. Families usually only wanted women teaching their daughters, and to date, women teachers have not been as well educated as men. But the new Madrasat al-Salihat—the Madrasa of Righteous Women—was a hope that things might change. In a generation or two, education might erode long-standing codes.

Sitting with Akram at a fusion restaurant in Oxford, sipping lattes and eating nachos, it was hard to imagine just how smothering the gentle pressure of village custom could be. Life in Jamdahan confined people to a tight-knit group of Muslims, living much as their ancestors had. The warm press of such an environment made it far too easy for local traditions to get tangled up with faith. Akram—like many Muslim migrants to Europe and the United States—felt that life in the West had helped him tease out which traditions were simply a part of North Indian culture and which were a part of Islam. Living in Britain allowed him to mix with Muslims from various countries and schools of law. Far away from his village and madrasa, he found a neutral space where he could reexamine the original sources afresh.

"Going to Nadwat al-Ulama was a shift, but it was really when I came to this country, and started reading more hadith, that I could focus on the main things in the religion—like piety and fear of God— rather than on things that are just culture," he said. But villagers, with limited education and no experience of the outside world, wouldn't welcome being lectured on his discoveries.

"But you let me give a lecture," I fished. "Speaking of which, how did people respond?"

Apparently, my visit was the talk of the village. "People don't have much to do," explained the Sheikh. "For about two weeks, whenever people sat together, they must be talking about you. They are not necessarily saying bad things, but they'd be talking. A lot."

"I never really understood what a risk you were taking, just having me there," I said.

"All the people around there, they cannot imagine an *alim* and a woman," he agreed. "Even now, people must be telling about it to their friends. It's something in the memory of the village."

"So did anyone say anything nasty?" I pressed.

"Nobody made a big problem about it," he said, sounding mildly surprised. "Nobody doubted our piety."

"But it was so clear that they really didn't like the United States," I said. "They were lovely to me, but all those questions about policy . . ."

"They don't like American policy," he nodded. "But they didn't connect those policies to you."

What's more, he added, the audience questions might have been less about political ideology and more about showing off: "They might have been asking about Palestine and Israel because they don't know anything else about America."

I wouldn't find hard-line anti-Western rhetoric in the village, the Sheikh assured me. "They are very simple people," he said. "They praise British rule more than Indian rule, because all they care about is who makes their lives better." Urban elites might have the luxury of thinking big thoughts about colonialism and the struggle for independence, but for Jamdahanis, what mattered was the fact that the railway track that took them to Jaunpur was British, just like the BBC they listened to on their battery-operated radios.

If Jamdahan was Akram's ancestral home, Nadwat al-Ulama was his intellectual one. As an undergraduate at Lucknow University, he'd studied Arabic and economics, but it was the years he spent at Nadwah, in Lucknow, that shaped him most. Visiting the campus, Akram was as nostalgic as a former quarterback returning for Homecoming—and just as feted. On seeing him, older professors lit up, and younger ones darted awed looks in his direction.

"Did being away from the village make you homesick?" I asked the Sheikh.

He looked nonplussed. "I was so happy to be here, you could not imagine."

I could, actually, because the madrasa was like none I'd ever seen. Black and yellow butterflies darted across the quad's grass. The campus was green and spacious: outside his former dorm, the Sheikh pointed out a copse of trees he'd had his students plant. ("It was against the rules," he said with a grin. "But nobody said anything.") We paused at the lot where his badminton team used to practice. We paid tribute to the spot at the campus canteen where Akram and his friends would sip chai together, splitting the bill, a practice that, because of the individualism they'd heard reigned in the United States, was called "American tea." In the evenings, the madrasa held poetry recitations—Islamic poetry slams of sorts, with each student trying to best the others. The hub of the Nadwah campus was its original building, built in the nineteenth century in high Anglo-Indian style. Lemon yellow with white trim, it had scalloped arches and sculpted strings of delicately painted plaster flowers trellising their way around columns. It resembled an upmarket bridal boutique.

The decorative grandeur was deliberate. Nadwah was founded in 1898, more than a half century after the British had decided to push English-style education for the Indian elites. Madrasas had been declining for centuries, as had the prestige of Islamic scholars. "The whole idea behind making Nadwah so beautiful," Akram explained to me, gesturing up at a latticed balcony above us, "was so the ulama who were in training could feel proud. The men who founded it didn't want Muslim students to feel inferior to those who were studying in Western-style institutions."

He paused under a framed quotation and translated: "How many times have I wished I could return to childhood, so I could study in Nadwat al-Ulama, so I could breathe its air and take its knowledge." Nadwah graduates earn the right to put "Nadwi" after their names. Madrasa football matches pit "Nadwis" against "non-Nadwis." The "non-Nadwis" aren't an away team, just Nadwah students who haven't yet received their degrees. Scrolling down a list of alumni or the college magazine's masthead makes for repetitive reading: every name ends in "Nadwi."

Nadwah's great rival is Deoband, founded a generation earlier. The Deobandis opposed British rule and refused to include Western-influenced sciences or humanities in their curriculum. The men who founded Nadwah, by contrast, were keen to train young men both in the Islamic sciences and in secular subjects, carving a middle way between the strict traditionalism of the Deobandis and the secular education championed by the British. Akram's study of *fiqh* and the Quran, Arabic grammar and logic, was supplemented by reading Shakespeare, Freud, and Sartre—Nadwi students of his generation were very taken with existentialism. "Nadwah basically wanted to teach its students to think," he said. "At most other madrasas, it's not thinking, it's just copying."

There were limits, however, to how much of the outside world was allowed inside the madrasa gates. As undergraduates, Akram and his friends begged to be allowed to go off campus to see the circus. As future ulama, they petitioned, they needed firsthand knowledge of depravity, to see the evils pious folk were up against. Their argument failed to move the mufti, so they never saw the circus. Movies were banned, too. Sneak out to the Leela movie theater to see the latest Shah Rukh Khan or Tom Cruise, and you risked the standard Nadwah punishment: having your meals stopped for a week or two. "People say you can't be a Nadwi without having your food stopped at least once," grinned Akram. As a warden for a madrasa dorm, Akram patrolled the downtown movie theaters for Nadwis. "They don't want students to get corrupted," explained Akram. "People already think it's a modern institution, and they don't want it to get a bad name."

The madrasa's movie patrols didn't always work. Later, Akram was to find that he was the only Nadwi he knew to observe the ban: every other student, it seemed, had been to the movies.

Not all Nadwis end up scholars, as I discovered when I met Akram's old madrasa roommate, Waliullah. A broad man with bright eyes and a bushy beard, he resembled a South Asian Ernest Hemingway. He'd shared Akram's dorm room but not his studiousness. After bungling his final exams, Waliullah went into construction, where business was good. It showed, too, in the easy way he greeted the waiters at the tandoori restaurant he treated us to, and in our transport for the day: a Chevrolet SUV, complete with a driver and air-conditioning. We drove through central Lucknow, past the bone-white Tila Mosque, where Akram once celebrated a friend's memorization of the Quran with Cokes from a nearby café. We wove down the Malihabad Road, past once-gracious bungalows built by the British that were now rotting slowly under exhaust fumes and monsoon rains. A group of young Muslim women passed, wearing scarves tied around their heads and faces, like guerrilla commandos. It's a look that's developed since his time in Lucknow, said Akram, one less about piety than about belonging to a Muslim identity group. "Identity," he said, shaking his head.

The land bordering the road was lined with low-slung warehouses and shops, but back when Akram had been at Nadwah, it had been forest. On Fridays, Akram and his friends used to hunt in nearby fields before midday prayers. Akram would use the old German rifle that his father had a hajji bring him back from Mecca. The Sheikh wasn't quite as good a shot as his dad. "He'd draw a 5 on a piece of paper, go back a long way, and still hit the stomach of the 5," recalled Akram, suddenly the slightly awed son. But the Sheikh himself was pretty good. Some weeks, he and his friends would bag sackfuls of doves that they'd take to a nearby madrasa, run by a fellow hunter, and they would have them for lunch. "We could get twenty-five to fifty birds in a morning," he recalled. "My friend's wife would cook them in a curry. Very tasty."

"What was Akram like when he was at Nadwah?" I asked, swiveling around from the front seat to look at Waliullah. "He studied hard," said Waliullah. "Once, after our rector gave a lecture, Akram was so inspired he went into our room and kept reading for three days straight." He chuckled. "He'd heard somewhere that it was healthy to eat the green sprouts off chickpeas. So all he ate for those three days were chickpeas, soaked in water, with those little green sprouts." I recognized the ascetic streak: the Sheikh was rigorous about his workouts at his Oxford gym, and a couple of years ago he had embarked on a weight-loss regime, eating only fruit in the evenings.

Just off the road, we stopped to look at land Akram had bought while a young Nadwah professor. Back then, he'd imagined staying in his beloved Lucknow, teaching and raising his family on the two plots of land he'd purchased. In the two decades since, a suburb of white cinder block houses had sprung up around them. But Akram's land remained undeveloped. Waliullah managed it for him, building a neat brick wall around it and planting a grove of poplars. The trees were now tall, monuments to Akram's twenty-two years away from India. They cast a welcome shade, and as we got out of the SUV and stopped in it for a moment, I thought of how much Akram had given up by moving away from home.

5

A Migrant's Prayer Mat

When I worked at the Oxford Centre for Islamic Studies in the early nineties, it was a flimsy prefab building off a back street in Oxford—not the sort of place I associated with giddiness of any sort. But one spring day, it seemed to hum. A tent had been erected, a red carpet unrolled, and fruit juices and cookies ordered. For on that day, a prince was due. Prince Charles—or, as the Centre newsletter would call him, His Royal Highness the Prince of Wales—was to visit. The Centre's administrators had spent weeks in preparation. Invitations were printed and caterers engaged. The phone lines were clogged, and fax machines spat out security clearances. All this bemused Akram, as did the breathless speculations of the young secretaries planning the event. The day itself had the vibe of a costume party for well-connected old men. Oxford dons assembled in their black academic gowns. Limousines from London disgorged mustachioed Arabs in flowing white *thobe*s, the Gulf's traditional ankle-length gowns. British businessmen with slicked-back hair and tailored suits consulted one another in clumps, craning their necks, searching—in vain—for the sherry. When the prince and his entourage arrived, a hush fell, and heads bobbed in uncertain half bows.

Not Akram's. He stood ramrod straight in his gray karakul cap and his *shehrwani*, the buttoned black frock coat that is the traditional garb of an Indian *alim*. Standing a few paces back from the red carpet, he watched the prince mingle with courtiers. I was awed at Akram's cool. Like many scholars before him, he believed that the ulama should stay independent from royal courts of any kind. But his dignity derived from somewhere deeper, I later realized. It wasn't just that he was unmoved by office politics or royal celebrity. Islam, for him, flattened worldly hierarchies. There was just a single power he cared about: God's. "To behave differently just because someone is weaker or stronger than ourselves," he later wrote, "implies a weak understanding of our equality of being as creatures of the . . . Creator."

His imperviousness to Prince Charles was particularly impressive, since he'd grown up in living memory of British rule in India. Born in 1963, he spent his childhood on a subcontinent where Britain and its royals still commanded considerable respect. When his own sheikh, the principal of Nadwah, had selected him to go to take up a fellowship in Oxford, Akram agreed, not because of Britain, but because of his obedience to his sheikh. He was a slave of God. In Akram's world, when your sheikh asked something of you, you did it, provided it didn't interfere with your faith.

During his first autumn abroad, Lucknow felt very far away indeed. He bought a bus pass and a bicycle and applied for a reader's card at Oxford's Bodleian Library. He invested in stout shoes and a parka to withstand the British winter. He borrowed books on Christianity from the Oxford public library, and he was shocked to read the way people wrote about Jesus, "either as a god, or as just another human being." In the spring, when Lucknow's famous mangoes ripened, he found an Oxford supermarket selling mangoes and bought every last one. He found a halal butcher and taught himself to cook Lucknawi *yakni pulao*. At the mosque in North Oxford, his prayers felt the same, of course, but he couldn't help missing his Lucknow routine. At Nadwah, he'd follow his dawn prayers with a stroll beside the Gomti River, debating Greek logic with friends or discussing how the Arabic grammar schools of Kufah differed from Basra's and Baghdad's. At Nadwah, worship and religious study had shaped the days into a continuum of faith. In Oxford, his fellow worshippers prayed and left, rushing off to their classes or their taxis or their corner stores. Once, I asked him what he missed most about Lucknow. "True friendship," he replied.

The Atlas team provided conviviality. One tea break involved a half-serious debate over how a Muslim astronaut would time his prayers in outer space. (The assembled scholars finally settled for allowing him to pray on Meccan time, once he was free from the earth's atmosphere.) David Damrel, a long-haired American expert in South Asian Sufi orders, would engage in a sort of duel of graciousness with the Sheikh, each trying to one-up the other in South Asian–style courtliness.

"You, Sheikh," David would begin, in his soft Southern drawl, "are the sun."

"Ah, Sheikh, you are so bright that you blot out the sun and the moon together," Akram would reply.

Since the two men shared an office, the Sheikh would frequently ask David about the oddities he kept discovering in Western culture. British women's propensity to wear what the Sheikh saw as "such small clothes" could be disconcerting. How, he once asked his officemate, did he handle the distraction? "I just figure, 'it's none of my business,'" David told him—an attitude that Akram readily embraced. British music was another puzzle. A street musician habitually played under the window of the Atlas Room, every day at the same time. After a few days of listening, over and over, to the same three songs, the Sheikh finally asked: "Is that good music?" Some Muslim traditionalists frown on music; the closest thing to songs the Sheikh had ever listened to were recitations of the Quran. Once, after he'd lectured in Liverpool, I asked him whether he'd heard of the Beatles. "When I came to Britain, I read many British philosophers," he said. "But no, I don't know these Beatles."

Akram stayed on in Oxford, and after a couple of years he managed to get visas for his wife and his two daughters, Husna and Hala. Four more daughters were born in England, British from their first breaths. At the Centre, other researchers came and went, from Europe or America, to help research the atlas of South Asian Islam. All were diligent, but progress on the project remained glacial. The research team kept changing, for one thing. Moreover, the Centre's director was frequently taken up with plans for a grand new building for the university skyline: a center that would marry the best of Oxford with the finest traditions in the Islamic world. The director would write funding letters to Gulf sheikhs and princes and have Akram translate them into Arabic. Akram did this uncomplainingly, just as he would translate the Centre's glossy newsletter into Arabic. Because he was asked, he attended seminars on topics he'd never even heard of at Nadwah, like Islam and the Environment or Islam and the Media. Because he was asked, he'd sip tea with the latest visiting scholar, or stand beside a benefactor while the visitor inspected the blueprints for the new building. He performed these chores without complaint. He may have missed Lucknow, but he lived in Britain without an ounce of self-pity. His self-discipline was prodigious, this man who would pray deep into the night, then rise before dawn to pray again. Once, I called him on his mobile and found him on a bus to London.

"I'm going to the eye hospital," he told me. He'd had a headache that had lasted for several weeks.

"Weeks?" I asked. "But how have you managed to work?"

"It's not so very bad," he said. "It is painful, but I can still read."

Just then, for example, he was rereading the medieval theologian Ibn Taymiyya.

Once, the Atlas team went down to London for a day to look at the antique map collection at the India Office Library. We watched as a white-gloved curator unfurled a yellowed strip of paper, which turned out to be a Mughal strip map showing the road between Delhi and Kandahar. Whereas standard maps show places in relation to one another in a plane, this one showed a road, and almost nothing but the road. Two elegant lines in spindly black ink, it included the occasional marker—a boulder or a tree, a shrine or a town. These were signposts, but the road was the real thing. What lay beyond it was of little concern. It was a map for a traveler who chose not to indulge in his peripheral vision, for someone who had no use for distractions. That, I remember thinking, is a map for a man like Akram.

· · ·

Oxford's prestige didn't daunt Akram. It was just the place he found himself in, and he was neither hostile to it nor particularly impressed. The manicured lawns were just grass, the spires and courtyards mere stone. For Akram, it was simply a place to work, as his sheikh had suggested, and pray, as God commanded. Nobody else I knew in Oxford had such a steady compass. The project we worked on was massive and multivolumed, lavishly funded by prestigious American grants. The Centre touted it to visiting dignitaries as a happy marriage of high-tech methods and high-minded scholarship. Eager to cross the chasm between the university and their fledgling institution, the Centre's administrators would put on their black academic gowns to dine at High Table with their fellow dons. Every couple of months during my two years working at the Centre, I'd done so as well, crossing town for an evening of the traditional trappings of Oxford: lectures by scholars I'd seen on TV, dinners with good port, bright silver, and the tense and shiny exchanges of insecure students. Akram never ventured out of the Centre and into the university except to use its libraries. As Akram focused on his books, the Centre tunneled into the heart of the British establishment. Prince Charles became a patron not long after he visited, and he later awarded it a royal charter. The Centre's director was eventually made a Commander of the Order of the British Empire. The Sheikh remained impervious. He would perform his duties at the Centre, then go home to his real work.

At twenty-four, I found Akram's indifference incomprehensible. I was ambitious in the standard mold of a privileged American—for myself, for my career, for "experience," whatever that was. At work, I wore my skirts as short as I could get away with, fancying myself pretty daring for bringing the outside world into the Centre. "You'll be good for them," a silver-haired Centre administrator assured me when I asked whether the more traditional Muslims might mind me, a woman, around the place.

As I ran around Oxford, scrambling to assemble a self, Akram seemed curiously content. His calm acceptance of his exile from Lucknow baffled me. If he missed Nadwah so much, why not move back?

Surely his sheikh's directive didn't mean he should leave his family and suffer homesickness? No doubt there'd be a professorship waiting for him in India, if he wished. He'd be closer to his parents, his wife would be nearer hers, and he'd have the camaraderie of Nadwah he so adored. Raised on the doctrine of the pursuit of happiness, I found his unwillingness to move entirely mysterious. The daughter of an American nomad, I just figured a person could always cut loose and move on until he found contentment. I had never doubted the centrality of the self in one's own life. As a toddler, I had lisped along to the *Sesame Street* song, a true believer: "The most important person in the world is you—it's you, and you hardly even know it!" My parents and teachers had drummed into me how intensely special I was, just as millions of other darlings were told they were special, too.

Akram did not subscribe to the American cult of specialness. Once, he had asked me to help him write a letter of recommendation for a former Nadwah student of his who wanted to do graduate work in Scotland. Akram's English remained pretty rudimentary, so he'd supply the facts, he suggested, for me to render into a reference. The details he offered were sketchy: the student in question had done well in his classes in *fiqh*, hadith, and the other madrasa subjects. "All the usual things," said Akram. "A good student."

Just "the usual things" wouldn't dazzle the admissions committee. We'd need originality, I'd explained earnestly. At the very least, we should convey a sense of this person's unique intellectual gifts, the ones that would make him stand out from a tall pile of applicants. Was this student, perhaps, extraordinarily perceptive about currents in Islamic philosophy? Did he have a particular feel for medieval jurisprudence? Akram looked puzzled. I tried another tack. Perhaps he'd enrich university culture, I prompted. Did he have interesting hobbies? Any sporting prowess? Akram smiled, and shook his head. My forays went further. Given the chance, would he perhaps help build cultural bridges between Muslims and non-Muslims in Scotland? Had he overcome any particular hardships in his past?

Nothing. Akram didn't quite see the point, all this scrounging for his student's individuality. Trying to plot the salient points of a Nadwah seminarian's life on my own neat little graph of American-style achievement just didn't work. For Akram, it was simple enough. His student had mastered the curriculum. That should suffice, surely, to allow him to continue his studies.

But I felt we needed a story of sorts. I lived in the age of Oprah. My passion for personal narrative came as easily as breathing. To get into a good school, to land a prestigious job, or to be valued at all required presenting the world with something new and unique. I was musing on this one day with my former colleague Iftikhar, whose University of Chicago days had exposed him to the American quest for originality. In traditional madrasas, the groves of academe weren't quite the same, he explained. Islamic cultural history prized continuity and precedent, not rupture. Most Muslims believed that the best generation had been the Prophet's, and each successive generation had gone downhill from there. He went on to tell me a story about an Islamic scholar who, after years of work, had at last finished his magnum opus. "And what's more," proclaimed the scholar proudly, "there's not one original word in the whole thing!"

Why on earth, I remember wondering, would Akram remain in Oxford, suffering loneliness and the British rain and working on a job that wasted his scholarly gifts? It was only years later, when I heard the Sheikh teach the sura on Yusuf, the Quran's chapter on the Prophet Joseph, that I began to understand. What I'd first dismissed as passivity was revealed as something far more purposeful: a muscular submission. Yusuf, one of twenty-five prophets mentioned in the Quran, was the Bible's Joseph. My own vague sense of his story, culled from an old DVD of Donny Osmond in *Joseph and the Amazing Technicolor Dreamcoat*, was of a man with great clothes and horrible brothers. Akram read the story rather differently. In it he found the tools to endure wherever he happened to find himself: humility, patience, and adaptability.

The Sheikh gave his Yusuf seminar at a university in Liverpool. Waiting for the lecture to begin, I skimmed through the Joseph sura.

I could see why Andrew Lloyd Webber saw a hit in it. A noble and handsome hero endures family breakups, treachery, murder plots, lust, and sudden reversals of fortune. A synopsis of the Quranic sura: As a young boy, Yusuf has a dream of the planets and the moon and sun prostrating to him. The vision is a sign, realizes his father, that the child is a prophet. Jealous over what they see as their father's favoritism toward Yusuf, his brothers try to kill him, throwing him in a well and claiming he'd been devoured by a wolf. A passing caravan rescues Yusuf, and when it reaches Egypt, he is sold as a slave to a rich and powerful man. The handsome young slave catches the eye of his master's wife. When she attempts to seduce him, he resists: "He desired her, but for the fact that he saw evidence of his God." The women of the city begin gossiping about the grandee's failed seduction of a poor slave boy. To save her reputation, she has him thrown in jail. There, Yusuf interprets the dreams of two fellow inmates, and when word of his ability to read the meaning of dreams reaches the palace, he is called to interpret one of the king's own dreams. Impressed, the king grants Joseph a high position in government. By the sura's end, Joseph is eventually reunited with his family. He forgives his brothers and restores his blind father's sight.

The Quran tells the story vividly, particularly the scene in which the master's wife attempts to seduce Yusuf. So vividly, in fact, that one Muslim scholar forbade women to learn it. Luckily, Akram disagreed. The fatwa against reading sura 12 was unsound, he said, likening it to other fatwas designed to limit women's rights, like the one banning women from learning to write on the grounds that they could write love letters, or from living on high floors lest they be seen from outside. "Nothing in the Quran is for the men or for the women," he emphasized, peering out at the crowd. "It's for men and women both."

We opened our Qurans. From being a slave and a prison inmate to being a king's right-hand man, marveled Akram. Such a change in circumstances—and all because of piety. On the whiteboard next to him, the Sheikh drew a line. Next to it, he sketched a circle. The line represented your space, the environment in which you find yourself. The space could be anywhere—a well, a prison cell, a state ruled by a despot, or a foreign country. Next, he pointed to the circle. That symbolized the cycle of a Muslim's life, the steady beat of night and day, ticking away, for as long as God chose to keep you on this earth. The space you found yourself in was not in your control, said Akram. The cycle was. Your circumstances were given to you by Allah; using the cycle of your days to practice *taqwa*, or love and awe of God, was your job. Tend to this cycle of faith, said Akram, rather than worrying about your circumstances: "Any condition, even the worst condition of life, will result in something better if you keep the cycle going on," he intoned. "Whatever circumstance. You are in prison, you are a slave, you are a master, you have parents, you don't have parents, you are married, you are not, you speak Urdu, you speak English. Whatever space you have been given by Allah, thank Him!"

Consider Yusuf, he went on. "He was in the well. Did he complain? He was sold into slavery. And did he complain? He was sold as a slave in Egypt, then put in prison, what could be worse than that?" Yusuf taught us stoicism whatever happened. When he was thrown in prison on a trumped-up charge, "Did he write something in the newspapers?" asked Akram. "Did he go to the media?" To change your situation, tend to the cycle, resist temptation and pray to God. Once you do that, "any space will be turned in your favor." To be sure, he added sternly, *taqwa* takes work. "If you want *taqwa* to come to your house, you will make effort," he said. "It's not magic. Every value is connected with labor. You work hard, you get it."

Herein lie the seeds of political quietism and a docile population, I thought to myself as I tried to copy down Akram's torrent of words. Akram's formula felt entirely alien to someone raised to believe she was more or less master of her own fate.

We broke for lunch, and I went for a sandwich with a group of women from the audience. Most were all British-Asian and British-African students, the daughters of parents who had migrated from South Asia or East Africa for better lives in Britain. They were confident young women, most pursuing medicine or dentistry degrees. One student, Aisha, was Chinese, a recent transplant who wore tights under microshorts and no hijab. Exceedingly cheerful, Aisha assured me she adored Liverpool. Finding the university's Islamic society, she said, had been vital. When I asked her if she was homesick, she shook her head vehemently: "Not at all."

Reflecting on it, I could see how Akram's space-cycle model could comfort a migrant, homesick or not. In recent decades, terror analysts have suggested that the dislocations of the migrant experience helped create conditions for breeding extremism. Ripped from their ordinary contexts and networks, migrants are often vulnerable to being recruited by Muslim extremist networks. Greatly simplified, the theory goes as follows: The children of the migrants, at home neither in the culture of their parents' homeland nor in the West, find a cultural home in the mosque. Radicals, savvy to the vulnerability of this in-between generation, target these lost youths as recruits.

Yet here Akram was proposing an entirely different response to the challenges posed by a fragmented world: prayer and acceptance. Reading the sura, I could see how Yusuf's endurance, as he is bounced from slave market to jail, spoke to millions of Muslim migrants. To the Mumbai-born day laborer in Dubai, or the Punjabi gas station attendant in Texas, or indeed to the Lucknawi sheikh missing his old madrasa, the *taqwa* cycle gave control over circumstances. The conscious practice of patience and faith lent dignity, comfort, and meaning to lives spent far from home. For those who had to tell themselves that it would be just one more year before they went home, it served as an engine. The men who'd promise themselves daily that they'd quit the Gulf after just one more season, after earning just another thousand dollars, got strength from *taqwa*. "Every time when the sun rises, think what Allah is," said Akram. "Do what he commands. And the space will be changed."

To do otherwise, he went on, was to court disappointment. The problem with many Muslims today: they were too concerned with their immediate conditions, and not concerned enough with their *taqwa*. "For a long, long time, Muslims have been very concerned with the space. We think, 'If I had a better space, it would be better.' The Muslim reformers think, 'If we had the caliphate, it would be better. If we get a Muslim state, it will be better.' Are there Muslim states?"

Nods from the crowd.

"Are we better?"

Silence.

In Egypt, Muslims said that when the Muslim Brotherhood took charge, all would be well. All is not yet well in Egypt, said the Sheikh.

Or, he said, just as sternly, there are the Muslims who contemplate *hijra*. The term, which means emigration, refers to the Prophet's flight from Mecca to Medina, to try to find a place where his Companions could worship freely. Today, some Muslims invoke the concept of *hijra* in their own lives, aspiring to move from non-Muslim environments to Muslim ones. "We think, 'The people around us, they are not Muslims.' We think, 'If we go to Saudi Arabia, it will be a better country.' Go to Saudi Arabia . . . and you'll see there's no freedom!"

He went on. All the complaining, all the protests that the Muslim world had seen over the last century were counterproductive. India's Muslims thought they'd be better off when they got a proper space of their own? Well, they got Pakistan—and look how well that turned out. After the great struggle by Indians to get the British out, after the traumatic slicing up of territory to create Pakistan, what did the children of these freedom fighters do? "They're all running away!" he said. "They all want to leave Pakistan and come to live in the UK!"

All this energy spent looking for the perfect space in which to create the ideal Islamic state, and yet the Muslims living in so-called Islamic states were desperate to get to the West. Only last year, he'd met a scholar from Mecca—the epicenter of Islamic civilization—whose great aim was to go work in the United Kingdom. All time wasted: "When you come to the space given to you by Allah, don't complain!" he exhorted his students. "Learn how to use it. Think!"

Besides, he pressed, did living in the West prevent you in any way from being a good Muslim? "Tell me," he persisted. "Is any government stopping you from being pious? When you are in the mosque, is anyone stopping you from being pious? Do you really need an Islamic government to make your house pious?"

Days after the lecture, when we talked on the phone, he continued on this theme. The real problem, said the Sheikh, was not the British, but the Muslims themselves. Without the purity of intent of the Prophet and his followers, *hijra* was a hollow gesture. The other day, he said, a French Muslim asked him about the French government's ban on the *hijab* in public places. Would it be better, he asked Akram, if French Muslims emigrated someplace where they could practice their faith properly? Akram sighed. "These people are making a big thing out of nothing," he said. "I ask these people, 'Is the French government coming into your home? Into your heart? Preventing you from fearing God? Is it stopping you from being pious?'"

For Akram, the Yusuf sura was a primer on how to live a God-centered life in a secular world. Just like Yusuf, who managed to stay pure even as his master's wife gazed at him in a most improper way, Western Muslims needed to practice mindful pragmatism. A *hijab* was important, but even if one was banned from wearing it in an office or school, as French Muslims were, nobody could take away what was far more important: your faith.

With this in mind, he tried to be flexible when people approached him for fatwas on life in Britain. To be a skilled mufti, or legal expert, you needed two traits. First, one had to remember that "if people come to ask you for a fatwa, they're not criminals." They've come either to repent for something they've done, or to ask for guidance on how to do it. A mufti's job, believed Akram, is to provide solutions, not obstructions. "To say *haram* [forbidden] is easy," he said. "Everyone can say '*haram*.' What's harder is to find a solution."

To live in Britain—indeed, to live anywhere in the world today—required a certain flexibility about Islamic laws. He drove a car. Technically, he shouldn't. Cars weren't *haram*, obviously, but drivers' insurance was. Most interpretations of sharia law see insurance as just gambling on the future, and thus it is forbidden. But British law required drivers to have insurance. So here was his fatwa: British Muslims could indeed get drivers' insurance and still be good Muslims. As long as one observed the cycle of *taqwa*, necessary compromises on issues like insurance weren't a big deal.

The Sheikh had little patience with showy gestures of piety. Too often, sharia laws and other draconian measures were simply showcases of religiosity rather than the real thing. Elaborate Islamic finance schemes promising to avoid *riba*, or interest, were exercises in finding loopholes, not practicing piety. A woman who wore a *niqab* but wasn't nice to her neighbors had missed Islam's point: true belief comes not from the right clothes, but from submitting to God. Purifying the heart, that was crucial, not loud proclamations of Muslim identity.

In his own life, the Sheikh worked to avoid excessive display. Even as his acclaim grew, Akram refused any hint of showiness, a striking attribute in an age when the TV and the Internet have made some of the ulama into celebrities. "When other sheikhs give lectures, they often come on first-class tickets, with entourages, staying in the best hotel in town," Akram's student Arzoo had told me. Akram arrives alone, via bus or train, or he drives himself. "He's so humble," she remarked admiringly, "he almost goes unnoticed." Many scholars dress in specialized attire marking them out as sheikhs—turbans or robes, or frock coats and karakul caps. Akram rarely wears such garments. "I don't like to wear clothing that sets me apart from the people," he told me. He doesn't say so, but he's keeping with the Prophet Muhammed's habit of dressing in the same coarse and simple cloth as his Companions.

The Sheikh thought that all this energy expended on showy Muslim identity, on Islamic political parties, on worrying about the requirement for beards and hijabs, was proof of just how far many had strayed. "When people come far away from the purity of the religion, the outer aspects of the religion become identity," he explained. "When you have *taqwa*, you don't need fatwas." Change yourself, he counseled, not the system. It really doesn't matter where you are, whether you're in Liverpool or Lucknow. Pray. Reach out to non-Muslims. Work. Smile. Don't complain. Use the space you find yourself in wisely, and Allah will take care of the rest.

This call to endure sounded downright countercultural to me, trained as I was in the West to strive for More, Better, New, and Now. To accept your circumstances, uncomplainingly? Such virtues hadn't been fashionable since before the French Revolution. Where I come

from, claiming dissatisfaction with the status quo was just something everyone did. "Think Different," counseled Apple ads. "Question
Authority," said the bumper stickers.

When I got off the train from Liverpool and crossed King's Cross
Station, I saw a young man who reminded me that one could practice
piety and accept one's place despite modern distractions and Western
dissatisfaction. People streamed off trains toward heaving city streets
and poured into the station's restaurants and chain stores. The man
was silent, standing apart. Under an arch in a corner of the station, he
had put down his overnight case, rolled out a mat, and begun praying.
The crowds hustled by. Credit card machines whirred. Glasses clinked
in cafés. On his mat, with his prayers, he had found a separate peace.

As I watched the young man in King's Cross, I realized how Akram
had made Lucknow, and now England, his home. Prayers were a home,
even far away from one's homeland. A five-times-daily return to
origins, no matter where in the world one found oneself.

PART TWO

THE HOME

6

Pioneer Life in Oxford

Home is where one starts from, said both T. S. Eliot and the Sheikh. A good Muslim home makes for a good Muslim life, said the Sheikh, whether in Las Vegas or Lahore. Particularly since the era of Western imperial expansion, the home has remained perhaps the most hotly contested arena in Muslim cultures. For centuries, there have been tensions between conservatives and modernizers revolving around family life, and women's and men's roles in it. Almost invariably, the issue is framed around women's rights. Muslim societies might build glittering skyscrapers, depose their despots, retool their banking and trade laws, but customs and laws regarding women's roles remain largely unreformed. Whether in debates over women's dress or their rights to go to school or work or to choose their husbands, women have been the front line in the jihad, the struggle, between tradition and change.

Protecting women's honor proves an emotive rallying cry for traditionalists, from the Taliban to conservative Saudi clerics. At times, Western powers have used the cause for their own agendas, making much of liberating Muslim women during foreign wars. For both modernizers and traditionalists, the status of women is a barometer for a country's mind-set. Conservatives have long cast women's liberation as a newfangled import from the West—or, worse, an imperialist plot. Women, opined a postrevolutionary Tehran weekly, are the stealth weapons of colonialists, "the best means of destroying the indigenous culture to the benefit of imperialists."

The Sheikh's masterpiece collapses the opposition between women's rights and Islam. All forty volumes of his work, *al-Muhaddithat: The Women Scholars in Islam*, stand as proof that women's freedoms are intrinsically part of Islamic traditions, and have been for centuries. Much like the work of Islamic feminists, his discoveries underscore that it is often patriarchal culture, not Islamic tenets, restricting women.

My conversations with the Sheikh about gender roles were by turns reassuring and disconcerting. On women's rights to study and work, and on disrupting outdated gender roles for housework, the Sheikh's beliefs nearly matched my own. Sometimes, the limits of his vision could shock. Other times, examining his worldview forced me to reexamine my own. If my readings of the Quran showed me what the Islamic tradition allows, spending time with the Sheikh and his wife and daughters allowed me to see how one family actually lives that tradition.

We needed to take gifts, of course, the day I took my two daughters for lunch at the Sheikh's. I'd learned that lesson in Jamdahan, where the largesse of the Sheikh's sisters had overwhelmed both me and my suitcase. I'd returned to Britain with diamanté jewelry, embroidered shawls, and *shalwar kameez* sets, but reciprocating had been tricky. I wanted to send toys to his nephews and nieces, but I didn't want to contravene Islamic restrictions on representations of the human form. The ban on idolatry made the toy section of Amazon.com a minefield. Anything involving action figures was out, and everything for tweens seemed drenched in icky pink suggestiveness. The Jamdahan adults would take a dim view, I was sure, of the Amazing Makeover Barbie. I chose coloring books and crafting kits. As it turned out, I needn't have worried: I later found a fatwa from a respected sheikh waiving the usual strictures on idols and statues in the case of children's toys and dolls.

Unlike their cousins in Jamdahan, the Sheikh's children speak English, which made picking gifts easy. I'd seen the Sheikh's youngest, nine-year-old Aisha, reading a Horrid Henry book during her father's lectures. My own nine-year-old, Nic, was a fan, and so we brought her a few. I also packed a copy of *Little House on the Prairie*, not merely for the pleasure of inflicting a childhood favorite on others, but because the Sheikh's Oxford life frequently reminded me of Laura Ingalls Wilder's tales of American pioneer life. Like the Ingalls family, the Sheikh and his wife, Farhana Khatun, were raising a family in an uncharted landscape. All immigrant parents do this, of course, but the couple's moral code made the similarities more striking. It wasn't simply that the Akram family's entertainments—from playing I Spy to making checkerboards out of cardboard and buttons—were nineteenth-century wholesome. Both the Akrams and the Ingallses had a moral architecture built of privation, hard work, endurance, and above all, a fear of God.

On the appointed day, we marched up to the brick house with white trim, past the family Volkswagen, and rang the bell. I'd briefed Julia and Nic on the bus from London. We'd just be seeing the Sheikh's two youngest daughters and his wife. There wouldn't be video games, or pasta on the menu. I trotted out the standard speeches about being on their best behavior and remembering their manners.

They did, bless them. The only gaffe I detected came not from rudeness but an excess of enthusiasm. At the last minute, Nic had decided to bring her own gift for the Sheikh's daughters: a palm-sized snake figurine she had won the day before on the two-penny game at the amusement arcade on Brighton Pier. As we walked in the door, she pulled it out of her jeans pocket and thrust it toward a perplexed Aisha. "This is for you!" trumpeted Nic. "And I got it"—arms thrown out, legs planted in a conquering hero stance—"from gambling!"

I winced. Gambling is *haram*, the Quran explicitly warning that "Satan only wants to sow hostility and hatred among you with wine and gambling." Yet here was Nic, barely inside the front door, bragging about her takings like the whole cast of *Ocean's Eleven*. Boasting, too, was un-Islamic. "Don't swagger around on earth," cautioned the Quran, "for God loves no pompous braggart / And moderate your stride, and lower your voice."

To my relief, Aisha and Fatima either didn't notice or were just too polite to comment. Besides, Nic's bumptiousness was soon drowned out by our admiration of the house. My eleven-year-old daughter Julia exuded high-gear politeness, like a Victorian vicar's wife hopped up on sugar. "So much light!" she exclaimed. "So lovely! And you have a garden! Isn't it lovely?"

It was. They'd redone the living room since last I'd visited, and the effect was unwittingly chic. Dingy carpet had been stripped away in favor of wooden floorboards. Teacups dangled neatly on hooks in a china cupboard. The bright white of the walls glowed in the sun, making the room's sole decoration mesmeric in its simplicity. It was a single word, in elegant calligraphic black: Allah.

"Their house was so clean!" Julia later exclaimed. "So tidy!" So spoke a kid whose own home was filled with the noisy chaos of a patchwork aesthetic, a place stuffed with oriental carpets and Egyptian copper and Pakistani mirrorwork. All beautiful, but also all testimony to the magpie tendencies I'd inherited from my father. The simplicity of the Sheikh's house shocked Julia. It reflected a sensibility of certainty; the surroundings suggested the residents' streamlined spirit. Like a magazine devoted to simplifying your life, or one of those stores selling organizers for your closet and kitchen, the Sheikh's worldview had an appealing promise of order about it.

Looking at the luminous "Allah" on the wall, I was reminded that this order was built solely out of words. Among non-Muslims, it's a cliché to say a writer or poet is immersed in language. But a secular relationship to words, passionate as it may be, doesn't begin to touch Akram's. His life is built of them. The divine words of the Quran provide the bedrock of his existence. Growing up in a village without TV or movies or billboards or museums, he received all information of the outside world verbally, either on the radio or on a page. As a young boy, Akram learned about the world from the Quran, and later, from books of Persian poetry. When he went off to Nadwah, his immersion in words only grew, through his study of classical Arabic grammar. A core subject in any madrasa, it provides the Islamic scholar tools to parse the meaning in Allah's pronouncements.

Poetry was his sole artistic pleasure—his *Star Wars* and his *Citizen Kane*, his *Sergeant Pepper* and his *Mona Lisa*. His memory stored reams of verse, so he'd often lace his lectures with a couplet from Saadi, or a bit of a Hafez *ghazal*, to drive home a point or revive flagging attention. And daily, after dawn prayers, he allowed himself a few moments to read a poem or two. "Poetry," he once told me, "makes the heart soft, especially when read in the morning."

The Sheikh's wife, Farhana, was in her forties, with a moon-round face. She struck me as having the solid air of a woman who has shouldered her lot in life and trudged with it uncomplainingly. She spoke little English, so we relied on fourteen-year-old Fatima to translate. After we arrived, Farhana appeared briefly, hugged me, then hustled back into the kitchen to prepare lunch. We sat on sofas opposite Fatima and Aisha, both in pink, with their long hair left uncovered, since there were no men around. Julia and I flapped and jabbered and queried. Yes, they were enjoying their holiday. Yes, Aisha liked Jacqueline Wilson books, just like Julia.

To cultivate modesty, the Sheikh was sparing in his praise of his daughters. Whenever the girls came home with good grades, he would tell them they'd done well, but then he'd invariably ask: "Is there anybody better than you?" He wasn't acting on the competitive instincts of a Tiger Parent, but rather from a concern with God-consciousness, *taqwa*, and the humility it required. "Don't be proud of your children," he counseled. "Never be proud. If they do well, just say, 'You have done this favor upon me, O Allah. Everything is from You anyway.'"

The lunch table was quiet; there was only the sound of clinking plates and cutlery. Farhana had filled the dining table with platters of curried fish and rice pilaf and mini-pizzas. She sat at the head of the table, not eating herself until she saw that we had started. Watching her, I thought fleetingly of the Angel of the House, the self-sacrificing Victorian wife that Virginia Woolf conjured: "If there was chicken, she took the leg . . . If there was a draught, she sat in it." When my

daughters went upstairs with Aisha to see the family hamster, I tried
to find out more about Farhana, with Fatima's help as translator.

Farhana had grown up in a village about a half hour from Jamdahan. "What did your parents do for a living?" I asked. "Were they
shopkeepers, like Akram's, or farmers?"

"Farmers."

"And did you go to madrasa, like your husband?"

"There was no madrasa in her town," translated Fatima. "The
school stopped at year four."

That meant that her education had ended at age nine.

"How old were you when you married?"

She held up ten fingers, then another six. She'd never seen the
Sheikh before her wedding day: their elders had arranged the match.

Farhana's life had begun in a village, then had been stretched
across the earth. Her story was not dissimilar from those of hundreds
of millions of other modern lives. But that didn't diminish the enor-
mity of quitting the green fields of Jamdahan, boarding a plane, and
emerging into the hustle of Heathrow Airport. I thought of the lonely
heroism it must have taken to leave her life in the courtyard in Jamdahan and to be set down alone in the unforgiving gray of Oxford, to
raise her daughters in a strange culture, one whose language she didn't
speak.

I tried another angle. In Jamdahan, I said, I'd heard that after
dark, when nobody could see them, the village women used to go visiting by scrambling over the rooftops from house to house. "I bet
Oxford must have seemed a bit . . . lonely, at first."

A leading question, I knew, but I was dying out there. What, I
pursued, did she miss most?

Her answer came, quick and sure: "My parents," she said softly.
"My brother."

Both mother and father were now dead. Her brother was in Saudi
Arabia.

"Ah," I said, delighted at this nugget of information. "What does
he do in Arabia?"

A quizzical look.

"I mean, what job?"

A short burst of Urdu. "She's never asked," said Fatima.

Was Farhana's reserve cultural, personal, or both? Whichever it was, my curiosity about her life must have seemed to her to verge on the obscene. To display parts of oneself like shopwares, to allow a casual visitor to rifle through memories, to pick them up and inspect them—this was an alien culture of individualism. Hoping that she'd get to reminiscing about her childhood, I asked what sort of games she'd played as a kid. She regarded me warily.

"Is this going to be in the book?" she asked, smiling in sweet exasperation.

"Um—no, not if you don't want."

I knew I should have drawn the interview to a close but could not resist asking which of her husband's lectures had been her favorites, which themes spoke to her most deeply.

"She doesn't really understand them," said Fatima. "They're all in English."

I left lunch with a neatly framed image of Akram and Farhana's marriage. I'd read the news stories about first-generation South Asian women in Britain, ground down by isolation and tradition. I was certain I knew what was at work here: a busy husband with a spouse cut off from her home and culture. Farhana, I decided, was suffering from the misery of exile. Weighed down by domestic drudgery. Imprisoned by tradition.

Such was my attempt to stuff her into a grand cultural narrative. Not long after, I realized that my vision of her as Virginia Woolf's Angel of the House was a flight of fantasy.

As it turned out, she had a headache that day. I would later learn that instead of the dutiful housewife I'd imagined I'd seen, she was a lively and respected member of the Muslim community who did charity work, ran her own sewing business, and possessed an impish sense of humor.

As it turned out, had I spoken Urdu, I could have enjoyed her quick wit. ("Mmm, this pasta is delicious," a lunch guest once told her. "Who made it?" "The Sheikh," she said. "Really?" said the student. "No, not really!" Farhana quipped. "You think the Sheikh would have cooked this?")

The next time I came to stay, Farhana's face glowed. Downright girlishly. She chortled as she tickled her grandchildren, rewarding them for good behavior with tenpence coins from her purse. I was staying the night, so when I unpacked and showed her the new pajamas I'd just received for my birthday, she wheedled me into modeling them for her.

It took a meeting with Akram and Farhana's second-eldest daughter, Sumaiya, to get a sense of the fortitude it had taken for Farhana to raise her six children in Britain. When Sumaiya was young, it was Farhana who took the girls to school and who was home waiting for them when they returned, who cooked their meals, washed their clothes, disciplined them. "My dad's work wouldn't really have been possible without her," observed Sumaiya. "He would have had less time to write the books, to travel abroad, to teach or lecture. She's made lots of sacrifices."

Sumaiya, a confident woman in her late twenties, was proof that the sacrifices have paid off handsomely. Married to a medical student, she was the mother of a nine-month-old boy, Asim. When I went to visit her at the family's suburban house in London, she was dandling Asim while cooking a multicourse lunch for us, just having run batches of food over to her ailing in-laws. All this while helping her father organize lectures and debating rival offers to pursue master's degrees at two prestigious London colleges, one to study Arabic, the other to study history.

Though the Sheikh had six daughters, there was never any question as to whether his ambitions for their education were in any way diminished because they were girls. "The Prophet," he told his students, "never liked anyone who treated women differently from men." Then he'd tell them about the time Muhammad saw a man arrive with his two children at one of his lectures. The man set his daughter on the ground, but then he kissed his son and sat the boy on his lap.

The Prophet went up to the man and pointedly asked, "Why did you not treat them equally?"

The Sheikh began teaching the girls Islamic subjects while they were still in grade school. Mornings, they studied Arabic for an hour, and in the evenings they would study hadith and the Quran for two or three hours, on top of their regular schoolwork. The Sheikh would sit with them from five to eight every evening while they completed their work.

It helped that they always came directly home at the end of the school day. Akram saw school as a place one went to learn, not somewhere to loiter around doing gymnastics or drama club. There were no birthday parties for the Akram girls. To throw a party for something that Allah did—making a year pass—was to take credit for the divine order. Real achievements were celebrated, so the girls got parties in the backyard when they finished reading the Quran. Aisha, the Sheikh's youngest, made it through the scripture at the extraordinarily young age of five, so her party featured a bouncy castle and cupcakes. She shared the festivities with Fatima, who is six years her senior: "Yeah, she was reading it, and I was too, and when I heard she'd finished it, I thought I'd better hurry up," grinned Fatima. "Everyone said the party was for both of us, but . . ." Fatima's face suggested she knew better.

On weekends, the family used to pick a place out of the *Road Atlas to Britain* and get in the car to explore. There were picnics, and once, horseback riding. In the summers, after dawn prayers, the family would walk to the local park to play badminton or tag. In the evening, they'd have Chat Time, when Akram and Farhana would sip tea and the girls would come down from their rooms to join them. For a time, there was a TV, and the children would watch cartoons and Farhana would watch Indian soap operas. After a while, Akram began noting loudly that nobody had time to talk with one another, or to him. "One night, after one of these comments, my mother took the TV out of the wall and decided to get rid of it," recalled Sumaiya. She put it outside with the garbage, for collection.

The next morning, thinking better of it, Farhana went to retrieve the TV, but it was gone. "As always, my father got what he wanted without having to say or do anything!" laughed Sumaiya.

The TV incident was the Sheikh's modus operandi at work: suggest, don't demand. "He'd never shout," she recalled. "He'd be quiet, which was worse. And he never told us to do things directly, but somehow we'd end up doing them anyway."

In parenting, as in other matters, the Sheikh's watchword was *sabr*: patience. "People should not expect what they want at the moment that they want it," he told me. "Things should happen at the moment that God wants. If I want my children to behave properly, even if I become annoyed, I have to think, 'Okay, if not today, then tomorrow, and if not tomorrow, then sometime.' The fruit should come when God wants. If you can control your desire, then you will get what you want."

There were no real rebellions anyway. "My sisters and I didn't have teenage-hood," shrugged Sumaiya, who thought perhaps she might have slammed a door a couple of times. "At school, I had no clue what went on. When girls talked about how they'd been out the night before at a club, I used to just ask, 'How did your parents allow you?'" she recalled. "And when they would tell me that their parents didn't allow them out and they just snuck out, that was shocking. I would be like, 'But your parents would be so worried about you! They must have been waiting up for you!' And they'd be like, 'It's just normal to not tell parents where you are.'"

There was never any question of the Akram girls going clubbing or dating, but the Sheikh did believe that children needed freedoms. Just as Islamic governments will inevitably fail when they try to legislate piety into their populations with sharia laws, parents won't teach their children morals by being ultrastrict. "People should have the right to do wrong," he explained. "You need to give children their space, and to teach them well. And it is up to them whether they do good or not."

When Sumaiya graduated from university, her parents began pointing out a young student in her father's weekend hadith classes. "My dad sort of told me to check him out," grinned Sumaiya. "Every Sunday, my mom would say, 'Go see how he looks! His beard is this length! His glasses are like that.' And I was like, 'It doesn't matter what *you* think of him, Mom!'"

The couple married five years ago. "I don't think anyone else could be better for me," said Sumaiya. Had she been engaged back in Jamdahan, she would have been lucky to be allowed a single glimpse of her groom before the wedding: her parents didn't meet before theirs. Sumaiya was allowed a few chaperoned meetings before the engagement, during which she couldn't find any basis to reject him: "We ended up together on the basis of, 'How could I say no?'"

She could have, of course. Islam does not allow forced marriages. Like her father, Sumaiya believed that everyone has the right to make individual choices. But like him, she was conscious that people needed limits, and she was skeptical about the culture of individualism that dominates Western life. It starts so early, she marveled: "Even in nursery, in Show and Tell, there's a sense of 'Look what *I've* got.' There's all this emphasis on the fact that it's *your* thing and *you're* showing it off."

I'd never thought of Show and Tell as baby's first building block of individualism, but seen through Sumaiya's eyes, it suddenly seemed like an early foray into the culture of the self. The monogrammed towels, vanity license plates, and sloganeering tote bags would follow—a lifelong parade displaying one's own distinctiveness. If Western culture has the laudable goals of speaking up and standing out, these values also bring collateral damage: the cult of personalization.

"In this country, we're constantly getting drilled, 'This is your life, and you do with your life what you want,'" said Sumaiya. When she was in the hospital giving birth to Asim and the doctors wanted her permission for a procedure, "They kept saying, 'We need your consent,'" she recalled. In the middle of labor—"not in the frame of mind to go through the pros and cons!"—she referred them to her husband. "But they kept saying, 'It's what *you* want.' And I was like, 'I *want* you to ask my husband!' But they wouldn't: they needed my consent! You can be a woman in labor, or a drunk person—someone hardly fit to answer—and they still ask for your consent!"

For Sumaiya, the incident showed the chasm between the Western secular worldview and her own. She was puzzled by anyone who thought they had a sense of ownership over their own fate, or even absolute ownership over their own body. Everything belonged to Allah. "You don't have this attitude that 'I do what I want, because it's my life,' because the first thing you're taught is that it's not your life," she said. "We believe you've been given this body to look after."

That said, Sumaiya isn't beyond making temporary adjustments to the body that's been entrusted to her. Recently, she decided she wanted to color her hair, something her father, when asked, had said he'd prefer she didn't do. Still, Sumaiya, like every Muslim, was free to seek out any scholar's opinion that she wanted to, and so she went to see a sheikh who took a more relaxed view on hair dye. On receiving his fatwa, she colored her hair.

Sitting and gnawing his fist, Asim gurgled. His first year had been hard for Sumaiya. Wide-eyed and round-cheeked, he was a beautiful baby, but a colicky one, whose cries, much of the day and much of the night, meant that Sumaiya hadn't slept much over the past year. "My mom says she's never seen a baby like him," she said. "He just cries and cries. No remedy seems to work." Sometimes, she'd put on a recording of Abu Bakr al-Shatri, her favorite Quran reciter, which seemed to calm him. Sumaiya herself would find her own peace when she read her favorite sura, "Al-Rahman," or "The Benevolent One." "When I'm stressed, it just reminds you of how much you have," she said. During that year of being shut in with a baby in a London suburb, the sura provided Sumaiya a window to wider vistas. Detailing the creation of the universe, it stretched her vision past baby bottles and colic remedies. "The way our lifestyle is here, you don't often see the sky," she said wistfully. "With all the modern technology, we sometimes forget the original things. If the electricity went out, Europe would grind to a halt. But listening to "Al-Rahman," you're reminded of how much you have. How perfect it is." It's simpler to remember this bounty of nature back in Jamdahan, "where the sun is hot, and the day's timetable works with it," sitting in the courtyard, or watching dawn or dusk from the roof.

When I get home from Sumaiya's house, I open to the sura "Al-Rahman," whose steady beat mirrors its stern logic:

> And the Benevolent One has set the earth for creatures,
> with fruit there, and date palms with spathes,
> and grain with stalks, and fragrant herbs.
> Now which of the blessings of your Lord do you deny—
> having made man from clay, like earthenware,
> or having created the sprites from a mixture of fire—
> which of the blessings of your Lord do you deny?
> Lord of the two Easts and Lord of the two Wests—
> which of the blessings of your Lord do you deny—
> having loosed the two bodies of water to meet
> without overflowing a barrier between them—
> so which of the blessings of your Lord do you deny—
> owner of the ships under sail over the sea, like mountains—
> which of the blessings of your Lord do you deny? (55:10–25)

The Quran is known as "A Book of Signs." *Aya* means "verse" in Arabic, but it also means "sign," and just as every verse of the Quran is a sign, so, too, is nature. The Milky Way, a birch tree, a breeze, all are made to guide humans toward belief. To read these signs was not just to believe, but to appreciate, just as "Al-Rahman" demanded.

Spending time with the Sheikh and his family, I was struck at how grateful they were for small things, and how often. In Sumaiya and her sisters, I saw none of the vague dissatisfaction I'd seen flourish around me—indeed, in me, growing up. As a member of the American middle class, I was raised in a nation of strivers, a nation founded on the right to pursue happiness. Our discontent was productive. It got things done. The drive to do better propelled you through graduate school and up career ladders. Through spin classes and salary negotiations. A world of infinite favors didn't yield reliable results. My secularist's do-it-yourself existence did not get me into the habit of being grateful for date palms, fragrant herbs, and seas.

The Sheikh's sense of gratitude was altogether more muscular, perhaps because it had somewhere to go. His consciousness of God as a creator took gratitude to a whole new level, cosmic in scope and near-constant in presence. Akram was a man who could find God in the act of making a cup of tea. "Everyone says, 'Any child could make a cup of tea,'" he said. "But every cup of tea depends on the whole universe being there. For the tea to exist, it needs the sun and the moon. It needs the earth to be there. He made water, He made the container to hold it, He made the leaves to grow. When we were born, everything was there, just waiting for us. Every cup of tea depends on the whole universe." I couldn't decide whether this logic was oppressive or inspiring. I rather thought it was both, like the satisfying ache of stretching after a session hunched over a laptop.

Studying with a man who saw everything from tea leaves to algebra as gifts from God, I was struck by a new seam of gratitude running through me. I'd emerge from a lesson not with faith, but with what I suppose a fashionable guru would call mindfulness. On the bus ride home, particularly when the sun lit up the green hills beside the highway, I found myself, for a second, seeing them as the Sheikh might: not as something pretty, or as expensive real estate, or as the space between me and London, but as a connection to something larger. There were moments, while I was reading a sura, or carting the kids to school, or chopping an onion, that I sensed what this radical gratitude must feel like: a constant reminder that you're alive, but just for now.

The Sheikh's gratitude didn't afford him laziness, either for himself or for his daughters. Quite the opposite. He had always expected the girls to work hard, both in their secular education and in their Islamic subjects, and his discoveries of the achievements of women scholars throughout Islamic history only raised his expectations. "He's seen so many women do so many things," said Sumaiya. "He can't understand why we can't do it all. Those women scholars had families. Their children had colic. They had to look after ill people. They had money problems. With all that to handle, they still managed to do a lot, so he doesn't see any reason why we should be behind."

Many traditionalist Muslims educate their daughters, but when the girls hit puberty, they often opt for madrasas, not mainstream education. At first, the Sheikh did the same with his own daughters, sending the eldest three up north to board at an all-girls' madrasa in Bradford. "But I found out that it wasn't really serious about education," he said. "Most people just send their daughters to madrasa to keep them safe from . . ."

"Boys and nightclubs?" I offered brightly.

He nodded. After discussing the matter with his own sheikh in Lucknow, he decided to send his daughters to the local school in Oxford and teach them Islamic studies himself. "Too often, girls' madrasas don't have good teaching," he tells me. "Many people don't want their daughters taught by men." Since men have traditionally had access to the best education, the girls get second-rate teachers.

That will change gradually, he hopes. A few days before we spoke, he'd held a graduation ceremony for graduates of the Nadwat al-Ulama course in Islamic sciences he'd taught in Oxford. Of the six, four were women—Arzoo and Mehrun, and his daughters Hala and Husna. There are also plans for him to open his own madrasa in the UK in a few years, when the Cambridge group organizing it completes the fundraising. When he does, women and men will be taught together.

The next time I saw them after the family lunch, Akram's daughters told me that the whole family had sat in the living room testing one another on the riddles in the joke book Nic had given Aisha. The Sheikh, mysteriously, had known all the answers. Asked how, he smiled: "It was really very easy," he said. "I waited till the end, and so I was tested last. By that time, they'd been through the whole book."

Quietly biding his time as the answers unfolded, the Sheikh had let his daughters test out their answers. Then he offered his own.

7

Nine Thousand Hidden Women

In 1998, I went to Afghanistan to report on life for women under the Taliban. During their five-year reign in Kabul, the Taliban's major policy initiative was to ban anything that they deemed to be un-Islamic, including flute music, kites, nail polish, and the public display of women's faces. The most devastating of the Taliban edicts, however, was the ban on women's education. When I visited, it was illegal for girls over eight to attend school. Girls' schools were closed, said Taliban leaders, to halt the rot of secularized education. I'd met women defying the ban by running secret classes, and women university graduates so terrified the Taliban would discover their diplomas that they'd traveled with the documents under their burqas, next to their skin. Whenever she saw her old textbooks, a former law student in Kabul said, she got headaches and anxiety attacks, so she had to hide them. At one point during my trip I had asked a father of a ten-year-old girl whether she ever went out. His answer: "For what?"

In the years that the Taliban were busy protecting Islam by keeping women at home and uneducated, Akram was uncovering a radically different version of Islamic tradition. Its luminaries included women like Umm al-Darda, a seventh-century jurist and scholar who taught jurisprudence in the mosques of Damascus and Jerusalem. Her students were men, women, and even the caliph. Another woman in Akram's research discoveries: the fourteenth-century Syrian scholar Fatimah al-Bataihiyyah, who taught both men and women in the Prophet's mosque in Medina, drawing students from as far away as Fez. She leaned against the Prophet's tomb while she taught, reported one of her rather dazzled male students, who couldn't resist adding that she leaned on the most revered spot: right beside the Prophet's head.

I first heard of Akram's finds on my way back from reporting in Kabul. "I'm working on something you will be interested in," he mentioned over tea in an Oxford department store. "It's about women."

"Women?" I replied.

It had begun by accident, he explained. Reading classical texts on hadith, he kept running across women's names as authorities. He decided to do a biographical dictionary—a well-established genre in Muslim scholarly culture—that included all the women experts of hadith.

"A short book, then?" I teased. Researching the atlas at the Centre, I'd toiled through some biographical dictionaries of scholars: cover to cover, they'd been all about men.

"That's what I thought, too," said Akram. "I was expecting to find maybe twenty or thirty women. I was planning to publish a pamphlet. But it seems there are more."

"Really?" I said. "Well, like how many more?"

"Thousands."

"*Thousands?*"

Who knew? Learned women were well known, of course, throughout history, stretching back to the Prophet's wife Aisha. A couple of historiographers had written about women hadith experts. But the prevailing perception was that women's Islamic knowledge always functioned as a kind of cottage industry: if women studied, it was generally in the purdah of their own homes. And if women taught, they taught only women.

Akram's work, *al-Muhaddithat: The Women Scholars in Islam*, would challenge such myths. A decade after he'd begun work on his "pamphlet," Akram had a dictionary spanning forty volumes and containing nearly nine thousand women scholars, stretching from the day of the Prophet to the twentieth century. His work stands as a riposte to the notion, peddled from Kabul to Mecca, that Islamic knowledge is men's work and always has been. "I do not know of another religious tradition in which women were so central, so present, so active in its formative history," Akram wrote. In traditional Judaism, women didn't learn or teach the Torah, and though feminist scholarship is now uncovering the fact that women had a greater role in early Christian history than previously believed, Christianity's clergy was until relatively recently an all-male affair.

In medieval Mauritania, the Sheikh found evidence that hundreds of girls could recite *al-Mudawwana*, a famous book of *fiqh*, by heart. In twelfth-century Egypt, a woman scholar was lauded by her students for her mastery of a "camel-load" of religious texts. In Samarkand during the medieval period, Fatimah al-Samarqandiyyah, trained by her father in hadith and *fiqh*, would judge court cases. She also issued fatwas—and advised her far more famous husband on how to issue his. In an age when many women never enter mosques, let alone teach in them, it's bracing to read about these historical female scholars enjoying such freedoms. Women scholars taught judges and imams, issued fatwas, and traveled to distant cities on horse- or camelback to study with scholars. Some particularly learned ones made lecture tours across the Middle East, like the tenth-century Baghdad-born jurist who traveled to teach women in Syria and Egypt, or the fifteenth-century Meccan scholar who taught across Arabia. Or Fatima bint Yahya, a thirteenth-century jurist whose husband, also a jurist, used to consult her on his tougher cases. "This is not from you," his students would say when he'd bring back one of her fatwas. "This is from behind the curtain."

Like the Sheikh himself, many of the *muhaddithat* led cosmopolitan lives. Among my favorites was the eleventh-century scholar Fatimah bint Sa'd al-Khayr, whose travels in Asia deserve a book in themselves. Born to a Spanish Muslim father in western China, she was an itinerant student, moving through madrasas in Bukhara and Samarkand, studying with another celebrated woman scholar in Isfahan, settling for a time in Baghdad, teaching men and women in both Damascus and Jerusalem, and dying in Cairo at the age of seventy-eight.

To find such women, the Sheikh haunted the margins of Islamic history. He found traces of them tucked away in biographical dictionaries, in travel books and private letters, and in the accounts of mosques or madrasas. The lost history he searched for was scattered across continents, genres, and languages. Friends and fellow academics sent him copies of manuscripts from libraries in Turkey, Pakistan, and Saudi Arabia. To write a single entry, the Sheikh could hunt through half a dozen texts, some in Urdu, others in Persian or Arabic. Like the craftsmen who decorated Islam's mosques, working entirely with colored squares and triangles of tile, Akram seized on pieces that had until now been isolated and arranged them to reveal a dazzling pattern.

The work was achingly slow, and for nearly a decade unrecognized. At his day job, the project was met with indifference at best. The director at the Oxford Centre for Islamic Studies seemed far keener for him to concentrate on the atlas project and tasks like translating business letters into Arabic. Like the women scholars he was chronicling, the research was pushed to the margins: the Sheikh's *muhaddithat* project was confined to his evenings and weekends.

By the standards of modern biography, the facts he turned up were pretty bare-boned: dry lists of books and teachers, the odd dutiful notation of a scholar's virtues. The life of a prominent eleventh-century hadith scholar, Umm al-Kiram Karimah bint Ahmad ibn Muhammad ibn Hatim al-Maarwaziyyah, for example, is sketched out in *al-Muhaddithat* through tantalizingly brief details. We learn that she was a popular narrator of the famous book of hadith *Sahih al-Bukhari*, and that she was based in Mecca, where she died at the age of one hundred. Students came from all over to study with her, including great imams and the well-known historian al-Khatib al-Baghdadi. She traveled "in the path of knowledge" to the Iranian cities of Sarakhs and Isfahan, and to Jerusalem.

For Akram, these details are a mine of information, much as the briefest of descriptions—"Upper East Side, pre-war," or "Varsity Lacrosse, Harvard"—conjure whole worlds for an American. "In Islam, after the Quran, the most important book is Bukhari"—one of the six key compilations of hadith. "If she is teaching Bukhari, you can imagine how great she is," the Sheikh said. "In any madrasa in India or Pakistan, the most important teacher is the person who is teaching hadith. It is the source of law, and the source of life."

At first, I blithely assumed that these women's names had been forgotten in much the same way that Western women's lives had been ignored. For most of Western civilization, men wrote history, and they wrote what they knew. Until feminist historians began unearthing women's achievements after the 1960s, women's contributions were left unsung.

In the context of Islamic culture, the erasure of women was rather more complex. "Muslim society prizes female modesty," Akram explained one day on the phone. "Traditionally, many Muslim families didn't want the names of their wives or their daughters published." Keeping women's names out of classroom, madrasa, or mosque records was just a broad interpretation of the concept of hijab. The term, commonly used to refer to women's headcoverings, in fact referred more generally to the modesty required by both men and women. In an effort to keep women shielded from public view, the lives and works of learned women were simply left unrecorded.

The broad interpretation of hijab still persists today, he said. "Even now, some people don't want the names of their wives and daughters printed or announced in public," Akram told me. "Once, I wrote an article about going on hajj for an Urdu newspaper. I wanted to include the names of the people in my pilgrimage party, but all the men told me not to use the names of the women in their family."

"So how did you refer to them?"

"As 'the wife of so-and-so' and the 'daughter of so-and-so.'"

A generation ago, my own mother had done the same. Her address labels from the 1960s read "Mrs. Richard W. Power." Then came feminism, and the labels were consigned to a drawer. By the eighties, one of her women's studies students would ask, in utter seriousness, whether she'd taken the name "Helen Power" as a feminist tribute to Helen of Troy.

Given the tradition of the unnamed woman, the nine thousand women the Sheikh had found were probably just a fraction of the female Islamic scholars through history. "If I've found nine thousand of them, there are many, many more," he said. At the end of each volume of *al-Muhaddithat*, he had included citations of scores, sometimes hundreds, of women who weren't named in sources but were identified—in heartrendingly brief descriptions—simply as "Sister," "Wife," or "Daughter."

He hasn't found merely quantities of scholars, but quality ones. The women hidden in the sources, he enthused, were excellent authorities on hadith, well-versed in the traditions. "In the history of Islamic scholarship, no woman has ever been accused of fabrication or inaccurate reporting of hadith," Akram said.

I laughed. "I don't believe it," I said. "Much as I'd love to believe in the moral superiority of women over men, I can't believe that!"

"No, really! It's true!"

"But how can that be?"

"They didn't need to make up hadiths," explained Akram. "Hadith wasn't a source of income for them, and they didn't do it because they wanted to become famous. When they decided to learn, their reasons to do so were just for learning."

Purdah, argued Akram, kept their scholarship pure. For women, scholarship was a spiritual vocation rather than a career.

Men, on the other hand, had to earn their living. The cut-and-thrust of court life meant that they had to pitch their scholarship to appeal to the powers that were. "Many times, Islamic scholars in the service of kings would invent hadiths," said Akram, "because they flattered or aided the ruler." One Central Asian scholar managed to "find" a hadith stating that the Prophet Muhammad said that the rivers of Central Asia were just like the rivers of paradise. Another savvy scholar-courtier, noting that his boss tended pigeons as a hobby, "discovered" a hadith stating that whoever looks after pigeons has a place in paradise. The pious caliph, recognizing flattery and faked Islamic tradition, promptly killed all his birds.

After the seventeenth century, with the rise of European colonial rule in many Muslim countries, women's scholarship declined. The Sheikh explained its dilapidation, in part, by the more general decline in Muslim intellectual confidence. The madrasa system languished, so patriarchal customs filled the vacuum. Flabby leadership from the ulama, many of whom have turned to politics rather than scholarship, left Muslims ignorant of their own history. "Our traditions have grown weak," the Sheikh once told me, "and when people are weak, they grow cautious. When they're cautious, they don't give women their freedoms."

Insecurity made the issue of who can claim religious authority particularly fraught. Some ulama deemed a woman's voice raised in public to be *haram*. For these men, a woman speaking authoritatively about religion was particularly offensive. When a woman comes to the mosque from the local government to speak about mundane matters, like flu shots or community relations, the men will listen to her, Akram told me. But a woman speaking about religious matters rankles many men. "If it's about religious knowledge, they say, 'Oh, a woman's voice is *haram*, and this, and that!'" said the Sheikh glumly. "It's because it's their field!"

Male insecurity about what they saw as their own traditions meant women often suffered. A friend of the Sheikh's was traveling with his wife in England, and when it came time for prayers, the couple stopped in the local mosque. The imam refused to let the wife pray there, claiming that women weren't allowed to pray in mosques, even when they were far from home. Who finally gave the woman space to perform prayers? A Hindu merchant. "He opened his shop to let her pray there," said the Sheikh approvingly.

Denying women access to the mosque, like denying them other rights, was simply clinging to customs, not faith, said Akram. In the case of education, he'd gone further: preventing women from pursuing knowledge, he said, was like the pre-Islamic custom of burying girls alive. Stifling their potential makes the current status quo no better than the *jahiliyya*, the Arabic term for pre-Islamic ignorance. "I tell people, 'God has given girls qualities and potential,'" he said. "If they aren't allowed to develop them, if they aren't provided with opportunities to study and learn, it's basically a live burial."

By digging up the buried tradition of women scholars, Akram has prepared the ground for radical social change. For Muslims, the Islamic past is not just a source of interest for historians but a blueprint for the present. Precedent, not innovation, guides the devout on how to live and behave. So Akram's discovery of these women scholars isn't simply an interesting bit of long-buried history, but a quietly eloquent argument for changing the status quo.

"What he's doing is revolutionary—which is perhaps an odd word to use in connection with a traditionalist scholar," says Asma Sayeed, a history professor at UCLA and the author of *Women and the Transmission of Religious Knowledge in Islam*. While other Muslims—progressives and feminists—might question the Islamic patriarchy more forcefully, the Sheikh chips away at it from inside its traditions. He's a madrasa-educated man, a conservative, whose interest in women scholars was formed by the tradition itself, starting through the lens not of gender, but of hadith.

His findings inadvertently make him into something of a spokesman for women's liberation. When news of *al-Muhaddithat* emerged, Muslim women passed it around via email. "We were ringing one another up that Sunday morning the story about his findings appeared, telling each other, 'Can you believe it?'" one Muslim woman told me. Suddenly, the Sheikh's name was being touted on such unlikely blogs as Badass Muslimahs and The Fatal Feminist. (Full disclosure: the Sheikh had no interest in publicizing his research. I, however, did. Word of his work spread widely only when I wrote a piece on it for the *New York Times Magazine*, leading the Sheikh to tease me that he had me to blame for his growing fame.) Now groups from New York to Kuala Lumpur have invited him to speak on women. Muslim graduate students come to Sayeed in her office at UCLA eager to do their dissertations on Islamic women's history, citing the Sheikh's book as inspiration.

One night, he spoke at the Idea Store, the public library in Canary Wharf, London's financial center. His audience was nearly all women, with their BlackBerries buzzing and their backpacks and briefcases sitting beside them. To sit in a forest of skyscrapers housing the world's biggest banks listening to Islamic scholars might seem incongruous— but only to non-Muslims. Indeed, a theme of the evening was fluidity, and the range of roles and venues afforded Muslim women scholars. Akram and his fellow presenter, the scholar Aisha Bewley, sketched a history at odds with the confinement of many contemporary Muslim women. In medieval times, women bazaar merchants held classes in their shops. Some learned women taught courses in parks. The Sheikh reminded his listeners of the woman who publicly dared to correct a caliph—the leader of the Muslim community. When he told them about Fatimah al-Bataihiyyah, the scholar who taught while leaning on the Prophet's tomb, the women gasped. "Whoa!" exclaimed the young woman next to me, shaking her head disbelievingly. "Leaning on the Prophet's tomb!"

Despite the excitement rustling the grassroots, the details of most of Akram's nine thousand women remain buried. With the exception of a single-volume introduction, published in English, his research lies dormant in the hard drive of his computer. Forty volumes would prove too expensive, said his usual publishers in Damascus, Beirut, and Lucknow. Despite entreaties from his students, he wants to see it as a book before publishing it on the Internet.

For a time, there was interest from Prince Turki al-Faisal, Saudi's former ambassador to Washington. Sheikh Yusuf Qaradawi, whose TV sermons on Al-Jazeera helped make him one of the most famous Sunni scholars in the world, expressed his admiration for the project. Some of his students have started a *Muhaddithat* fund, attempting to raise money for publication. But the research remains unpublished, in part due to the Sheikh's lack of worldly ambition. "Some man from the United Nations called me," he said one day in passing. "He said they want to help me with my work." But Akram misplaced the caller's name and number, and when I pressed him, he couldn't remember the name of the section the man worked for. He wasn't concerned: "He'll call back."

Until he does, Akram spreads news of his research by lecturing to women's groups and on university campuses. But the differences between his findings and contemporary mores gape depressingly wide. The day he lectured on women at Cairo's Al-Azhar, the Sunni world's venerable university, which has both women students and even female professors, the audience was all male.

At moments like that, Akram lamented how change arrives too slowly. "All culture," he would say, frowning. "It's all culture." Great scholars like Abu Hanifa and Malik—founders of schools of religious law—"They never had problems with women! They were learning from them!" He once described reading Thomas Gray's "Elegy Written in a Country Churchyard," the eighteenth-century poet's lament for dead English peasants, whose horizons were constrained by village life, which denied them the education to develop their natural talents. "Gray said that the villagers buried there could have been like Milton" with the right education, Akram observed. "Muslim women are in the same situation. There could have been so many Miltons."

8

"The Little Rosy One"

If there was ever proof that a pious Muslim woman need not be a muffled and submissive wife and mother, it is the life of Aisha, the third of the Prophet's eleven wives. The Prophet's most controversial wife, she has divided opinions ever since the seventh century, among both Muslims and non-Muslims. A top Islamic scholar, an inspiration to champions of women's rights, a military commander riding on camelback, and a fatwa-issuing jurist, Aisha stretched the role of Leader's Wife far beyond the usual job description of comeliness and decorum. By the standards of both our own time and hers, Aisha's intellectual standing and religious authority were astonishing.

She knew it, too. Ten things, she said, set her apart from her co-wives. An excerpt from an early Islamic account of her words: "He did not marry any other virgin but me . . . The revelation would come to him while he was with me, and it did not come down when he was with any of his wives except me. Allah took his soul while he was against my chest."

Aisha is not the only wife of Muhammad whose life explodes notions of what constitutes a "traditional" Muslim woman. Khadija, whom the Prophet married first and loved deeply until her death, ran a caravan business in Mecca. A wealthy and successful trader, she was also a twice-widowed single mother, fifteen years Muhammad's senior, and his boss. Her marriage proposal to the future Prophet was forthright: "I like you because of our relationship, your high reputation among your people, your trustworthiness, your good character and truthfulness."

Khadija emerges as an impressive presence, but it is Aisha who shimmers, lifelike, on the pages of the early Muslim histories. Her voice carries across the centuries, preserved in 2,210 hadiths. And what a voice: bell-clear and courageous, one can hear it, should one we choose to listen, pronouncing on Islamic traditions on matters from prayer to trade to sex. That we know so much more about Aisha than Khadija comes down to timing: most of Khadija's life predated Islam, so it was not chronicled with the same care as Aisha's. Born four years after Muhammad's first revelation, Aisha grew up while the verses of the Quran were descending on the Prophet. We are privy to extraordinary details of his youngest wife over the course of her sixty-odd-year life: her penchant for wearing safflower red, her gift for poetry, her knowledge of medicine. We hear accounts of her spirited debates with other intellectual luminaries, and her fatwas on topics ranging from breast-feeding to inheritance. After the Prophet's death, her fatwas were highly respected, pronouncements that remain crucial to Islamic law to this day.

Some fourteen hundred years on, Aisha remains not just a role model but a red-blooded human, at once laudable and yet reassuringly flawed. We see her giving away the last scrap of food in her house—a grape—to a beggar, but we also hear her jealousy of her co-wives. Here is her crisp account of a quarrel with Safiyya, a Jewish convert and the Prophet's tenth wife: "I insulted her father, and she insulted mine."

Reading about Aisha—how she'd fret over the Prophet staying out too long in the sun, or how she'd recite scores of poetry verses from memory—I was exultant. So much of Aisha's life closed the gap between Islamic traditions of womanhood and my own feminist sensibilities. In Aisha we find a woman, and a woman's interpretations, at the core of a religious tradition. "Take half your religion from Humayra [the Little Rosy One]," Muhammad advised his Companions, using his nickname for the fair-skinned Aisha. For Leila Ahmed, in her authoritative book *Women and Gender in Islam*, it is the centrality of women in Islam's core texts that sets Islam apart from other monotheisms: "How many of the world's major living religions incorporate women's accounts into their central texts, or allow a woman's testimony as to the correct reading of a single word of a sacred text to influence decisions?"

But while Aisha showed how close my beliefs were to the Sheikh's, she also showed how far apart they could be. It was the subject of Aisha's life that led to our most distressing conversation.

She was betrothed at six or seven. As Aisha described it, she was playing outside, oblivious, at the time the marriage took place. "The Messenger of Allah married me while I was playing with the girls," she recalled. "I did not know that [he] had married me, until my mother took me and made me sit in the room rather than being outside. Then it occurred to me that I was married."

It was marriage, but not, at first, as we know it: she wasn't to live with the Prophet until she was nine. "I was playing on a seesaw and had become disheveled," she said. "I was taken and prepared and then brought in to him. He was shown my picture in silk." The silken image appeared to the Prophet in a dream. The Angel Gabriel appeared holding the portrait, and said, "Marry her. She is your wife."

The marriage was an extremely happy one, full of playfulness and intellectual debate. Muhammad's love for Aisha was "like a firm knot in a rope," he once told her, ever constant. Even today, she is known by the epithet "the Beloved of the Beloved of Allah." Still, Aisha's description of the short route from seesaw to silk picture unnerved me. My temptation, when I came across it, was to snap her biography shut in disgust. Islam's detractors have done that for centuries, dismissing the marriage between the fifty-year-old Muhammad and the little girl as pedophilia. But to shut the book, so to speak, would reduce Aisha to merely being a bride. To focus only on her age at marriage, rather than what came after it, I'd miss the best bits of the story, the ones that add tone and texture, not just to the marriage, but to Aisha herself.

For the child bride grows into a heroine for grown-ups. After the Prophet's death, when the jousting began over what Muhammad actually said and did, Aisha proved an agile debater against misogyny. When one man claimed that Muhammad had said that prayers were invalid should "a dog, a donkey, and a woman" cross in front of the person praying, Aisha retorted: "You have compared us [women] to donkeys and dogs." Nothing of the sort invalidated prayers, she said: "By Allah! I saw the Prophet praying while I used to lie in bed between him and the Qibla." In the political arena, her boldest move came after the murder of Uthman, Islam's third caliph, or successor to the Prophet. She demanded that the new leader, Ali, hunt out Uthman's assassins. When he refused, Aisha undertook the Battle of the Camel, so named because she directed the troops from camelback. Her side lost, but she went to nearby Basra to teach women from both the winning and losing sides about Islam. Some scholars have read the Battle of the Camel's defeat as proof that women aren't meant to be leaders. Not the Sheikh. Aisha's tenacity, and expansiveness to the women of the victors suggested another lesson to him: "When you make a mistake, move on!"

One evening in London, I set out to hear the Sheikh deliver a lecture on Aisha. The lecture was to be held at Imperial College, one of Britain's premier science and engineering universities. For an evening in midweek, the audience was huge. The Sheikh was expecting as much, he later told me: the subject of Aisha always draws big crowds, particularly at universities. She inevitably steers the discussion toward marriage—a popular topic with students. The Sheikh was late, stuck in traffic, so as I waited, I scanned the auditorium from my perch at the back, in the "Sisters" section. The Sheikh didn't believe that male and female students should be segregated at his lectures, since they hadn't been in the time of the Prophet Muhammad. Still, the people organizing the Sheikh's lectures often seated men and women separately. Divisions were signaled in a range of creative ways. Sometimes there was a white plastic curtain, or a hanging sheet, drawn down the center of the room. Other times, though there was no formal division, the men and women automatically gravitated to opposite sides of the auditorium. Whether visible or invisible, the gendered seating created an atmospheric shift, like a change in cabin pressure in a plane. Dividing the room gave it its own set of rules, at odds with those governing the streets outside.

That night, the division was innovative: a desk with bottles of Pepsi Max and plastic cups separated the men, in front, from the women, in back. I minded this, not merely for the message it sent about women's second-class citizenship, but because it made it difficult for my Black-Berry to pick up Akram's words clearly. It could be worse, of course: in many mosques, women aren't even allowed in the main room with the men. I've been crowded into dank basements with the other women, trying to make out a *khutbah*—the mosque imam's lecture—over the squall of babies and the loudspeaker's crackle.

Rarely, in my experience, does this gender apartheid seem to do what it's designed to: turn one's thoughts away from the opposite sex during lectures. As my mother once reported, on returning from an orthodox Jewish wedding, where women and men sat on separate sides, barriers actually seemed to heighten one's awareness of the opposite sex, rather than tamp it down. I remember hearing a story about a Pakistani scholar who was asked why Islamic cultures were so intent on keeping men and women separate. "Why?" he asked. "Why, to boost the birthrate, of course!"

As we waited for the Sheikh's arrival, the scene morphed into two parallel parties, one all-male, the other all-female. Nothing gets people thinking more about sex than gender segregation, I muse, watching a guy in a checked shirt sneaking glances at the women's section from under thick-fringed lashes.

At last, the Sheikh did arrive, having made his way through London's traffic. After apologizing for keeping the audience waiting, he began to talk about Aisha. Because the Prophet knew Aisha both as a child and as a wife, he said, her life serves as a guide for good Muslims on how to raise pious children, and how to have a happy marriage. Both children and wives, he continued, need the freedom to explore, learn, and pursue happiness.

Aisha enjoyed far greater freedoms than many twenty-first-century Muslim women. She debated with men, and she went to the mosque and to the battlefield. Once, when Muhammad received a dinner invitation that excluded her, he refused, three times—until finally the evening's hosts agreed to include her in the invitation, too. When she wanted to see a public sporting event, he hoisted her up so she could see, even though "the Prophet was not so interested, because he was old," explained Akram. What's more, the couple would run races with each other—some of which Aisha won. "You can't imagine any *muhaddith* [expert in hadith], or *faqih* [jurisconsult], or someone like me, having a race with their wife? Their young wife?" Approving chuckles from the crowd. "They have a race, and she beat him! And he did not mind! Nobody does this now! Why do we not follow the example?"

These anecdotes stirred mixed feelings in me. They suggested a tender, respectful union. But the stories—of races run, of Aisha's enthusiasm over a sporting event, of unabashed questions—seemed only to underscore that unavoidable fact: Aisha was very young.

Akram read them differently. For him, Aisha's life suggested something all too often overlooked: that happiness was crucial for a good Muslim family. "People, when they marry, they don't want to make their wives happy," he said. "When they have children, they don't want to make them happy." Why ever not? demanded the Sheikh. "Make them happy!" Aisha shared the Prophet with many other women, and yet, he pointed out, Muhammad managed to make all his wives happy. Admittedly, not every minute was blissful. Once, Muhammad's wives began to grumble about his propensity to give away the household's food to the poor. "The wives would say, 'Why do you give to everyone else, but not to your family?'" noted the Sheikh. This carping meant that Muhammad slept separately from his wives for a month, and he received a revelation that appears in the Quran, giving them a choice. They could either stay married to the Prophet, living simply, or they could leave him, but leave as rich women:

> O Prophet, say to your wives, "If you desire the life of the world and its
> finery,
> come then and I will provide for you, and divorce you on the best of
> terms.
> But if you want God and God's prophet, and the home of the hereafter,
> God has prepared a tremendous reward for those of you who do good."
> (33:28–30)

This verse answered anyone concerned that the Prophet was keeping Aisha in a marriage against her will, said Akram. "Many people think Aisha was forced to be married," he said. "But when the revelation came, she said, 'I have chosen you.'"

The Sheikh lingered over what is the most famous anecdote of Aisha's life, one so important that it appears in the Quran. The so-called "Incident of the Lie" triggered a marital crisis for the couple, political tensions in the young Muslim community, and a revelation proclaiming Aisha's innocence. Muhammad and his followers were returning to Medina from a campaign against a hostile tribe. When the caravan stopped, fourteen-year-old Aisha hopped off her camel to relieve herself. On returning, she realized that she had lost a necklace and so decided to retrace her steps. Since the girl was light, and the curtains of her canopied seat on top of the camel remained closed, nobody had noticed she wasn't there when the caravan moved on. On discovering she'd been left behind, Aisha waited for someone to return and escort her back to the others. Nobody did, but a young man happened by and brought Aisha back to Medina, setting her on his camel and leading her by the reins.

Back in town, the gossips began whispering. Aisha's young rescuer was awfully handsome. And she was so playful and pretty. What on earth could have happened out there in those secluded dunes? Even the Prophet himself became unsure of what had taken place that day in the desert. He grew distant and a bit chilly to Aisha, and his revelations stopped. Aisha herself had fallen ill after the incident and had moved back to her parents' house to recover. Eventually, the Prophet confronted her. Her parents were crying, and so was she, said Akram. "The Prophet said, 'Oh, Aisha, listen, if you have done this thing, it is a mistake,'" continued the Sheikh. "'Repent to Allah, and he will forgive you.'" Aisha, however, remained resolute. "I was a young girl at that time, and I had not read much of the Quran," she later recalled. But having seen that Muhammad thought the accusations might be true, she couldn't say anything. "If I say to you that I am quite innocent—and Allah knows that I am innocent—you would never believe me to be true," she said. "If I confess to the allegations . . . in that case, you would take me to be true." Her only course, she decided, was to be patient and to ask for Allah's help. She turned her head away and lay down on the bed.

The Prophet, in turn, began to sweat, and beads of moisture were "dropping from his body like pearls, though it was a wintry day," Aisha recalled. He fell into a sort of trance and began to receive a revelation. The words that came down denounced the gossip as slander and the gossipers as sinners. The verses not only confirmed Aisha's innocence, but stipulated that if a husband accuses his wife of adultery and she claims her innocence, she should be believed. Later in the verse come the key Quranic passages for Islamic laws on adultery, invoking the famous "four witnesses" of the sex act needed to prove the guilt of the accused:

> When you heard it, why didn't the faithful men and women think
> the best on their own and say, "This is an obvious lie!"
> Why didn't they bring four witnesses to testify to it?
> If they didn't produce witnesses, then *they* are the liars in the sight
> of God. (24:12–13)

Muhammad was hugely relieved, said Akram. "When the revelation came to him, the Prophet became very, very happy," he said. "And his face shone. And he said, "Oh, Aisha, your purity has been revealed to me by the heaven." The girl's mother immediately urged her to thank her husband. Aisha wouldn't. "She said, 'No,'" said Akram, admiringly. "She said, 'I'm not going to thank him. I'm going to thank my Lord.' She was so bright, no doubt, that she had learnt that Islam is about the connection to her Lord, and every word, every deed should be to please Him." A husband, even if he was the Prophet, was not the dispenser of grace. Allah was.

And here, Akram laid out a powerful principle, one that had battered against man-made hierarchies from the start of Islamic history. No matter who you were, and what your situation, you were given an implicit dignity by faith in your God. *Taqwa* (God-consciousness) and *imaan* (belief) made you answerable not to the power structures around you, but to a higher power. You could be a teenage bride, refusing to be cowed by small-town gossip, or by your parents' pleas, or even by the suspicions of your husband—who just happened to be God's Messenger on earth. Aisha's faith gave her the strength to withstand such pressures, to turn from earthly power structures in favor of something much, much larger.

Akram could draw a huge, approving laugh from the women's section whenever he mentioned the counsel he gave women contemplating divorce: "I always tell women who are having trouble with their husbands, 'You think your life is married life? Husbands can come and go, but your Lord is always there.'" Akram's vision of *taqwa* also provided a key for combating oppression within marriage. To the husbands in the audience who might be tempted to mistreat their wives he'd state its corollary: "You don't rule her! You didn't create her! If your wife is happy, thank Allah and be happy. We did not create our wives, and we did not create our husbands. Allah did."

His reasoning was framed in the language of submitting to Allah alone: no human should have control over any other one. It sounded bracing, liberating, and as stripped of gooey romanticism as any second-wave feminist text.

After Akram finished his Aisha talk, he opened the floor to questions. From the men came questions about marriage. A young man asked advice for "the brothers here who are looking for wives": What should they look for in a wife? Not a household slave, held Akram. "It is the duty of the men to look after the house. Men have to cook the food! Men have to clean!" The Prophet, after all, would sweep the floors, patch his own clothes, and repair his own sandals.

From the women's section, applause. From the men's, nervous laughter.

"The wife's job," continued Akram, "is to educate the children. So the primary criterion to look for in a wife, is to look for someone educated."

Akram went on, warming to his theme. In Muslim societies nowadays, women seldom got the respect they deserved. The Quran and the early life of the Prophet show just how much authority Islam gave them. Modern Muslims needed to turn back to these basic sources, to recognize all the rights they had lost.

And then came the question I was desperate to know about but was glad I didn't have to ask.

How, asked a young man, would the Sheikh address the question of Aisha's young age when she was married?

Well, responded Akram, Aisha was the Prophet's only child bride: all his other wives were mature women, widows or divorcées when he married them. Aisha was exceptional. Aisha did indeed go to the Prophet's house when she was nine, but different people mature at different ages. "Some girls, they are, from the beginning, very bright, very intelligent," he said. "And they also, you know, they grow very quickly. Some girls are different from most other people . . . God has made some people like that. There are other people who are thirty or forty years old, but they're not mature."

I thought I'd misheard him. Hoped I had.

What's more, he said, "We have never had any single report that she was unhappy." Like the Prophet's other wives, she was given a choice whether or not to leave his house, and she chose to stay. What's more, we had her word on her happiness in the marriage, for it is her account of it that has been passed down from generation to generation. Unlike so many women, Aisha got to tell her side of the story.

My chest felt tight. I had utterly expected—and now fervently wished—that Sheikh Akram would have taken the cultural relativism route. Things were different in seventh-century Arabia, I wanted him to say. Life was short, and girls grew up fast—not just in the Muslim community, but among Jews and Christians, too. One Jewish tradition holds that Rebecca married Isaac when she was three; scholars estimate Mary gave birth to Jesus around the age of twelve. Besides, we need to refine our definition of what it means to be married: across the Near East, marriages were often political alliances used to link families and tribes—a custom that continued for hundreds of years in Europe, too.

That was how I would have framed the issue, and how many Muslim feminists do.

And then, I wanted the Sheikh to say, "Look, we can acknowledge that Aisha's marriage was of its time and place, and that, because of the extraordinary personalities involved, it worked out very well. But that doesn't mean we shouldn't condemn the marriage of young girls today." I wanted him to criticise child marriage in places where it remains common, like India and Yemen, and to call it one of the greatest drags on Muslim society today. I wanted him to tick off how it ruins women's health, chokes off their education and employment, and bodes ill for the future of their kids and communities. For Muslims, followers of a faith deeply concerned with justice, child marriage today should be an abomination, just as it should be for every other human being on this earth.

That's what I wanted him to say. I wanted him to denounce child marriage in loud and ringing tones.

He didn't.

He didn't say it later, when another student, a young man in the front, raised the issue again. Those hadiths about her playing with dolls and swings, he said, didn't they bring up the issues of consent?

"She was a child, but she was a bright child, very bright," responded Akram. In Islamic law, issues of consent only arise when a girl is married by someone other than her father: "Other people don't have the love, but a father has the love," he said. "He has full wisdom, and full love."

(And the mother? I wondered. Where's the mother in all this?)

Of course, he continued, if a daughter doesn't want to marry, she should never be forced. A girl once knocked on Aisha's door, crying that her father was trying to marry her against her will. Aisha took the girl inside, and when the Prophet heard the girl's complaint, he declared the marriage invalid.

That was calming. And yet, still, the questions kept coming about Aisha's age—polite, but pressing.

How, one young woman asked, should one explain Aisha's marriage to non-Muslims? It was one of the things they always asked about. When they do, she said haplessly, "I don't know what to reply."

Forget defending it to non-Muslims, said the Sheikh. "*You* should be convinced," he said. "And if you believe that the Messenger is so pious and so pure," he said, "then you must know that the marriage was, too."

One culture could never understand another "unless they appreciate the main foundation of the culture." Non-Muslims, who may not know the Prophet's honesty and purity, might never be able to understand some of his actions. "When you read the story in light of our time, it looks bad, but when you read it in light of the Prophet, then it's understandable."

Soon after, I went to a party and ran into Hans, the intellectual who'd dismissed my arguments about Islam guaranteeing the same human rights as secularism. How was the book going? he asked, refilling my glass with champagne. The lessons with the Sheikh?

I told him a bit of what I'd been learning. How studying with the Sheikh constantly surprised me. And then I rapidly changed the subject.

Of course, I wouldn't keep off the subject of Aisha's marriage when I next met Akram for a lesson. One member of the Aisha lecture audience had praised him for his courage in "not shying away from the marriage issue," and I couldn't ignore it, either.

"Look," I said, "I understand that it's one thing for a very young girl to have been married in the seventh century. But I wasn't quite clear on whether you thought that behavior was acceptable now. Could you unpack that?"

Context was important, the Sheikh agreed. It put him in mind, he said, of a saying of Mahatma Gandhi's that he'd learned at Nadwah, "something about, 'If you're not in that person's situation, it is difficult to imagine the whole situation, and difficult to judge wisely.'"

And the context was? "Well, in the Western world now, there is university education, and people cannot plan to marry if they don't have jobs. But imagine Europe, three or four hundred years back. Imagine a farmer's house—you know, these people have nothing to do, other than marry. A farmer's boy and a farmer's girl—there's nothing to stop them from these things, even very young."

"But now, in the modern world, people basically see children marrying as child abuse!"

"Abuse is also happening, you will see abuse," he nodded composedly. "But not everyone who marries like this is thinking about child abuse. If you grow up in a certain context, and your mind is so much thinking one way, you can't think of things like this in any other way."

It was a point of pride for me, as a pluralist and a journalist, to try to see things from another cultural point of view. I could see that Aisha was an exception, could allow that seventh-century Arabia had an entirely different set of codes. But the Sheikh's unwillingness to offer a blanket condemnation of child marriage rankled. True, he didn't believe children should be married, but he still didn't challenge the fact that traditional interpretations of Islamic law—like those of Hinduism and Judaism—allowed it. For the Sheikh, marriage, even relatively young, was far preferable to the Western phenomenon of unmarried teenage motherhood. "Without marriage, people are having kids at fifteen, sixteen, and so the woman is left alone," he argued. "That's worse, surely!"

Intellectually, I could see his point, within traditional societies where single women are outcasts. Emotionally, I couldn't, not least because of the memory of Nujood. She was ten when I met her, in Sana, Yemen. I'd been sent by an American magazine to interview the girl, whose courage in the face of local culture had made her Yemen's most famous divorcée. A child with a passion for Tom and Jerry cartoons had been married at nine and divorced at ten. After one sister was kidnapped and another raped, her unemployed father, who had sixteen children and two wives, figured an early marriage would keep Nujood fed and safe. On her wedding day, she got a twenty-dollar ring, three dresses, and two hijabs, but the excitement wore off by the evening, when, she said, her thirty-year-old groom raped her. A year later, she made Yemeni history by taking a taxi downtown to the courts and demanding a divorce. Asked by her future lawyer why, she responded: "I hate the nights."

Nujood's case made headlines across the world. When a law in Yemen was passed raising the minimum marriage age to seventeen, it met with so much opposition from conservatives that it was repealed. In 2010, the Associated Press reported that Yemen's Muslim leaders had issued a statement declaring that any supporters of the new law would be denounced as un-Islamic, and apostates. It took until 2014 for there to be a concerted push to pass a law banning child marriages.

In classes, the Sheikh would caution his students not to repackage Islam to make it more acceptable to Westerners. His lectures on Aisha—and the issue of polygamy—were proof that he practiced what he preached.

"So Sheikh," I ventured one day. "My understanding is that you're only allowed two wives as long as you treat them equally."

I was talking about the verse that qualifies the fact that you can "marry women who please you, two, three, or four; but if you fear you won't be equitable, then one."

Muslim feminists had pointed out that in affairs of the heart and house alike, being equitable was impossible. They argued that the verse actually discouraged, rathern than promoted, the pre-Islamic practice of polygamy.

Nope, responded the Sheikh, to my dismay. "A man can have two, three, or four wives, as long as he provides each of them with separate accommodation and expenses. But people cannot love them equally— what's in your heart, this is more difficult."

"But wasn't the revelation about polygamy really about taking care of widows, after the Muslim battles?" I asked, hoping that he'd agree with the reading of a Muslim woman activist I'd once met. She'd said that the verse had descended after Muhammad and his Companions were faced with military losses, which had left lots of widows behind. The spirit of the law, she suggested, was not about picking young and gorgeous second and third wives for fun. Rather, it was meant to provide vulnerable older women with protection, sorely needed in patriarchal seventh-century Arabia.

"No doubt, after the battles, when there were people killed, it was beneficial for society for people to marry widows," said the Sheikh. "But no, the reason was not for this. Arabs used to have more than one wife anyway—there was no limit!" Islam simply capped the number at four.

"So it wasn't really about protecting widows or orphans?"

"No, not just that. Some Muslims just want to show Islamic law as acceptable to a larger audience."

In the case of polygamy, I couldn't accuse the Sheikh of that.

But the Sheikh saw polygamy as something else, too: an acknowledgement of male weakness, and an efficient system for minimizing its damage. "Many men cheat," he said. "It's so easy for them to fool a woman, and leave her, maybe with a child." Marrying a second wife, he argued, gives women protection: the relationship is made public, and the man's responsibilities to provide for the woman are, too. "A second marriage is better for the woman," he said. "They get a house, and they get expenses."

Within a traditional worldview, I could see the institution's logic. But my worldview couldn't stretch to see it as the Sheikh did, so I hung up despondent. Championing women's rights within a conservative Muslim matrix, the Sheikh saw such arrangements as logical. I, however, saw them as aspects of the patriarchy that he was unwilling to touch.

By assuming the Sheikh wouldn't revise his views, I'd underestimated him. It took Arzoo and Mehrun, the two Oxford housemates studying with the Sheikh to become Islamic scholars, to make their teacher rethink his position on child marriage. One Sunday, in an advanced course on *fiqh* in Oxford, the class was tackling a legal text by Imam Kasani, with a chapter called "The Marriage of Minors." "There were about forty guys in the room, and just a few women," recalled Arzoo. As the day wore on, with the class placidly taking notes on the finer legal points of marrying children, the two women "were turning pink, and purple, and blue with anger," said Arzoo. As a doctor and public health consultant, Mehrun had worked in Kenya and Zambia and had seen the dire costs of the practice up close. "She was imploding," said Arzoo. "The more upset she gets, the quieter she goes."

"I could not understand how an eight-year-old could be expected to stand up to her elders and explain to the court what is in her best interests," recalled Mehrun. "I was too flustered to ask the questions myself, so I prodded Zoo"—her nickname for Arzoo.

Arzoo raised her hand and asked the Sheikh how Islamic law could possibly condone anything that led to such suffering. She spoke of Yemeni girls; of parents marrying off their kids for money rather than protection; of internal bleeding and prolapsed uteruses, those all-too-common results of underage intercourse and girls giving birth. She went on, saying she knew the jurists said a girl could refuse a marriage, but how, she asked—slightly breathless now—could one expect a little girl to challenge her parents like that in a court of law, or to even know her own mind?

The Sheikh listened, and nodded. Without the proper mindset—and monitoring from the state—such practices were no doubt common. They were unjust, and un-Islamic. Islam would never condone anyone being married, or having sex, without their consent.

For weeks, the women continued to debate the issue with Akram, watching his position evolve. At first, the Sheikh held that while child marriage was permissible, the parents must have the best interests of their daughters in mind—and that governments should monitor such arrangements to ensure that neither the parents nor the husband abused the girl. He could find no evidence that marriages could legally be consummated before puberty, and he said no girl should have sex before she begins menstruating. "What is needed for the child is a contract," he told Mehrun and Arzoo, "not consummation."

Such debates went on for weeks, with Arzoo making the legal case, and Mehrun telling the Sheikh of child brides she'd treated in Africa. Then, at the morning Hadith class one Sunday, the sheikh told the two women, "Make sure you try to come to the *fiqh* class today," he stressed. "It's an important one."

It was indeed, for it was at that class that he made an announcement that, as Mehrun later put it, "lifted us up to the clouds."

"He said, 'I have been talking to Arzoo and Mehrunisha over the last few weeks about the issue of the marriage of minors,'" recalled Arzoo, in a Skype conversation. "'And I've revised my position.'" Having heard their arguments against the practice, he had gone back to the sources, and had found an eighth-century judge and jurist, Ibn Shubruma, with a sound fatwa against the practice of child marriage. Ibn Shubruma argued that the issue hinged on a woman's autonomy. When girls reached puberty, they could choose whom to marry. By being married in childhood, this choice was taken away from them. Akram added to this argument, stating that the oppression and injustice occurring within child marriages today emphasises the need to oppose it at the juristic level. The classical legal argument, bolstered by the modern examples of injustice that Arzoo and Mehrun had brought to his attention, changed his mind: "I've learned from these girls," he said.

The mostly male crowd was stunned. For a sheikh to declare that he was changing his mind was unusual enough, but for him to do so after debating with two women students?

"The boys were shocked," recalled Mehrun.

"The guys' hands all shot up immediately," laughed Arzoo. "For weeks, none of them had said anything during our classes to challenge the marriage of minors. And now suddenly, they were spurred on by the turn of events."

"The men were very quick to form a dissenting voice," agreed Mehrun. "It wasn't that any of them practiced child marriages in their own lives or that they even agreed with it. But they clearly felt that this was an attack on their role as males, and their ability to make decisions for their children."

"Their reactions just motivated me more," added Mehrun.

The pursuit of justice, the Sheikh told the two women, needed to be informed by women's voices and experiences. Muslims shouldn't merely look to classical texts to understand their faith. Today's scholars needed to write new ones, taking into account women's viewpoints on the true spirit of the Quran and the sunna. "Write a book," he urged Arzoo. "Women were not so present when these legal opinions were being written. You must write a book."

How ironic, I later mused, that so many outsiders see Islam as a matter of cast-iron rules, of binding fatwas and unforgiving bans. As the year went on, I was repeatedly surprised by the broadness of its intellectual framework. This intrinsic flexibility could be used for good and ill alike: Islamic laws were only as humane as the Muslims interpreting them.

9

Veiling and Unveiling

One morning, Sumaiya Akram had come down to the family car for her ride to school wearing a *niqab,* and her father was so shocked, he refused to start the car. She was now a figure with her head and face covered, a slit left for her eyes. "He thought I was mad," Sumaiya recalled. "He just sat there waiting for me to go back into the house, to change. He wouldn't turn the car on."

On first seeing the *niqab,* the Sheikh thought that she had fallen under the sway of some hard-line group. He worried that she hadn't made the choice to wear it for herself. Could she have been influenced by somebody? "I was thinking that she was perhaps impressed by someone," he said. "That she wanted to copy someone."

Wearing the *niqab* had been entirely Sumaiya's choice, though she wasn't completely sure what, exactly, prompted her to take it up. She was sixteen, so there were hormones to consider, both her own and other people's. As a teenager, she felt that she shouldn't be looking at men, and men shouldn't be looking at her. "I thought the hijab might be a constant reminder for me," she said, to help control temptations. But a decade on, her decision remained vaguely mysterious, even to her. "I don't know what it was," she said pensively. "I just thought I'd try it."

Watching this straight-talking, self-possessed woman bustle around her suburban living room in East London, I wondered how much her *niqab* had been a halal form of teenage rebellion. Had it been a version of a Goth hairdo or a heart tattoo? A declaration of self, a gentle press against the boundaries of her childhood? But then I checked myself: simply flattening the *niqab* to an adolescent fashion statement stripped it of anything sacred. Not that all hijabs are about submitting to God. Those with fake Calvin Klein logos on them suggest a submission to the market. For the women wearing both hijab and skinny jeans, a headscarf is not necessarily about modesty but perhaps represents a personal style signature.

But a *niqab* was different. It was not a "choice" in the manner of the consumer economy. A visual obliteration of the self, a plain black *niqab* was a refusal to engage in everyday modes of self-expression. The woman who wore it chose to wear it because it connected her to something bigger than the self. It could be God. It could be a Muslim identity. But it wasn't a simple case of a teenage fashion choice, that was certain.

Whatever it was that made Sumaiya don the *niqab* in 2005, it took courage. Sumaiya's *niqab* was among Oxford's first. What's more, she attended a high school without many Muslims, so she wasn't getting support from her peers. Her classmates, she crisply observed, must have expected her "to blow up the class or something." Her favorite teacher asked if there was a festival of some sort. Not at all. "This is me now," replied Sumaiya. The woman never mentioned it again: that appeared to be that.

Non-Muslims didn't tend to comment on her new attire—"the English are very reserved." It was fellow Muslims who seemed most unnerved by this bold declaration of piety, and in class they tended to keep their distance. "For some of my teachers, it must have been, 'What do we do with this girl now?'" But she took care to stay "normal," to continue speaking up in class, to sit where she'd always sat, to keep her grades as high as ever.

As for her father, he accepted the *niqab* as soon as he understood that it had been her choice and hers alone. Muslims, men and women both, must be modest. On that Akram and his daughter agreed. Both

agreed, too, that a *niqab* was optional, not required. Like many classical scholars, the Sheikh believed a woman should cover her head,
arms, and legs and wear loose-fitting clothes so as not to draw attention to her form. But her face and hands didn't need covering. If a
woman wanted to wear a *niqab*, that was her choice. If she wanted to
wear black gloves with it, as some *niqabi*s did, that was her choice,
too. But in the Sheikh's opinion, neither was required. For the Sheikh,
modest Muslim covering was not to render a woman absent or invisible, just "that they be present and visible, with the power of their
bodies switched off."

Few garments, if any, have been freighted with more debate than the
Muslim veil. Mullahs pontificate on the proper sheerness, length, and
style. Governments, both Muslim and Western, have used it as a plank
in policy strategies. Even using the word "veil" can be controversial, as
it can conjure an orientalist fantasy of alluring harem girls. Despite
this, I've opted to use the term "veil" in this chapter, not to perpetuate
an image of the Mysterious East, but because it's the broadest term I
could find to describe the concept of Muslim women's coverings, which
can range from filmy headscarves to all-enveloping burqas.

There's debate among Muslims as to whether the Quran says explicitly that a woman must cover her head. The verses most frequently
quoted as arguments for veiling appear in the chapter "Light," or "Nur":

> Tell the believing men to lower their eyes and guard their privates.
> That is more innocent for them; for God is fully aware of whatever
>   they do.
> And tell the believing women to lower their eyes and guard their
>   privates, and not to show their ornaments except the obvious
>   ones, and to draw their coverings over their breasts. (24:31)

The verse's wording is so vague that it's been ammunition for both
champions of the veil and their opponents. Akram and many classical jurists believe that the line allowing women to show "the obvious"

ornaments suggests that women can show their faces and hands. Others say that the verse merely encourages dressing modestly. Some have even read the verse as a simple caution against innuendo-laced banter between the sexes, which historians say was common in pre-Islamic Arabia. Some conservatives read it as prescribing the burqa. One controversial Quranic translator even renders the verse to read that women should only allow the palms of their hands to show, along with "one eye or both eyes for necessity to see the way."

Characteristically, Akram managed to be both aware of the range of readings and respectful of them. "There is an opinion that covering the face with a *niqab* is obligatory, a requirement on every woman," he said diplomatically, when asked. "But," he went on, "we know that the wives of the Prophet didn't ordinarily cover their faces, from a story about Aisha." Once, having heard about a beautiful woman who wanted to offer herself in marriage to the Prophet, Aisha's co-wives urged her to go survey the woman's charms. To do so without being recognized, Aisha donned a *niqab*.

What's more, the wives of the Prophet were more covered than the other Muslim women in the community. The Quran ordered as much, in the verse that's sometimes called "The Verse of the Hijab," which an early account says was revealed after one of Muhammad's weddings. When the celebrations had wound down, some guests had lingered in the bride's room rather longer than was polite. A verse descended:

> Believers, don't enter the houses of the Prophet unless you are
> > given permission to come for a meal, and then without waiting
> > around for its time.
> But when you are invited, then go in;
> and when you have eaten, then disperse, without socializing for
> > conversation;
> for that annoys the Prophet, so he shies away from you.
> But God does not shy away from truth.
> And when you ask the ladies for something needed, ask them from
> > behind a screen:
> that is purer for your hearts and their hearts. (33:53)

The part about addressing the Prophet's wives from "behind a screen" spoke to the situation in the household of Muhammad, whose stature in the community meant there was a constant flow of traffic. The more people came to see the Prophet, the more it became necessary to find ways to give the Prophet's wives privacy. The curtain mentioned in the verse allowed this. During the Prophet's lifetime, "veiling, like seclusion, was observed only by his wives," writes historian Leila Ahmed. The veil's prevalence in the Muslim community came later. It may have spread in part, surmises Ahmed, in imitation of the Prophet's wives, or after Islam spread to regions like Syria and Palestine, where veiling was an aristocratic custom. Later, medieval scholars made these customs into law.

Nobody should force women and girls to cover their heads, believed the Sheikh. Modesty, like piety itself, should come from within, not be imposed from above. "Laws don't make people pious," he observed. "They protect piety when it is already there." Governments couldn't legislate their citizens into submission: Iran and Saudi Arabia proved that. Just as trying to impose sharia law wouldn't make people into good Muslims, imposing the hijab wouldn't automatically confer modesty. Without fear of God and a true submission to Him, these outward displays of Islamic identities were just about showing off an identity, he explained, not about faith. "There could be people who follow sharia law, but they're not believers," he said. "Or there could be someone who doesn't cover, but they are believers," he said.

Covering your head required true commitment before it truly worked. "Clothes don't make you pious," he told his students. "If you're pious, the covering can protect you. But trying to force women into the house, or into the hijab, it's not going to make them pious." Nor could one presume to judge what a particular woman's headcovering meant. Veils, like other public displays of Islamic faith, meant little without true Islam. For the Sheikh, the issue of hijab was a bit beside the point compared to the more trenchant matter of true piety. In this he was in agreement with a very different type of Muslim thinker, the African-American feminist Amina Wadud, who had said, "If you think the difference between heaven and hell is forty-five inches of material, boy, will you be surprised." She quotes the Quran's assertion that "the best dress is the dress of *taqwa*," or God-consciousness.

Knowing *taqwa* couldn't be dictated, the Sheikh left his daughters to decide how to dress. When his younger girls reached puberty, the age at which many Muslim women begin wearing the *jilbab*, the flowing, long-sleeved robe, they asked whether they'd need to wear it, and Akram's response was mild. "I'm not going to force you to wear it," Sumaiya recalled him saying. "I think you should. But it's up to you."

"Because he didn't force us," she shrugged, "the *jilbab* stayed."

So did her devotion to modesty. Sumaiya's decisions on what constitutes modesty varied from day to day. She was not a veiled woman, but a woman who chose how she veiled. Some days she wore the *niqab*, a choice that often hinged on geography. When she and her husband moved to their East London neighborhood, she found the mood there to be "very anti-Islamic." It was nothing overt, but she couldn't help but notice little things: chilly nods in the street, terse notes left on the doorstep reminding the couple to trim their grass. When she and her husband first moved in, somebody complained to the local government authorities about the fact that there was furniture on the sidewalk. "Of course there was furniture outside," Sumaiya sighed. "We were moving in!"

Whether her neighbors were being Islamophobic or merely rude, Sumaiya decided to forgo the *niqab* in her own neighborhood in favor of a simple hijab. She still wore the *niqab* when going to more Muslim-friendly parts of London. The day we spoke about it, she was unsure as to whether she would wear the *niqab* while attending graduate school; she'd stopped wearing it when she was an undergraduate and had resumed wearing it—when she wanted to—only after leaving the university. "I feel more comfortable wearing it," she observed, "rather than not wearing it."

One day, midway through the Sheikh's seminar on manners, I looked up to see a late arrival, a woman in a *niqab*, trundling in with a stroller. I nodded and smiled, moved my backpack so she could sit, and turned back to the lecture. A nudge, a whisper—"Hi, Carla"—and possibly, I inferred from the warm eyes, a smile. Sumaiya was now a voice and a presence rather than a face. Later, during lunch break, I watched as her son Asim toyed with the face veil. "He's used to it," she said. "He loves playing peek-a-boo with it."

For centuries, male leaders have played veil peek-a-boo, too. But their game is less about clothes than about power. "All the problems Muslims have faced in recent decades are more or less boundary problems," wrote the Moroccan feminist writer Fatima Mernissi. In the Islamic world over the last two centuries, the biggest boundaries crossed have been territorial, in the form of Western imperialism. But these incursions into Muslim lands frequently led to skirmishes over more intimate boundaries: those related to women, and how they covered, or didn't cover, their bodies. From the French in nineteenth-century Algeria to the Americans in twenty-first-century Afghanistan, Western military invasions of Islamic countries have been accompanied by rhetoric about liberating Muslim women from their hijabs. To "modernize" or subdue a country meant to unveil its women. "The Arabs elude us," noted General Bugeaud, the French administrator of Algeria in the 1840s, "because they conceal their women from our gaze." After 9/11, in the run-up to the American bombardment of Afghanistan, politicians and pundits linked the country's liberation from Taliban rule to the liberation of women from their burqas. In the months after the Taliban's fall, the Western press would rush to capture women shedding their veils. It was as though this transition from burqaed lump to woman was a twenty-first-century Pygmalion myth: a breathing of life into Afghanistan's people.

The extent to which a Muslim country's women veiled—or didn't veil—has long served as a sort of litmus test for its relationship to the West. For the Middle Eastern dictator, making your women take off their veils was a cheap and easy way to prove you were moving toward Western-style "progress." When the Iranian dictator Reza Shah, father of Iran's last shah, banned the chador as part of his modernizing drive in 1936, police were told to rip the coverings off women's heads if they persisted in wearing them. The edict was soon followed by a sort of regional dance of the veils. Rulers from Afghanistan to Turkey encouraged women to uncover their heads; traditionalists fought back, either in the mosques and streets or in parliaments. Making women take off their headcoverings signaled assertive Westernization, or secularization. Orders to veil sent a countermessage, telegraphing a commitment to traditionalism and independence from the West.

It's an epic struggle that continues to this day, not just in the Muslim-majority countries but also in Europe. The judgments—for wearing a hijab, for not wearing a hijab—rain down on women as well as nation-states. Too often the meaning of the hijab is taken as clear and unequivocal, like an on-off switch, a neat binary code. A Muslim woman is "traditional" if she wears one, "modern" if she doesn't. "Oppressed" if she wears one, "liberated" if not. Scarf on: "devout." Scarfless: "moderate," or, who knows? Perhaps even "secular." Much like my efforts to locate the Sheikh on a spectrum modeled on the American scale from left to right, such conceits are doomed to fail. Sumaiya's confidence is palpable—indeed, has grown—under the *niqab* she chooses to wear.

In the Taliban's Kabul, veils weren't about choice, but submission. Under Taliban rule, women shrank against the walls when the Vice and Virtue squads rolled by in their red Toyota trucks. While there in 1998, the photographer Nina Berman and I both wore burqas so as to sneak into Afghan homes undetected as foreigners. But a burqa couldn't hide the bulge of Nina's Nikons and lenses, nor did it hobble her strides. Even shrouded, she looked like what she was: a Manhattan woman in a hurry. "Baby steps!" I hissed at her from under my burqa. "Remember, you're oppressed!"

In societies where women themselves decide what they wear, a hijab can mean any number of things. It can suggest a woman's relationship to God, or peer pressure. It can signal obedience to her state or to herself, or can just mean a bad hair day. The Cairo commuter may don a headscarf to avoid harassment on crowded buses. The Lebanese villager may wear her headscarf to signal that she's a Muslim, not a Christian. An American feminist Muslim could don her hijab to demonstrate a defiance of consumer culture. But her sister, whose hijab has a Nike swoosh on it, embraces it. Sumaiya thought perhaps she took up the *niqab* against sexual temptation; another woman told me she felt like "a right sexy bitch" when she put on her red-and-white-flowered *niqab*.

I was only five when my parents bought me my first chador in Iran, but I still remember the charge of excitement it gave me whenever I wore it. Its soft polyester gave it a spooky warmth and stretch. To put it on was to be folded in an oversoft, overclose embrace: cozy but cloying, like the moist hug of a great-aunt. I stood beside my mother at a merchant's stall in the Tehran Grand Bazaar, finally settling on a print of peacock greens in swirling paisley, chosen from hundreds of bolts, from the palest dove gray to the fieriest orange, stacked floor to ceiling. I remember the *kiss kiss* of scissors blades as the merchant cut into the fabric. The pleasure of watching him fold it into a squashy bundle, wrapped in brown paper. Even then, I knew that sometimes a length of cloth was not just a length of cloth. A veil was special, I recognized, a strong signal of something about adulthood, and its dangers.

To a kid with the luxury of not having to wear it, the chador meant power, not submission. There was glamor in its sweep, drama in its drape. I'd seen *Sleeping Beauty* and knew what real femininity entailed: flowing garments and, if not a trancelike sleep, then at the very least a mysterious silence. When my friend Tara and I spent afternoons playing Iranian Ladies, dandling our baby dolls while wrapped in our chadors, there was a tacit agreement that the women in chadors held far more dramatic potential than our American mothers. With their jeans and uncovered hair, American women lacked the force field of femininity that the women in chadors possessed. In 1972, with our feminist mothers jettisoning their heels and lipsticks, it was chador-clad Iranians who embodied a five-year-old's vision of what it meant to be a woman.

I was a child then, and I have since put away childish things. But when it comes to the veil obsession in the West, many haven't. Why is it that the hijab seem to obsess non-Muslims so much? Muslim men are supposed to wear beards, but this covering of chin and cheeks is seldom described as a human rights violation. Under the Taliban, Kabul's men would nervously pull and fluff their facial hair, worried it would not meet the "fist and a half" standards required by the Virtue and Vice squads.

But it's the veil that gets all the attention, drawing a near-fetishistic interest by religious zealots and Western media commentators alike. Sensational legislations by strident secularists like the French, or religious zealots like the Taliban, make veils into news, of course. But more fundamentally, the veil wreaks havoc on the standard secular notion of what is private and what is public. When a woman puts one on, her head is suddenly signaled as an erotic site. What secular society deems public is now made private, while one's religion—what is in many Western societies considered to be private—is exposed for everyone to see. As the Moroccan feminist Fatima Mernissi observed, modern tensions between Muslims and non-Muslims come down to boundaries.

Once, back working at the Oxford Centre for Islamic Studies, I'd accidentally walked in on my Pakistani colleague Iftikhar while he was praying. Mortified, I quickly turned and left, shutting the door behind me. Later, he brushed away my apologies. "That's the difference between us," he said, waving a hand breezily. "You Westerners make love in public and pray in private. We Muslims do exactly the reverse."

At a lecture by the Sheikh in Manchester one Sunday, I felt profoundly dowdy amid a sea of hijabs. Mere hair can't compete. My mousy-brown pixie cut made me as invisible as any *niqab*, surrounded as I was by heads swathed in scarves draped as carefully as Chanel gowns, with fabric covered in leopard print, roses, bright plaids, or stripes. Pearl and diamanté clips secured headscarves, some folded so voluptuously that they resembled cloth crowns. The irony of the fashion for lavish hijabs wasn't lost on the Sheikh. "Many Muslim women make them so they become more attractive!" he told me later, with a rueful smile. "That's not the function. Islam wants to develop simplicity of the clothes for the woman. You can't just put a hijab on your head while you're wearing tight jeans. You should wear it to show your purity."

To be fair, it wasn't just women who'd indulged in pre-lecture primping that morning in Manchester. Riding the elevator up to the auditorium, I caught one youth raking his fingers through his beard, patting and tugging it for maximum length and heft. The Sheikh's theme that day was how to create a good Muslim marriage. The crowd—young, and largely single—packed the lecture hall, which hummed with possibility. The Sheikh chose his words to chill any romantic illusions in the room. "Very often, people think, 'I have fallen in love with someone,'" he began. But all too often, love proved to be mere desire. Allah had put sexual impulses into the hearts of humans in order to continue the propagation of our species. But like other basic human urges, the desire for sex with someone can't last. Once it is quenched, warned the Sheikh, it subsides: "If you marry someone because of desire, your desire will go down. Just like when you are hungry, and you eat, the desire for food goes down. Desire, by nature, is something that diminishes. Love, by nature, grows."

Marriages born of desire are destined for failure. "If you marry a woman because she has a good character, you will see more and more of her qualities. If you marry a woman because of desire, the marriage will fail. If you marry a woman because she is a twenty-year-old, what will happen? The next day, she'll be more than twenty years old."

The difference between desire and love, said the Sheikh firmly, was like the difference between a meal at a fast-food restaurant and a home-cooked meal. The hungry man passing a McDonald's might eat, but it would be bad for him. Far better to forgo that burger and go home instead to eat healthful food prepared with care. "Force your desires to listen to you!" he exclaimed. "If people just have what they desire, then they will ruin their health. If people marry someone just for enjoyment, that marriage will never last. When the desire for sex comes, don't rush. Think properly: 'Am I ready for marriage?'"

Returning home from the lecture, I passed through Victoria Station. I heard the din of chanting men, stumbling in packs from a rugby match, wafting beer and testosterone. A hen party tottered out of a suburban train, the bride-to-be trussed up in a fat pink sash with the word "Bride" on it. Her friends hustled after her in high stilettos and low necklines. Above me, a poster of two breasts, and behind them their owner, hawked beer. How curious, I thought, that so many Westerners think it's just the Muslims who mark out the differences between the genders, through segregation and the hijab. At the Sheikh's lecture that day, men and women both had been so modest that the differences between them seemed smudged and muted. Everyone had been so demure that the sexes seemed to blend.

But that's exactly it, the Sheikh exclaimed delightedly when I told him. "Uncovering makes more clear who are men and women," he said. "And when they cover their differences, they are more like the same."

The big issue was whether they were at home or in public. "God has made men and women both as human beings, but with certain differences," said the Sheikh. "Inside their houses, they can meet as men and women." Out in the street, they should meet as humans. "Covering those differences," he said, "helps people to be treated as human beings."

Talking to Akram and his wife, I found that the veil seemed to keep moving. Suddenly, the curtain dividing public and private would close, covering up topics I'd assumed were perfectly proper for public discussion. Farhana's childhood games were to be left off-limits in print. No amount of probing could get Akram to speak with any nuance about moving from India to Britain. But sometimes, just as suddenly, the hijab would be lifted off, often exposing surprising revelations. Nowhere was this curtain raising more dramatic than on the subject of sex. Figuring out when the Sheikh would draw the curtain and when he'd raise it felt as befuddling as desire itself. Once, I simply happened to ask whether Aisha ever had any disputes over a hadith with a particular companion of the Prophet, Abu Huraira. Suddenly, without warning, we were on the topic of ejaculation—or rather, the lack thereof. Akram said that Aisha did voice her differences of opinion with Abu Huraira on reporting sayings of the Prophet. "For example, Abu Huraira used to say 'If someone has relations with his wife, and nothing came out, there was no need for a bath upon him.' But Aisha, she said 'No, he is wrong.'"

Islam has a clear-eyed acceptance of sex as part of life. Early Islamic texts declare it a good part, so long as it occurs within marriage and between a man and a woman. "Your women are a field of yours," the Quran tells Muslims. "So come to your field as you wish." (That's Thomas Cleary's translation: other English translations sound even more macho: "Your wives are a tilth for you, so approach your tilth when or how ye will," reads one.) When I first read that oft-quoted line, I was taken aback at the comparison of women to soil, and at the implication that men were entitled to free and open access to it whenever they wanted. That was until Lily Munir, an Indonesian Islamic feminist, helped me tease out the metaphor's nuance. "Soil has to be prepared for the seed," she told me, eyes twinkling. "It has to be watered, it has to be made soft, and smooth, and ready."

The collections of hadith stress a married couple's rights not just to sex, but to enjoying it. "Don't come onto your wife just like an animal," the Prophet Muhammad is reported to have said, counseling kisses, caresses, and soft words to get her in the mood. In Cairo, I once interviewed an Egyptian religious scholar about Islam's attitudes to sex, and he was similarly enthusiastic on the subject of foreplay: "The woman is not a chair that you can just pull out and sit on!" he explained, slapping his knee for emphasis.

Done right, sex is an Islamic blessing. "A man's sexual play with his partner, when accompanied by sincere intent, causes him to be rewarded by Allah," wrote the sixteenth-century hadith scholar Ali Muttaqi. "As the Prophet is reported to have said, 'Allah is pleased with a man's playing with his wife, and records a reward for him and makes a worthy provision in the world for him because of it.'" Christianity links sex to sin, but the Cambridge theologian Tim Winter notes that Islam casts it as "a glimpse of transcendence." Islam doesn't endorse celibacy and has no mainstream traditions of monks or nuns. "In the Christian context," Winter once explained to a British newspaper, "sexuality is traditionally seen as a consequence of the Fall, but for Muslims, it is an anticipation of paradise."

Muhammad's biographies detail moving accounts of sexual tenderness between the Prophet and his wives. When Muhammad was unsure as to whether the Revelations were a sign of madness or a sign from God, Khadija asked him to alert her whenever he next saw the Angel Gabriel. When the Prophet did so, his wife asked him to sit next to her right thigh. Could he still see the Angel? Yes, just as he could when he sat next to her other thigh. But when she then opened her robe, the creature fled. For Khadija, that was proof that the being appearing before Muhammad was an angel, not a devil. Had it been a malevolent creature, it would have stayed to watch.

Within marriage, sex is a right for both married men and women. If either partner can't perform in bed, the marriage contract can be dissolved. "One of the classic reasons that a woman can go to the court and get a divorce is if a husband cannot have relations with her, or cannot satisfy her desire," Akram told me. Once, a student confided to him that after a year of marriage, she was still a virgin. "I told her not to be so shy. If he cannot do these things, it is important to find a solution. Now, she is married to someone else."

The Sheikh had a fairly low opinion of lust, which allowed him to talk freely about it. "Everyone wants passion," he conceded. But too much of it squeezed out room for God. "It means you are basically worshipping someone else than Allah." When it came to sex, his discussions weren't gummed up by romanticism or stifled by shame: lust was just an urge placed in humans by Allah for the sole purpose of procreation. I once asked him about the Quran's "tilth" verse. Where Lily Munir had read the verse about wives being tilth to cultivate as a call for lots of foreplay, Sheikh Akram emphasized its agricultural imagery. You till in soil, a place where things are planted to grow. "Some people think if they get desire, they can do it anywhere, like in the back place, or in the mouth," he explained. "But this desire is for a family purpose. You must do it in the right place. Any position they like, people can do, as long as they do it in the place that is meant for the purpose of having a family."

Lust required regulation: it was why the curtain hung in some mosques and classrooms, and why modesty was a cardinal virtue for all Muslims. Along with most classical scholars, the Sheikh considered sex outside marriage, or *zina*, to be among the gravest sins in Islam. Sex may have been regulated by Islam's moral dictates, but in this it was no different from prayer, eating, or giving charity. Since Islam was a way of life, and sex a part of it, one needed to ascertain whether one was approaching it in the spirit of piety. Shyness should never prevent anybody from finding out how to live as a good Muslim. Muhammad himself used to hold special women-only sessions, so there'd be no excuse for bashfulness. Good Muslims needed to ask questions about sex just as about other issues: "Shy people can never learn," Akram said with a shrug. "Arrogant people can never learn."

The Sheikh's ideas on sex were unlike any I'd heard firsthand. My own sex ed was fairly standard for the child of 1970s liberals. It began in the fifth grade at Linda Schuham's house, poring over the hairy couple doing nudie gymnastics in *The Joy of Sex*. Then came the day I overheard my mother discussing the So-and-So's, who were busy consulting divorce lawyers because their last-ditch experiments with whipped cream hadn't worked out. Hollywood played its usual role as erotic instructor. There was the flushed stillness required while watching *The Last Picture Show* next to my parents, and later, the damp thrill of Kathleen Turner and William Hurt's loveless couplings in *Body Heat*. Furtive flips through *Fear of Flying*. My mother's proud presentation, on my fifteenth birthday, of my first copy of *Our Bodies, Ourselves*. These rites imbued me with the orthodox sexual worldview of a modern Western feminist. Unshackled from marriage, pregnancy, and even love, sex was but another mode of self-expression. Provided you visited Planned Parenthood and pushed the specter of AIDS out of your mind, it was freedom incarnate.

The Sheikh had never read a *Playboy* or seen an R-rated matinee, but that didn't stifle frank discussion at his females-only day seminar, "What Every Muslim Woman Should Know." It was held at a Muslim primary school in South London, so I walked through hallways full of kids' drawings of London's Big Ben and Mecca's Kaaba before entering an auditorium with hundreds of young women and being handed the lecture notes. On the front page, in the discussion of *wudu*, or ritual ablution, was a hadith from the Prophet's wife Aisha that was so gamy that, certain I'd misunderstood, I had to read it twice: "I used to scratch the sperm off the Messenger of Allah's clothes if it was dry, and wash it off if it was still wet."

This information wasn't cordoned off from other advice in the notes, such as the number of shrouds required to wrap a woman's corpse (five), or the placement of women's hands when they pray (over their chests). Sperm, and its disposal, were simply seen as issues a good Muslim should know about, much as they knew about the rites of death or prayer.

The morning's lecture tackled wet dreams, both male and female— "a sign of desire, and becoming mature," said the Sheikh. There was a discussion of menstrual blood, and when precisely one could judge it had stopped so that one could resume sexual relations and return to the mosque to pray. To demonstrate the proper way to do *wudu*, the Sheikh came out from behind his desk. He slipped his feet out of his shoes to demonstrate where the water should go. Putting his hands on his head, he showed women how to cleanse their heads, how to place their fingers under their hijab to do so. He showed the subtle differences between men's and women's prostration: men touched their foreheads to the earth, with enough space that a baby goat could pass under them. Women keep their bodies close to the ground, for modesty's sake.

Nothing felt off-limits. "No doubt you will have certain questions different from men," said the Sheikh, looking out at the women encouragingly. "So many rules in hadith came because women asked questions!"

The crowd's main concern appeared to be makeup. Young women with open faces and open notebooks posed question after question. Could one wear toenail polish? Not during prayers, if the polish kept water from cleansing the nails properly during ablutions, responded the Sheikh. What if one wore socks over painted toes? What if the manicure had glued-on decals on it? Did waterproof makeup make ablutions invalid? Anything that keeps water from cleansing the skin, advised the Sheikh, would prevent a proper ablution.

The Sheikh's patience in fielding questions on Islamically correct beauty routines astounded me. Could one dye one's hair? asked one young woman. Pluck one's eyebrows? another pursued. The Sheikh replied that faith meant that you didn't need to spend your money on makeup and manicures. "You see," he said brightly. "Islam makes life cheaper!"

Besides, he said, launching into a speech nearly identical to the ones I'd given my daughters: "Don't just do things because other people do them. Always think that you're different, and you have to do things that are better for you, not other people! People are not going to respect you because you've got more nail polish!"

Before the lunch break, a woman with a microphone made an announcement, asking us to support HHUGS, a charity for the families of men detained under Britain's antiterrorism laws. "Close your eyes," she told the audience, and imagine that life as you knew it was taken away from you with a policeman's knock on the door. Your children are crying, she instructed us. "You're forced outside, without time to put on your hijab," she said. "You're in your nightgown." Your husband, or your father, is taken away, and you're never certain when you'll see him again. That, the speaker told us, was the experience of so many wives of prisoners, in Guantánamo or in British prisons.

When she finished asking for donations, I opened my eyes. I was now doubly dizzy from a morning spent careening between bodily functions and equality, nail polish and police detentions. Girly preoccupations had bumped up against the sacred; profundities were chased by trivialities. The flow of ideas simply didn't conform to my own logic. Edward Said's *Orientalism* argues that the Western study of Islamic cultures was in fact "a system for dominating, restructuring, and having authority over the Orient." I wondered just how much my own project was guilty of this: of trying to stuff the Sheikh's worldview into Western categories.

I wandered out, impressed with the Sheikh's sang-froid. Not many men could face an all-female audience to discuss sperm and menstrual blood. But Islam gave him a blueprint to discuss these issues. Few scholars of the Sheikh's stature would have tolerated teenagers asking question after question about toenail polish. It was a bit like having the head of the Mayo Clinic write you a prescription for your tickly throat. But the Sheikh's absence of vanity allowed him to swerve away from the hidebound masculinity that so often seemed to be expected of males, Muslim or otherwise. "Sheikh Akram's not a typical man," his student Arzoo once observed. "He's got a perfect balance of masculine and feminine qualities." In this, he was sticking to tradition. The Prophet Muhammad was gentle, affectionate with children, and did housework. Marriage was a partnership, believed the Sheikh: women had the duty to educate the children, and men the responsibility to provide financially. Even though Akram believed in those gendered roles, he conceded that the roles could be swapped, "although it would be difficult."

There were limits, however.

"You know, God has made a difference between men and women for a purpose: to make family. If you have two men in the house, that hurts the whole family. Some women are very strong, and some men are very weak. That's not a problem. But people should not exceed the limit."

The limit, of course, was homosexuality.

"But why, if God has created these feelings?" I ask. "Should they not enjoy sexual relationships too?"

Sex, said the Sheikh, is for just one thing: the continuation of the human race.

"But why is homosexual desire there, if we agree that some people are just born that way?" I pursue. "Surely if God created these feelings, they are fine."

"Enjoyment of the body is just for the purpose of the family. Nothing else."

"But if you have inclinations, Sheikh . . . ?"

"Well, just because you have inclinations does not mean you

should give in to them. That doesn't mean they should give in to those desires. These people should be supported to strengthen their faith."

My chest tightened, much as it did later that week when I read a newspaper story about persecution of Nigeria's *yan daudu*. An established subculture of men who act feminine, the *yan daudu* wear scarves and makeup, even as they live as husbands and fathers. Long tolerated, I read, they're now targeted by a Muslim religious revival in Northern Nigeria, and by renewed pressure on sexual minorities. "It hurts my heart that people say, 'May Allah reform you,'" one *yan daudu* said as he did *wudu* and made his way to the mosque. "A judgment belongs to Allah, so if we are different, it is because Allah made us different."

In a sentence, the Nigerian had succinctly summarized an emerging body of progressive Muslim theologies. In new readings of the Quran, whether from feminists, or Queer Theorists, or readers arguing for political pluralism, there is an emphasis that diversity is something not to be shunned, but embraced.

On this issue, I remained firmly in the Muslim progressive camp. Or rather, in the camp of most everyone but religious conservatives, be they Christian or Muslim. During my studies with the Sheikh, Christian evangelists in Africa were pushing through legislation to make homosexuality a crime. In a decade when new laws allowed gay marriage in many places, and when even the Pope said he was in no position to judge what consenting adults did in bed, Akram's views on homosexuality felt countercultural. Yet they were also a reminder that the fault lines we walked were not between Islam and the West, but between orthodox interpreters of the major faiths—and nearly everyone else.

✦ 10 ✦

Reading "The Women"

When I told a Muslim friend of mine that I was to be studying with a sheikh, she had one request. "Ask him," she said, "why Muslim men treat women so badly."

When I did, he said it was because men weren't reading the Quran properly: "If they don't fear God, then they oppress their women." And yet many of the men who deny their wives and daughters basic freedoms hide behind their Qurans. A favorite passage for patriarchs: the famous 4:34, the thirty-fourth verse of "The Women," the Quran's fourth chapter. These six lines must surely rank among the most hotly debated in the Muslim scripture. The Muslim women's group Musawah has called them the "DNA of patriarchy" for the Islamic legal tradition. For it is here that many scholars have claimed to find Allah setting out men's superiority and authority over women, an authority that can be backed up by force.

One popular translation, by the early-twentieth-century English translator Muhammad Marmaduke Pickthall, reads:

Men are in charge of women, because Allah hath made the one of them to excel the other, and because they spend of their property [for the support of women]. So good women are the obedient, guarding in secret that which Allah hath guarded. As for those from whom ye fear rebellion, admonish them and banish them to beds apart, and scourge them. Then if they obey you, seek not a way against them.

As debates on how to translate the verse rage online and at academic conferences, new translations suggest less sexist meanings than earlier ones. Thomas Cleary, whose work is used throughout this book, suggests a slightly more equitable arrangement—at least in the verse's first line:

> The men are supporters of the women, by what God has given one
>   more than the other, and by what they provide from their
>   property.
> So women of integrity are humble, guardians in absentia by God's
>   protection.
> As for those of whom you fear perversity, admonish them; then
>   leave them alone in bed; then spank them.
> And if they obey you, then seek no means against them. (4:34)

Another translation casts men as women's "protectors and maintainers," and yet another says that "men are to take care of women, because God has given them greater strength." The Arabic word that Pickthall translated as "scourge," and which other translations rendered as "beat," Cleary translates as "spank." But the word, notes Reza Aslan, can also mean "turn away from," or "go along with," or even to "have consensual intercourse with."

One may debate 4:34's meanings, but one thing remains certain: men's interpretations of the verse have made millions of women miserable. Muftis, or Islamic judges, cite it to excuse domestic violence. Husbands have hijacked it to stop wives from going to graduate school, to work, or to the bazaar. The Saudi Arabian government leveraged its message to legislate a "guardianship" system in the Kingdom wherein women could not, until recently, open a business or a bank account, travel abroad, or enroll at a university without a male relative's permission. A few days before my lesson with Akram, I'd received an e-flyer advertising a trip to go on a pilgrimage to Mecca. Under the price, the travel dates, and the assurance of four-star accommodations was a line derived from a Saudi reading of 4:34: "Females," it read, "must be accompanied by a *mahram*"—male guardian.

Like Akram, I had grown up in a household with many copies of the same book. In the Sheikh's case, it had been the Quran. In my parents' house, the multiple copies were not of a single scripture, but of a handful of seminal feminist texts. My mother taught women's studies at Washington University in St. Louis, and being a devoted professor but an erratic housekeeper, she littered the house with copies of her course books. One *Norton Anthology of Literature by Women* lived in my parents' bathroom upstairs, while another, annotated in my mother's spidery hand, sat atop the brass tray in the dining room between its trips to the university for classes. Toni Morrison's *The Bluest Eye* functioned as our household version of the Gideon Bible: you could find a copy of it in most bedrooms. And we seemed to have a shelf of copies of *A Room of One's Own*, in a paperback edition as slim and elegant as Virginia Woolf herself. It was as though my mother, heeding Woolf's call for her own room, had given Woolf the run of not just one, but many.

Growing up in a household with a Woolf in every room, I was trained to spot the signs of sexism young, in much the same spirit that pioneer kids were taught to hunt and fish. At abortion rights rallies, at seminars on *Thelma and Louise*, at Take Back the Night speakouts, I learned that only I could protect my own rights. When I was four years old and wondered aloud why my mother never served cookies to the ladies at her consciousness-raising group, I was told that the personal was political. Coffee was allowed, but anything more was banned at these events lest they trigger a carbs arms race brought on by competitive baking and hostessing. One Valentine's Day in St. Louis, sometime in my teens, my mother and I drove past a billboard advertising a suburban flower shop: it featured a pair of disembodied, naked female legs sticking out of a vase next to the slogan "We've got great stems." My mother reversed and drove to the florist in question, and together we went in and complained about the sign's sexism. Women's body parts sticking out of a vase weren't romantic in the least, my mother told the sales assistant. He looked bemused but promised he'd convey our concern to the owner. "Make sure you tell him that it was a mother and daughter, together, who came in to complain," my mother pressed sweetly.

Though she would often quote me that great feminist line about well-behaved women seldom making history, my mother was a well-behaved woman. She'd begun her academic career at a time when undergrads still wore white gloves on dates, and she only wholeheartedly embraced feminism during the Reagan presidency. Since she was happy to leave her teaching for years at a time to follow my father around the world, she'd missed the furor over *Roe v. Wade* and the Equal Rights Amendment and had sat out the sexual revolution. While her colleagues battled on the wilder shores of women's studies, like queer theory or feminist economics, my mother found her feminism in the essays of Woolf and Mary Wollstonecraft and the novels of Jane Austen and the Brontës. "Oh, I do love teaching all these kids about the possibilities out there for women, and how they shouldn't take equality for granted," she once exclaimed. And then, leaning forward, she offered a guilty confession, sotto voce: "But sometimes, I just want to close the book and tell them how fabulous it is to have children and a family."

Still, my mother applauded Virginia Woolf's critique of nineteenth-century family life. In class, she'd parse the writer's disdain for the Victorian ideal of the "Angel of the House," obedient, pure, self-sacrificing. At home, she'd press a copy of *A Room of One's Own* on me with touching urgency, echoing Woolf's call to young women "to go about the business of life," to shuck off the provincialism of confinement in drawing rooms and family life because "no human being should shut out the view."

During the Sheikh's classes, I detected a yearning for a broader view in some women's questions. Once, when a student asked him what he thought of feminism, Akram answered without hesitation. One cannot blame Muslim women who are attracted by feminism, he said, given the conditions many of them suffer under in the Muslim world. "People want justice," he said. "Feminism wants justice for women. Where Muslims aren't doing justice for the women, these movements will come. If women don't get the respect they deserve, we cannot complain if they seek it out in feminism. If women are suffering, they will."

Changing prevailing attitudes will take time, he advised me. "In Europe, when they comment on the rights of women in Muslim societies, they usually comment how they are all very bad," he said. "They talk as though it was always the way it is now in Europe for women. But in some places in Europe, women have only been voting since the 1970s."

On the day we met to discuss "The Women"—"An-Nisa" in Arabic—we sat at our usual table at the Nosebag. I was hunkered down over my latte, tense as a boxer before the championship bell. When I flipped through my Quran to find the passage, the Sheikh nodded resignedly, as though he'd known it was only a matter of time before I'd open it there. We both knew that it was all but inevitable, this squaring off over 4:34. We both knew that I'd point at the place in the text that I'd marked in ballpoint pen. I wanted to understand how a faith so concerned with justice seemed to have injustice written into its scripture.

"So—about this 'guardian' verse, where some translations claim men are superior to women—how would you translate it?" I blurted. "What does *qiwamah*, which I've seen translated as 'guardianship,' really mean?"

Akram paused. "Let us start by talking about the chapter as a whole," he said gently. "If you read the sura from the very beginning, you will find that it is actually defending women."

As Akram explained it, "An-Nisa" was a sura that protected women, not punished them. It laid out the approved treatment of weaker members of society, such as orphans, war widows, and women in general. Between its dictates, the sura reminds people to fear and to obey God. These warnings, embedded in a chapter concerned with the rights of the weak, are a rhetorical form of protection, explained Akram. "Clever people, or people with power, they always can interpret law in their own ways," he said. "So God reminds people, 'Fear Me.' Now we know, in your house, if you do injustice to your wife, maybe she cannot take you to court . . . but there's another court." He pointed upward. "The Lord knows what's happening."

The sura begins in the spirit of egalitarianism. "Look," said Akram, cupping his hands around the space in front of him, his fingers forming a neat oval. "At the opening, it says that men and women are created 'from one soul.'" He read, "O humankind, be conscious of your Lord, who created you from one soul, and created its mate from it, and propagated from the two many men and women."

So the Quran starts from the assumption of absolute equality in creation. So far, it felt more enlightened than the best-known creation story in the Bible, which casts Eve as a mere helpmeet for Adam, created from one of his ribs—and even then, created only after the Lord had given life to "every beast of the field and every fowl of the air."

The creation from a single soul, Akram pressed on, illustrates how Islam grants men and women equality in light of honor and respect before God. "They both have the same soul, and they both have the same Creator, so they are subject to the same laws."

In the context of seventh-century Arabia, the notion that women had rights of any kind, and were God's creations, on a par with men, was revolutionary. In pre-Islamic Arabia, girls were considered a liability. They were mouths to feed, and bodies requiring expensive dowries when they married, so they were sometimes murdered at birth, buried in the desert dunes—a practice the Quran explicitly condemns.

Those females who made it past childhood were nearly always prohibited from inheriting or owning property. Indeed, a woman was effectively part of a man's goods and chattels: if her husband died, she passed to his male heir, along with the rest of the property. With the arrival of Islam, women gained the right to inherit: the Quran states they are entitled to half as much as their male relatives. The formula may not meet contemporary Western notions of equality, but in seventh-century Arabian society, it was a model of fairness. In the traditional Islamic setup, it is the man, not the woman, who supports a family financially. A woman's inheritance is her own, to be spent as she wants; a man's duty is to use his inheritance to support his family.

By all standards but the most modern ones, the two-to-one inheritance ruling was extraordinarily progressive: until 1870, British common law operated on the principle of "coverture," which meant that married women, legally speaking, didn't exist. Since the law saw husband and wife as one, women couldn't inherit property or keep their earnings. "Their very being and legal existence is suspended during the marriage," wrote the eighteenth-century jurist Charles Blackstone. In the United States, it wasn't until 1900 that women gained the right to control their own property.

Unsurprisingly, men in the seventh century were less than enthusiastic on hearing that women could inherit property. Early Islamic histories report disgruntled men complaining to the Prophet, notes Reza Aslan. "How can one give the right of inheritance to women and children, who do not work and do not earn their living?" they asked. "Are they now going to inherit just like men who have worked to earn that money?" A verse in "The Women," suggests Aslan, gave them their answer, in no uncertain terms: "Those who disobey God and His Messenger, and who try to overstep the boundaries of this [inheritance] law, will be thrown into Hell, where they will dwell forever, suffering the most shameful punishment."

These verses have had a considerable effect on the Sheikh's family fortunes. He hadn't truly understood the inheritance verses properly until he was nineteen years old and studying at Nadwah. When he read, and then reread, the verse in Arabic, he was shocked. His grandfather, and his great-grandfather, had unwittingly cheated their daughters out of what was rightfully theirs. Like many Indian Muslims, Akram's family had followed village customs, under which women often don't inherit land. Akram's father and uncle had split it between them; his two aunts had received nothing. On his next visit home to Jamdahan, Akram confronted his father: he and his brother must give a third of this land away, dividing the share between their two sisters. Akram convinced his father, but when the two men explained to Akram's aunts that the Quran had granted them a share of their father's lands, they were too frightened to take it at first. "They used to come to our house and stay for a month, or two," Akram explained. "They were worried that if they took their inheritance, they wouldn't be able to come anymore. They worried that things would change."

His aunts fretted about their clever young nephew, just back from Lucknow, insisting on rearranging family affairs. Why bother with all this fuss when their brother took such good care of them? But Akram and his father persisted, and the two women eventually took what the Quran said belonged to them. Back then, they were among the only Muslim women to inherit land in Jamdahan. Now, Akram said, the village men have begun to approach him, asking what the Quran says about passing on property to heirs.

It's not only land inheritance that is changing in Jamdahan, said Akram. Over the centuries, the village Muslims had adopted the Hindu custom of the joint family system, in which grooms bring their wives home to live with their parents. But in Islam, every Muslim husband is required to provide his wife with her own home. Ever since Akram began advising the villagers of this, fewer Jamdahani Muslims were living in joint families. As he told me this, he allowed himself a smile of quiet satisfaction. "Even when I was young, they would listen to me," he said. "Even when I was young—still studying at Nadwah—they'd take my advice."

I thought for a minute about Akram's aunties, hesitant to grab hold of what their God—and their family—agreed was rightfully theirs. The warm and steady press of custom can provide a certain comfort even as it stifles.

"Change can be hard, huh?" I said. "Even when you're benefiting from it."

"Injustice has its own order," the Sheikh agreed. "After one or two generations, it can seem like injustice is the normal way of doing things. When you try to establish justice, it can create change, and for a time, it seems there is disorder."

Operating his household along Quranic guidelines, Akram used his salary to support the family, while his wife kept her own money for herself. What Farhana earned from her sewing business was hers. "Sometimes she sends it back to her family," he said. "But I never interfere with it. I never even ask her about it! It's hers."

Her *mehr* was hers to keep as well. The future groom gives this Muslim form of dowry to a woman before marriage. It's an investment in a woman's status, explained Akram: "If men have to give a *mehr*, then you think before you marry!" he exclaimed. "It means that marriage is not just for enjoyment!"

"Actually, in the Islamic context, the question is, 'Why do women get anything at all?'" said Akram. "They don't need to spend anything anyway!" He paused, letting this provocative statement linger for maximum effect before answering his own question. Women's inheritance rights had more to do with principle than practicality. Women need their own property "because money makes people look seriously at someone," he explains. "Women need to get shares of property so that they get a certain respect."

From inheritance, and the respect it accorded, came all sorts of other possibilities for women. Less than a century before Akram and I sat talking in Oxford, Virginia Woolf had mapped out some of them in a lecture she gave in Cambridge. In it she evoked the grandeur of Oxford and Cambridge's men's colleges, funded by kings and industrialists. She contrasted it with the grim little supper she'd had at a women's college—"Fernham," invented for the purposes of her argument—of beef and prunes, eaten off plain china and washed down with water. If only Fernham's founder, an energetic Victorian lady who'd laboriously raised the funds to build it, had possessed money: "Now if she had gone into business; had become a manufacturer of artificial silk or a magnate on the Stock Exchange; if she had left two or three hundred thousand pounds to Fernham, we could have been sitting at our ease tonight and the subject of our talk might have been archeology, botany, anthropology, physics, the nature of the atom . . ."

But they weren't. Instead, Woolf and her hostess were discussing why it was that there'd been no room "for partridges and wine, beadles and turf, books and cigars, libraries and leisure," and why "to raise bare walls out of the bare earth was the utmost [our mothers] could do." Women who could have left fortunes to Fernham had raised children rather than made money. (Before the 1870 act, of course, women couldn't inherit at all.) In Woolf's era, family life was exclusively women's work. Building an institution to rival the grand male Oxbridge colleges "would necessitate the suppression of families altogether."

Family life is laborious, agreed Akram. But it's made far easier by a neat division of labor—which is how he reads the controversial verse, 4:34. While many scholars had interpreted it as a broad endorsement of men's power over women because of their inherent superiority, Akram believes it has a far narrower application. *Qiwamah*—often defined as "guardianship"—was for him simply a matter of the man having financial responsibility to provide for his household. "You know, it's not that Islam does not want to give women authority," he said. "If a woman wants to become a mufti, if she wants to become a scholar, or wants to work: she can have all these positions. It's just in the house that the man is guardian. Under God's law, men and women have the same rights and responsibilities. The family is the only place where they have different ones. It is a secondary matter."

"Maybe secondary for him," I caught myself thinking. "Not just because he's a man, but because he's a believer." For Akram, equality didn't hinge on who does the dishes, but on equal grace from God: "In the Quran, man is the guardian. People think that the men are better than the women. It is not like that. When men are guardians, it does not mean that in the Day of Judgment, they are more pious. No! It could be that the wife goes to paradise, and he goes to the fire of hell!"

As a secularist, undecided as to what is to come after death, the only Day of Reckoning I'm certain of is today. Akram could content himself with a just God who would even things out after death. Yoked as I was to this life, I couldn't afford to see my justice deferred. I needed it now, in this world, in my own kitchen and bedroom: I wanted my dusting duties and school runs split down the middle so that I could then go out, see the world, and earn money, so that I could, if I chose, heed Woolf's advice and leave money to a women's college.

I must have looked unconvinced. "The idea of male guardianship," he hastened to add, "is just an organizational matter. It's just for the arrangements of the house."

"But for some people, how you organize the house is the starting point for justice, not just something incidental," I parried, thinking of my mother's cookieless consciousness-raising sessions. "For so many people, they say there can't be justice if one gender is given guardianship over another, even if it's just a matter of who does the laundry."

"But the one who is being a guardian, he does not make the law. He only implements it. If he has to make the law, then yes, that is injustice. Look, there's only one thing that is different, and that is that women get pregnant, so they cannot do some things as freely as men. The rest of the things are the same, really." Islam liberates mothers from the burden of certain duties that men can't escape. "Because of the way God has made the family system, men have all these collective responsibilities—they have to take part in active duties of society, but women have the right to decide whether they want to share or not. For men, it is a duty, they must do!"

"Well, like what?"

"When leaders call meetings in mosques, men have to go," he said. "Women can decide. Jihad—men must go; and women have the right to go or not to go. Friday prayers! It's the same thing—men must go, and women can choose."

Women's biology allows them certain respite from social duties, explained Akram. "They're going to be pregnant. They're going to be mothers. If women are given the same authority and duties as the men, it would really be much more difficult for them, no doubt really."

He grinned broadly and shook his head. "You know, I really don't understand why God does not divide things differently! You know, for ten years, woman can be mother, and ten years, man can be mother!" Suddenly, he was sounding like the head of a feminist collective in Vermont. "Because, you know, people always think that what men have got must be better! But I think it should be the other way around. Men should say, 'I want to leave guardianship of the house—give me motherhood!'"

"You remind me of some feminists," I smiled. "They talk about how society needs to value mothering, and how it shouldn't be undermined in favor of the male model of paid work and career status—that they're all about money. You sure you're not a feminist, Sheikh?"

By this time, we were both guffawing, perhaps a bit loudly. A bespectacled man at the next table shot me a hard look from over his teapot.

But Akram was in free flow. "God said, 'Paradise is under the feet of the mothers.' He never said the same thing about fathers! Mothers get so much respect!"

Besides, he continued, being a male guardian can be a drag.

"People enjoy power, but power actually limits their enjoyment," he said earnestly. "Administration is slavery. The Quran wants to free women from administration. A woman can sleep when she's tired. But I'm a father. Even if I'm tired, I know my duty. My wife, she can have a rest. But if I have a headache, I still have to teach."

The Sheikh shut his eyes for a second, a sign that a joke was coming: "If someone said to me, 'I am going to look after you, I am your guardian,' I would really feel so happy!" he quipped. "I would love that, really!"

Even hearing him jest about it, a Muslim woman's role sounded spookily similar to Woolf's Angel of the House, that powerless phantom creature that had to be stone-cold dead before a woman could begin to write well. Not that every woman, Muslim or otherwise, who stayed home to tend the children would end up powerless. But exemptions from duties can ossify into exclusions from power. In her famous essay "The Jew Who Wasn't There," Rachel Adler writes of how orthodox Judaism's exemptions for women, children, and slaves made all three groups "peripheral Jews." Allowing them to skip such rites as hearing the shofar on Rosh Hashanah or praying at the three daily services meant that they were "'excused' from most of the positive symbols which, for the male Jew, hallow time, hallow his physical being, and inform both his myth and his philosophy." In Islam, the dispensation that allowed women to pray at home worked, in practice, to deny many of the pleasures and support of communal mosque prayers. In many Muslim cultures, it had also morphed considerably, from being a rule allowing women to stay at home into a custom of confining them to it. Akram knew this better than most Muslims, having so often tried to persuade conservatives of women's right to go to the mosque or to attend university.

"Sometimes, a girl will come to me and say that her parents will not let her go to the mosque," the Sheikh said. "So I ask her, 'Do they let you go to the shops?' She'll say 'Yes.' So I say: 'They'll let you go shopping, but not to the mosque?'" To bar women from going to pray communally but then send them to buy groceries was not just inconsistent but unfair, and un-Islamic.

I knew that Akram was attuned to the dangers of overzealous confinement of women, for I'd heard him warn of them. A couple weeks after our "An-Nisa" discussion, he gave a talk on "Surat al-Jinn," a chapter at the end of the Quran dealing with unseen spirits, or jinns. Far too many people, he said, saw jinn possession as a major problem. Over the years, both Indian and British Muslims had consulted him on jinns, and usually it was women, not men, who were said to be possessed by them. These women were simply suffering emotional anguish brought on by overstrict interpretations of purdah. In the notes distributed to his audience, the Sheikh warned that these women's "jinns" were in fact mental distress:

They feel trapped in the lives they are leading, unable to escape conditions of confinement, terrible loneliness, emotional and even physical abuse. The conditions of their life are such that they have no hope of joy or happiness. They feel utterly powerless to change their circumstances, and so they do not want the life they have. After a time they find themselves, in extreme cases, unable to sleep, unable to eat, unable to move, unable to act or think normally . . . It is at this time that people around them, sometimes with the best of intentions, may say things like, 'She is not herself. She is possessed.'

The day we discussed "The Women," I pressed the Sheikh on how the whole "guardianship" system set out in 4:34 would work. "Okay, so assuming that we can limit guardianship to the man providing financially for the household. How is this system not going to be exploited?"

"People who take the power, they misuse it. There's no doubt about it. But the reason for suffering is that men are not implementing the Quranic way of justice."

"Sheikh," I began evenly. "I utterly understand how these arrangements were about justice in seventh-century Arabia. Women needed protection then. But now, in the twenty-first century, the socioeconomic conditions are changing. More women are educated. More women work and are shouldering economic responsibilities. Now that facts on the ground are changing, is it possible to change inheritance laws so that they're fair?"

"That's fine," nodded the Sheikh. "But they can only be changed if Islam changes their responsibilities."

"Well—on the ground they have, Sheikh! So can it?"

"Well, once this is changed, it means there is no guardian in the house," explained the Sheikh.

"What about having two guardians? Splitting the responsibilities and the power?"

Akram smiled. "If you have two guardians in the house, then, it's like there are two rulers in the same state: fighting will happen so quickly. Man should be supervising—otherwise, there's no way that they know who is going to decide things."

My face must have fallen, because he quickly added, "But he should consult his wife, and respect everybody."

"In some houses, it's the women who are actually ruling, even in the house!" he went on, eyes shining. "The Quran does not mind that. Actually, in the proper Muslim family, the house is always run by the women. My mother, she would decide how the household was run. But my father, he always earned the money and would go shopping . . . And now, it's the same thing in my house! It's not I who decides what we're going to eat: I just have to earn the money."

The Sheikh wasn't being disingenuous. Nor was he being patron-

izing, like the patriarch who nods at his wife while smirking and saying, "She's the boss!" Akram truly saw the twin spheres of the home
and the outside world as separate but equal. Family life was so central
to his understanding of Islam that he genuinely believed in the importance of a wife's main duty: educating the children. For Akram, this
business of the outside world, with its earning and getting and com-
peting, was really rather trivial.

Akram's faith created his very real respect for his wife's work.
My own, very worldly view was that economy was destiny. I had sat
and despaired with well-educated friends, bemoaning the fact that
family life meant cuts in our earning power. Whoever held the
purse strings of the house held the power, we agreed. Whether one
wanted a feminist household or a pious Muslim one, there was all
too often a chasm between theory and practice. I had watched my
own mother look up from marking her women's studies papers to
meekly ask my father whether she could buy a copy of the Sunday
New York Times.

"What prevents the guardian from being unfair about how he
provides for his wife and children?" I asked.

Akram assured me that in fact the Prophet had provided a loop-
hole for wives whose husbands were tight with money. Abu Sufyan,
the leader of the Quraysh tribe, was very stingy. His wife asked Muhammad whether it was allowed for her to take money from him without
his knowing it, just for basic household expenses. "The Prophet said,
'Yes, when a woman has a husband who does not spend properly, it is
okay to take what is fair.'"

"But suppose we agree that there needs to be one person who ultimately has the last say in a household," I said. "Why should it be a man?
What about women who earn more than their husbands? Or who are
cleverer, or better educated?"

"It doesn't matter if God has made men the guardian, or women
the guardian," he said. "Look, if women become it, what would happen? Go to any office where a woman is the boss, and ask people! It's
the same thing! It doesn't matter who's in charge: as long as people
don't fear God, these things are going to happen, really!"

"But is there not, Sheikh, an argument that the whole *qiwamah* system should be phased out, in the interests of justice?" I asked. "Since it opens the possibility for men to twist laws?"

"The basic thing is not who is *amir* (leader)," said Akram. "If people don't do justice, nothing's going to work."

For Akram, it all went back to piety and treating people with kindness and justice. It wasn't the *qiwamah* system that was to blame, but people and their flaws.

"So are there grounds that, since things have changed since the seventh century, we can now change the laws?"

"In the laws, there are certain things that will always be the same, that can't be changed. There is no doubt that Islamic law keeps changing, when the context of the people keeps changing."

In every society, agreed the Sheikh, people had to arrange their household affairs in practical ways. Marriages were partnerships and both men and women had shared responsibilities to make them work well. "But still, certain things are firm—certain realities remain the same. A mother being a mother—that can't be changed."

At last, we arrived at what remains the Quran's most contentious passage on marital rights. Specifically, the words that many Muslims claimed allowed husbands to hit rebellious wives.

"First, let us define the meaning," said the Sheikh. "The word used—*daraba*—means to strike someone. In any language, it has no other meaning."

"Not, 'to go away from?' or 'to advise'?" I said, ever hopeful. "I've read some Muslims who've glossed it that way . . ."

Nope. According to Akram, apologists might try to say it means all sorts of things, but they were wrong: "*Daraba* means 'to beat'!"

It was not advisable to hit—indeed, it was a mistake, but if it was absolutely necessary, he continued, there were steps a husband needed to take before hitting. "First, you must try to reconcile. Then, you can bring in the family—both of your families. Then if that doesn't work, don't sleep with them."

If that doesn't work, only then could you hit. But only on three conditions:

"Nobody in authority—whether in the state or in the family—is allowed to hit when they're angry. If you discipline when you're angry, then you're doing it for yourself. The second thing is, this must be in the interests of the person, not the hitter. If I am hitting my child, it should improve him, not me. The third condition is that it must just be a gesture. There should be no pain, no injury, nothing." Some jurists recommended using shoelaces, or a *miswak*, the twig from the tree that many Muslims used to clean their teeth, just as the Prophet had cleaned his. "If a husband, or a father, or a wife—anyone in authority—causes pain, then this is a grave mistake," said Akram. "If they hit, and cause injury, then jurists say you can take them to court."

So stringent were the limits on beating, he observed, that "there is no hitting happening in the Muslim world according to Islamic law," he said. "Most people are hitting out of anger—or out of their own pride or arrogance. That's not Islam."

Besides, he noted, the Prophet never hit his wives. Nor did most of his Companions. "The best among you," said the Prophet Muhammad, "is the one who is best towards his wife." As so often happened, the Quran's language was stricter than Muhammad's explanations to his Companions. "When the Prophet conveys the Quran, the words are so firm," observed Akram. "But when he teaches the message in his own words, he tells it so nicely."

Between this law and the Prophet's teaching of it, there was light: "The Quran puts down the boundary, but the Prophet did not go to the boundary. He did not hit his wives." Indeed, the Prophet strongly reprimanded those who did—"All the husbands beating their wives, those aren't good people among you"—and he cautioned men "not to beat any of Allah's woman servants."

"And you, Sheikh, in these matters, do you look to the Quran, or do you look to the Prophet's sunna?"

I thought I knew the answer, but I needed to hear him say it.

"In the way of normal behavior, I look to the Prophet. When I read something in the Quran, I then go, and look at the hadith, and at the

Prophet's *sira* [biography]. Remember, Aisha called the Prophet 'the walking Quran.' So it is always best to see what he did."

The Sheikh never hit his children, or his wife.

From the moment the first revelation—"Read!"—came down to the Prophet, Islam was established as a faith of the word, and the faithful as those who read God's signs, both in the Quran and in nature. The good Muslim must read the sources, and read God's signs. But with a text as intricate and powerful as the Quran, reading meant far more than mere literacy: Akram must have read "An-Nisa" dozens of times before he eventually realized that his father had to give away the land to Akram's aunts.

Across the world, Muslim progressives in places as disparate as Jakarta and Virginia have read 4:34 anew. They've been pressing this verse, and the rest of the Quran, for possible readings that can guide pious Muslims through twenty-first-century circumstances. In 1992, the American Muslim scholar Amina Wadud published the first woman's commentary on passages of the Quran dealing with gender roles. Until Wadud wrote the PhD dissertation that was to become her book *Quran and Woman*, modern Muslim women were all but voiceless in debates over Quranic interpretation. Through the work of Wadud and others, that's changing. Women are returning to the basic texts and chiseling off the man-made prejudices that have hardened into Truth over centuries. It's slow work, digging down to find the scripture's universal messages, ones that guarantee women and men justice and humanity. It takes courage to peel back the layers of misogyny that have grown over fourteen centuries. Many of the tools these Islamic progressives use are in the Quran itself. The seeming inequities of men and women in 4:34 can be countered with other verses, like Wadud's translation of this description of marriage as a shelter built of respect between man and woman: "Among His signs is that He created for you, from your own selves, mates. And He has made between the two of you love and mercy."

The Quran may say that men and women are "mates," but contemporary Islamic laws seldom reflect this. In many Muslim-majority countries, the modern laws governing marriage and divorce, inheritance and custody, are often based on the thinking of Islam's classical jurists, men in medieval Baghdad or Damascus, working between one and four centuries after the Prophet's death. Like any human interpretation of divine law, these medieval rulings bear the stamp of their time. One jurist went so far as to write that marriage "is a contract whose object is . . . dominion over the vagina." A millennium later, the frameworks set by classical jurists still underpin laws governing marriage rights in many Muslim countries. From Pakistan to Egypt, legal codes remain a far cry from the Sheikh's idea of partnership, or from the Quran's tender image of marriage as a comfort for both spouses: "They are a garment for you, and you are a garment for them."

Across the globe, Muslim women and men are challenging the misogyny that has crept into Islamic cultures. Pakistani schoolgirls are defying Taliban edicts in their quest for education. African activists are demanding that local mullahs point to where, exactly, the Quran advocates female genital mutilation. Indonesian feminist scholars are giving male mullahs gender sensitivity courses, while Malaysian campaigners travel to small-town mosques and schools, handing out pamphlets with bright red covers and provocative titles such as "Are Muslim Men Allowed to Beat Their Wives?" and "Are Men and Women Equal Before Allah?"

More and more people are realizing that the answer to that last question is yes. A few years before I started studying with Akram, I attended a conference organized by Musawah, the global women's organization devoted to reforming Islamic family laws, held at a glittering hotel ballroom in Kuala Lumpur. Activists from around the world gathered to celebrate the movement's goal: putting the justice and equality they found in the Quran back into Muslim laws and cultures. Scanning the ballroom, I saw Amina Wadud talking to Indonesian activists and Sudanese lawyers mingling with Thai anthropologists. Filipina development workers swapped business cards with Iranian feminists. A veteran of Malaysia's feminist movement chatted with an Egyptian éminence grise. On heads: hijabs, but also dread-locks and curls, African *geles*, combat-short buzz cuts. Toward the evening's end, the conversational hubbub dwindled as a loudspeaker proclaimed women full and equal members of humankind. The words were the Quran's, verse 33:35, revealed to Muhammad after one of his wives, the formidable Umm Salamah, asked him why, exactly, it seemed sometimes as though God only spoke to men, not women. The response came soon after:

> For the men who acquiesce to the will of God, and the women who
>   acquiesce,
> the men who believe and the women who believe,
> the men who are devout and the women who are devout,
> the men who are truthful and the women who are truthful,
> the men who are constant and the women who are constant,
> the men who are humble and the women who are humble,
> the men who give charity and the women who give charity,
> the men who fast and the women who fast,
> the men who are chaste and the women who are chaste,
> and the men and women who remember God a lot,
> God has arranged forgiveness for them, and a magnificent reward.
>   (33:35)

It was the promise of this forgiveness, of this reward, that drove the Sheikh. His scholarly critiques might have sounded muted next to Musawah's calls for equality and justice. Yet using the tools of his own madrasa tradition, he was working to excavate the Islamic prin-ciples of justice from underneath customs. I wouldn't call him a femi-nist, but within his conservative milieu, he waged a powerful campaign for women's rights. He wouldn't call himself a feminist either. Just a Muslim who has read his Quran.

PART THREE

THE WORLD

11

A Pilgrim's Progress

The multifaith prayer room in terminal 5 of London's Heathrow Airport was sandwiched between a cappuccino bar and the check-in for British Airways. Back when such airport facilities were called "chapels" and labeled with a cross, my father would often seek one out—not to worship, but to nap before flights. In these chapels, he found a quiet spot in a crowded airport. He'd usually have them to himself: in the 1970s, before the Iranian Revolution and the Islamic revival, nobody seemed to need them much.

They did now. When I arrived, panting and sweating from my run across the airport, terrified that I would be late to meet the Sheikh, I found terminal 5's prayer room full. The shoe rack was overflowing, and there were rows of Muslim men praying together.

I was at Heathrow to see the Sheikh and a group of fellow pilgrims off on *umra*. In Arabic, *umra*, or "the visit," is the smaller of the two Meccan pilgrimages. Unlike the hajj, which occurs on five days in the twelfth month of the Islamic calendar, *umra* can be undertaken any time of the year. One of the five pillars of Islam, the hajj is required for all Muslims at least once in their lives, if they are physically and financially able to perform it. Hajj requires stamina of the body as well as of the soul: pilgrims walk seven times around the sacred black stone, the Kaaba, run between two sacred hills, and pray on Mount

Arafat. As part of the symbolic renunciation of evil, "Stoning the Devil," pilgrims hurl pebbles at three pillars, on the spots where Satan was said to have tempted Ibrahim, telling him to ignore God's command that he sacrifice his son.

Hajjis perform these rituals in a state of purity, avoiding sex, quarrels, or unpleasantness, since both hajj and *umra* are meant to purify the soul and to bring pilgrims close to their God.

The Sheikh had performed two hajjs and several *umra*s before, but today he was embarking on his first teaching *umra*. He was leading thirty-seven British Muslims on the trip to Mecca and Medina, where he would head seminars with Saudi scholars. For many ulama, these pilgrimages can also serve as unofficial professional conferences, with Mecca and Medina serving as places to talk shop as well as perform rituals. When the Sheikh went on hajj in 2003, a top hadith scholar he'd always hoped to meet was in town for his own pilgrimage. On hearing the news that the man was in Mecca, the Sheikh said he had "jumped out of happiness."

The pilgrims on this trip were mostly young and mostly male: Saudi Arabia banned a woman going on *umra* without a *mahram*, a close male relative such as a brother, uncle, or husband to act as a guardian. Shabana, who had just finished her master's degree in human resources, had wanted to do *umra* ever since she began observing Islam devoutly, about six years ago. But she couldn't find a male family member who was willing to accompany her until she married last year.

"My family really doesn't practice, or pray or anything," she said. "So for me, the past six years, getting married, finding someone to take me to *umra* . . ."

"Women need a guardian to go," volunteered Shabana's husband. "A brother, an uncle . . ."

"To me it's so ironic that women can't go without men," I said. "What with the Sheikh having found women scholars in the earliest years of Islam traveling by themselves, on horseback and camels. If it's in the pursuit of religious knowledge, surely nobody can object to women going?"

"There are reasons that women can't travel alone," observed

Shabana's husband. "I'm not sure what the reasons exactly are, but there are reasons. There's a lot of travel involved. It would probably be a bit too much."

I stretched my lips across my teeth into a smile-that-wasn't. I remembered the "Step-by-Step Guide to a Successful Umrah," a chapter of the Umrah Course Handbook written for the pilgrims by the Sheikh's daughter Sumaiya and a friend. Throughout, the guide counseled *sabr*, or patience: "If someone annoys you—transcend it."

As a non-Muslim, I wasn't allowed in Mecca, but I had hoped to go with the group as far as Medina, where the Sheikh and other scholars were going to conduct seminars. For a month or so, it had looked as though I might have been allowed: the visa official at the Saudi embassy had been encouraging, at first. But the group's hotel, it turned out, was inside the Haram, the sacred area in Medina restricted to Muslims. Besides, getting my husband, Antony, to come along as my *mahram* would have been a fiscal, logistical, and ideological pinch.

Still, when the Sheikh's student Arzoo arrived, dragging a hot pink suitcase, I gazed at the *umra* visa in her passport enviously. "The last time I went, the officials stuck another woman's picture on my visa by accident," she said, laughing. She got into Saudi Arabia anyway, which surprised me. The dour face gazing out from her *umra* visa page looked nothing like sparkling, vivid Arzoo. To get the magic stamp in her passport this time, she and her sister had chipped in to pay her uncle's fare so that he would accompany them as *mahram*. Arzoo was lucky: her friend Mehrun had wanted to go, too, but all her male relatives were too busy to come. "I was so annoyed," Mehrun later recalled. "I didn't even ask them for their reasons; I didn't need to hear much more than the 'no can do.'" For a while, she wondered if she could contrive to go to Saudi Arabia for a professional conference or a consulting gig and then sneak off to join the Sheikh's group. Friends even suggested she claim one of the men on the trip was her "uncle"—a common ruse women use to flout the Saudi *mahram* rule. But unable to bring herself to tell a lie in order to go on a pilgrimage whose point was moral purity, Mehrun had resigned herself to staying at home and working on her master's degree.

The pilgrims were traveling light, at least on their way out. Many were planning to bring home water from Mecca's famous Zamzam spring; a ten-liter drum of water counted as half their baggage allowance. Zamzam water is widely regarded as blessed, and many pilgrims bring home bottles as gifts for friends or as a cure for illnesses, or for ablution during special prayers. Sumaiya swears by the water's nutritional properties, and its ability to clear up pimples. On her last *umra*, she returned from Mecca with a bottle, splashed it on her face daily, and found that her complexion improved.

As I stood in the group of milling pilgrims, a woman in a *niqab* approached who turned out to be Sumaiya herself. Through the slit in her *niqab* I saw dark half-moons under her eyes: she had organized the trip and hadn't slept for two days. Arranging the visas and lodgings had taken months, and writing the *umra* guide had meant lots of late nights. As Chaucer well knew, a pilgrimage is an uncanny mix of the logistical and the spiritual. Sumaiya's guide reflected this, combining practical tips with soulful quotes from medieval theologians. It advised on everything from practicing gratitude to hygiene in Meccan bathrooms to the importance of pacing oneself: "If you burn yourself out in the first few days, you put the rest of your days in the blessed lands at risk: tired minds and bodies will decrease your *ibada* [worship]."

Sumaiya even included emotional guidelines, such as what one might do when one first sees the Kaaba: "In that sweet precious moment, let the tears in your eyes melt the image of this majestic place that soothes your soul."

Wondering what the first glimpse of Mecca might be like for a believer, I asked the Sheikh's daughter Maryam, a solemn and beautiful eighteen-year-old, what she thought when she first saw the Kaaba. "I thought it would be bigger," she said.

Like the Taj Mahal or the White House for a secularist, I supposed. Of course it would be smaller. No structure that's been drummed into your dreams since childhood ever takes up as much space as it does in the imagination.

Aisha, the Sheikh's youngest, jumped from foot to foot. Even at nine, she was a seasoned *umra* pilgrim. The last time, she told me, she actually touched the Kaaba! But the crush of the crowds in the mosque could be a bit scary, too. During one trip, there was a time when she had been separated from her sister. At that point, she said, "I started crying."

I watched as a woman in the group dandled her toddler.

"Allah," she pronounced, moving her mouth slowly.

"Aya," hazarded the child.

"Al-lah."

"A-ee-yah."

"Aaaaalllllllaaaaaah."

"A-ee-yah."

The mother, Nadia, had spoken with Sumaiya daily over the past few weeks, consulting on the added challenge of taking a baby along on *umra*. "I almost expected Sumaiya would be a little bit on edge, or say 'Leave me alone,'" said Nadia. "But she always had time to talk, and was always patient and gracious—even when I could hear her baby crying in the background."

She admitted that she had been nervous about taking her child into the crush of a pilgrimage and the heat of an Arabian July. But then, she reasoned, where would God's protection be stronger than in Mecca? "The whole reason for going on the trip was trying to get closer to the Creator," Nadia said. "I thought to myself, 'I'm leaving my baby with my Creator. He created her; He will look after her.'"

Sumaiya, too, was worried about baby Asim in the Saudi Arabian heat. He had been sick the week before, growing so dehydrated he'd had to go on a drip in the hospital—"and that had been in Oxford," said Sumaiya. "So I was thinking, how is he going to respond to Saudi Arabia?" Her suitcase was crammed with sunscreen, baby aspirin, and rehydration powders, but Sumaiya's main protection for her son was faith in God.

By going on *umra*, the two mothers were traveling to the very spot where one of the great heroines of the Quran, Hajar, had trusted God to save her baby. When Ibrahim and Sarah couldn't conceive, Sarah gave the slave girl Hajar to Ibrahim in the hopes of their conceiving a child. Hajar bore a son, Ismail, but when God told Ibrahim to leave mother and child in the valley near Mecca, Ibrahim did so, depositing them under a tree with a skinful of water and a sackful of dates. Two nights later, with dwindling supplies and a fractious baby, Hajar ran between the hillocks of Safa and Marwa, begging God for aid. Seven times she ran back and forth, scouting the horizon for help.

It soon came, in the form of water, miraculously bubbling up from the sand. Hajar and Ismail drank deeply, becoming the first people to benefit from the Zamzam, Mecca's famous well. "To leave her kid, in the heat," marveled Sumaiya on Hajar's faith, "to walk in that rocky desert with no shoes. The more you trust in God, the more you're given."

Sitting on a bench beside the British Airways check-in, the Sheikh gave a short predeparture address. Half of the group had never been on *umra* before, so his opening remarks were cautionary. The trip would take *sabr*, he warned. Eat light: fruit and yogurt suit a hot climate better than heavy meals. One didn't want to be too sleepy to pray. Control your frustration. If you encounter trials on the trip, don't complain to anyone other than Allah. Don't backbite. Be nice.

But soon the Sheikh's tone changed to a new register, leading listeners away from travel-related stresses. He recited bits of poetry by the South Asian philosopher-poet Muhammad Iqbal on the glories of the hajj, and he waxed lyrical on the benefits of a journey: "Life becomes more and more pure by travel," Akram told the pilgrims. "With moving, and traveling, new blood comes to life."

After the Sheikh's speech, the group went to check in. From a distance, I watched them walk to gate G, receding into the brightly lit tube of the terminal, their wheelie suitcases bumping behind them. My eyes teared slightly as I watched them go, not least because I was envious. I disliked standing on docks waving other people off. I wanted to be the one leaving, the one whose "new blood" was stirred.

Alone in the airport, clutching my cellophaned fajita wrap, I waited for the glass elevator to ferry me to the Underground. For the Sheikh, Heathrow's terminal 5 was no different from the rest of the planet. He regarded this world much as many people do airports: a way station to endure in order to reach one's true destination. A place to navigate, as best you can, through its lines and officialdom, to get where you're really going. "We belong to God," says the Quran, "and to God we return."

As a journey to draw the faithful closer to the Creator, *umra* was a constant reminder of death. Repent all your sins, advised Sumaiya's handbook, before leaving for the "court of Allah" in Mecca. "Are you going to complete your Umrah or die on the way there?" asks the handbook. "Or die on the way back? Only Allah knows."

Sumaiya's step-by-step guide read like an antitravel brochure, upturning every convention of a glossy holiday guide. Instead of promising pleasures, it guaranteed trials. "Travel," read the hadith opening a section called "The Journey," "is a portion of punishment." The ten days were a chance for worship, and no time should be wasted in other pursuits. Don't spend time gazing at the famous clock that towers over Mecca (the biggest clock in the world, boasted Saudi souvenir guides). Bypass Mecca's shopping malls, and ignore the decorations in the mosques: they were mere distractions from prayer and the Quran. Watching TV in the hotel "would be an utter source of shame and regret," given that the Kaaba and the Prophet's mosque were so close, offering spiritual rewards. Travelers should be skeptical of soaring spirits: "A superficial elated feeling should not be equated with a rise in [piety]," wrote Sumaiya. "A rise in faith would lead you to perform more righteous deeds and abstain from sins."

The handbook urged the *umra* party to be polite, but the rigors of *umra*, and the stressful thrill of achieving a lifelong goal, meant that fellow pilgrims frequently weren't. Among the trials that awaited the pilgrims:

> People will push you, push ahead of you, poke you in the back, there are no proper queues anywhere—whether in the shop or the Masjid [mosque] toilets, or the hotel reception . . . The Masjid guards could shout at you, people can spit in your way and throw rubbish near

you. People will shout at you—constantly—even in the Masjid, even in *tawaf* [the seven circumambulations of the Kaaba]. People will shout and argue in languages you don't understand (or maybe do understand). People will smell next to you and make a mess in the bathrooms and the Masjid. Shopkeepers could throw the money back at you (this is normal) and you may not get what you paid for.

What to do in the face of such annoyances? "Prepare mentally for all the above and do not lose your temper," advised the handbook. "Just say *alhamdulillah* that Allah has invited you to the holy lands, and be beautifully patient." The chance to practice *sabr* was the chance to seek afterlife rewards.

At times during the party's stay in Saudi Arabia, the temperature reached 108 degrees. For Maryam, the Sheikh's eighteen-year-old daughter, the heat was *umra*'s biggest challenge. "We saw it as a way of learning to be patient," she said. "The heat added to the experience, and made it more exciting." To stay cool, everyone kept drinking Zamzam water from the beige drums around the mosque.

"We told people to bring lots of *sabr* with them," said Farhan, Sumaiya's husband. A compact, smiling man, he was a medical student and had taken his exams just before the trip. He'd helped as an organizer, wearing an "Al Salam Umra 2013" T-shirt at Heathrow and assisting pilgrims with their bags and papers, but it was his wife, he said shyly, who had shown "true commitment" to organizing the *umra* trip.

The travelers needed every shred of *sabr* they could muster. They needed it at the six-hour wait at the Jiddah airport's immigration zone after their flight, and on the five-hour bus ride through the desert to Medina. On arrival, the group discovered that many of them were without rooms, their reservations having mysteriously disappeared. After hours of calls home to England, and later to the police, it was alleged that some entrepreneurial soul, perhaps a travel agent on the Saudi end, had booked them in a day later, pocketing the cost of the night for himself.

"The guys at the hotel kept saying *sabr*," said Farhan. "But after a few hours, I was like, 'I'm doing business with you. We took money from these people for rooms, and so we need to provide them with rooms.'" *Sabr* didn't extend to botched business practices—or fraud.

While I listened to the Sheikh's daughters as they recounted their *umra*, I marveled not just at the physical rigors of the Arabian heat and dust, but at the mental toughness required to screen out worldliness. Some people didn't even bother to pray in the Grand Mosque, they told me, preferring the air-conditioned cool of their hotels. Others used the trip as a chance for shopping in Mecca's massive new malls. The handbook included a hadith for those tempted to shop on the trip: "The most beloved of places to Allah are the mosques, and the most disliked of places to Allah are the markets."

In Medina, it is customary to visit the Rawdah. A stretch of green carpet between the Prophet's grave and pulpit, it is a bit of heaven on earth, says one hadith from the Prophet: "That which exists between my house and my pulpit is a garden from the gardens of paradise."

Maryam had inherited her father's calm, but when she queued at the women's entrance, she was nearly overwhelmed by the crush of the crowd. The desert heat was stifling, and the guards' shouted directions were confusing. Pilgrims were divided into national groups for the duration of the wait, but Maryam was stranded far away from the Britons, squeezed in with the Pakistanis. Since she understood Urdu, she stayed, half-sitting on two strangers' laps, sandwiched between the Pakistanis and some Turks. "It was literally packed, and I was sitting with my legs out straight," she said. When the gates opened, some women began shouting at the guards: "All of these Pakistani ladies were quite desperate to get through," she said. "It must have been quite frustrating for the workers."

When the crowd finally surged forward, Maryam didn't push through. *Sabr.* "One woman looked at me really weirdly, like 'Why aren't you desperate?' But that's not what the Prophet taught." The melee at the grave contravened the Quran's counsel on how to speak to the Prophet: "Those who lower their voices in the presence of the Messenger of God are those whose hearts God has tested for conscience; there is forgiveness for them, and a tremendous reward."

At the Prophet's grave, many pilgrims cried. Maryam didn't, worried that tears might "seem like *shirk*." Worshipping anything other than God—*shirk*—is Islam's gravest sin, so mainstream Sunni Islam frowns on visiting graves as an act of religious devotion. For a scripturalist Muslim like the Sheikh, it was not permissible to travel simply to visit a grave, even the Prophet's. Making pilgrimages to graves and shrines was a superstition of unlettered village Muslims or Sufi mystics. The Prophet's grave was an exception: one could visit it, say "salaam" to it, but only if one happened to be in Medina anyway.

In Saudi Arabia, a Wahhabi fear of promoting idolatry had led to the destruction of many early Islamic monuments. When the al-Saud tribes entered Mecca in the 1920s, they destroyed cemeteries containing graves of important early Muslims. More recently, Saudi efforts to accommodate the growing number of hajjis have wreaked havoc on early Muslim monuments. The expansion of the Grand Mosque has turned the house of Muhammad's beloved Khadija into a bank of toilets; a Hilton hotel now sits where once stood the home of Abu Bakr, Aisha's father and Islam's first caliph. Strict Wahhabis may deplore sightseeing, but the Sheikh's party climbed Jabal al-Nour, the mountain Muhammad used as a retreat for quiet contemplation. "It took a good forty-five minutes to get up there," recalled Farhan. "I was struggling, and I'm in my twenties, I can't believe the Prophet Muhammad used to do it when he was forty years old!"

Mecca required even more *sabr* than Medina. To go to the city, the pilgrims had entered *ihram*, or the purified state of the hajj or *umra*. Women wear ordinary clothes but are forbidden to cover their faces, a ban that Sumaiya found "a bit strange," since it meant she had to take off her *niqab*. Men wear two pieces of white cloth, unstitched.

"Why can't there be stitches?" I asked Sumaiya.

"One should never try to comprehend the reasoning," she

responded. "Some of these things might not make sense logically, but there's a reason behind them, and one mustn't question it."

A good Muslim didn't ask for logic from the sunna, she said. One trusted Allah and didn't demand proof through science or reason. That Islam's ban on pork was later upheld by studies on trichinosis, say, or the discovery that fasting was actually good for your health—these weren't important. One avoided pork and fasted because that was true submission. God's laws didn't need scientific confirmations. They were God's, and thus the laws were the Truth. "Scientists could turn around tomorrow and say fasting is no longer healthy, and despite that, we should continue to fast," observed Sumaiya. "We should do it, because that's always been the sunna."

The *ihram* outfits made arriving in Mecca more stressful. "It's hard to faff around with luggage when you're wearing something you're not used to," observed Sumaiya. As in Medina, there was confusion over lodging. The pilgrims had paid for a five-star hotel, only to be told on arrival that the place they'd reserved had no electricity, since it was soon due to be razed to make way for a new hotel. This was plausible: the city was undergoing a massive modernization drive, and the Meccan skyline was a forest of cranes. But the group happened to drive by the hotel on their way to the Ramada Inn, and they could see other travelers checking in. The lights seemed to work just fine, and the excuse, they decided, had probably been the travel agent's ruse to swap their reservations on them.

In the section on *sabr* in Sumaiya's guide, she quotes a hadith: "Never is a believer stricken with discomfort . . . or even the pricking of a thorn, but that Allah expiates his sins on account of his patience."

The Ramada Inn was just a few minutes' walk from the Masjid al-Haram, the Grand Mosque. Farhana, the Sheikh's wife, spent nearly all her waking hours in Mecca there, doing *tawaf*, or the seven circumambulations of the Kaaba. Sumaiya reckoned her mother must have done *tawaf* about seven times—forty-nine circumambulations in all—but wasn't sure. Farhana would never have told her, since a good Muslim should never indulge in *riyaa*—showing off—about her pious actions on *umra*. However many *tawaf*s she'd completed, it was clear "she was on a roll," said Sumaiya. "Every time we were like, 'Where is she?'" invariably, she was at the mosque.

To avoid the heat of the day, Sumaiya did her own circuits around the Kaaba at three or four in the morning, when the temperature cooled to the high eighties and the crowds thinned. Even then, Sumaiya found the rituals harder than on her previous *umra*, before she became a mother. Asim wriggled as she held him and circled the Kaaba, and they frequently had to stop to let him drink some Zamzam water. Once, he even managed to toddle a circuit around the Kaaba on his own, wearing a tiny set of white cloths his grandmother had made for him. Farhana had sewn it, figuring that a ten-month-old was allowed a certain amount of stitching in his *ihram* even if adults weren't. On her Facebook page, Maryam posted a cute picture of the Sheikh with his grandson on his knee, both in their white garb.

Sumaiya's handbook warned that people might shout at the pilgrims in their party—and they did. Twice, Akram's daughters found themselves clashing with guards over Saudi norms on women's access to the sites. The Sheikh and Aisha were doing their circuits around the Kaaba when the Sheikh lifted her up to touch the black stone. "A man started yelling at us," Aisha recalled. "He grabbed my wrist. He said women shouldn't be allowed to touch it."

"The same thing happened to me," agreed fourteen-year-old Fatima. "Some man yelled at me for saying 'salaam' to the Prophet. He said women weren't allowed to stand where I was standing. He said I shouldn't say my 'salaam' from there." She beamed. "My dad said it was fine."

She shook her head. "Culture."

The hillocks of Safa and Marwa are part of the Grand Mosque: the rocky desert where Hajar ran between them is now an air-conditioned corridor with a cool marble floor, divided into lanes for the pilgrims. "Like an airport," explained Maryam. Green lights in the corridor indicate the stretch where Hajar lost sight of her son during her frantic search for water. Male pilgrims—not, strangely enough, female ones—run between them, symbolically tracing her route. The ritual encourages pilgrims to reflect on Hajar's faith in the face of hardship—and on one's own struggles. When Sumaiya's husband, Farhan, ran between the green lights, he thought of Hajar's strength of character—and prayed that he had passed his medical school exams.

So much of the hajj seemed to be about balancing one's own experience with those of the people around you. Today's pilgrim must negotiate her space in crowds and find a way to make her *umra* mesh with those of millions of others. In 2003, the Sheikh went on hajj with his parents, which compounded the pilgrimage's challenges. One afternoon, he spent hours searching for their tent amid the sea of white tents pitched on the plain of Mina. When it came to the day to renounce the devil by hurling stones at the three pillars, the Sheikh worried about how his parents would fare. Because of the crowds throwing stones, there were frequently deaths during this ritual. The Sheikh decided that his family should go late in the afternoon, and was glad he did: he later heard that nineteen people had been killed.

One could see why *sabr* could be a matter of safety as well as spirituality. Even a man as unflappable as the Sheikh had been known to get impatient with the crowds in Mecca. The second time he did *umra*, he and a friend went to visit the Cave of Thawr, where the Prophet Muhammad had hidden for three days while escaping Mecca for Medina. With space for just three people, the cave had a line of people waiting to enter it stretching down the mountain. Akram and his friend were going to be late for noon prayers back in Mecca. "It's such a big line," Akram's friend said, looking up from the plain at the mountain. "It's going to take the whole day."

"Don't say anything," said the Sheikh. "Come with me." Together, they crept around the other side of the mountain, approached the cave from a different direction, and hopped in—"ahead of everyone," recalled Akram, sheepishly. He'd never have cut the line, he was quick to add, had it been a proper hajj ritual rather than sightseeing. "It's part of hajj not to harm anybody or push yourself ahead," he added. "But the mountain's not part of hajj, so I didn't think about it in the same way."

The Sheikh's favorite moment during any hajj was the seven circuits around the Kaaba. Being there, so close to the House of God, as it was called, was a bit like being a teenager in love, he said, lingering outside the home of one's beloved.

A similar grace came the night Maryam left the hotel at 1:30 in the morning to do extra prayers before the *fajr* prayer at dawn. Despite all the fuss the Saudis made about women needing male protectors, it turned out that going out unescorted in Mecca was perfectly safe, even at that hour. Shop lights blazed, and people still strolled the streets. Maryam and her roommates walked to the Grand Mosque, where they prayed, then sat on the smooth marble courtyard with cool drinks. They splashed their faces with Zamzam water and talked softly until dawn prayers.

While I wasn't allowed to witness a religious gathering's potent mix of spirituality and logistics in Mecca, I did join a gathering in Cambridge a few weeks later. Toward the end of the Muslim holy month of Ramadan, I boarded a train with an overnight case, a half pound of cherries, and the Quran. Leaving Antony to look after Nic and Julia, I was going to sleep overnight in a mosque as part of *itikaf*, a spiritual retreat usually performed during the last ten days of Ramadan. The Sheikh was doing *itikaf* in a Cambridge mosque with seventy other Muslims, teaching and reading the Quran.

I took a hijab, a toothbrush, and a sleeping bag. The cherries were a hedge against the Ramadan regimen: no food or water for about eighteen hours a day, and prayer for most of the night. The dictates of the Muslim holy month required fasting from dawn until dusk. If the heat of an Arabian desert can make such disciplines tough, so, too, do the long days of an English summer. The day I went to Cambridge, British Muslims were fasting from around 3:30 in the morning until nine at night. I'm not Muslim, so I wasn't on a fast, but while in the mosque, I would respect theirs.

Though the Sheikh had asked Maryam to look after me, I was nervous about the lockdown during *itikaf*. Many of the Muslims confined themselves to the mosque for the whole ten days. The little rest they got was snatched in sleeping bags on the floor; bathing was done as best they could manage, under spigots. Night prayers could mean standing for an hour and a half at a stretch. The Sheikh urged us not to chat, and to avoid discussions of worldly matters. "Sleep less, eat less, talk less, mix with the people less," he told the assembled at the kick-off of the Cambridge *itikaf*, quoting an old saying by a Sufi sheikh.

Technically, I had nothing to be nervous about. I was going for only a day and a night, and just as an observer. A work deadline meant I was going to have to duck out of the mosque to write in a nearby café. But even with the prospect of panini breaks and clandestine phone calls home to check on the progress of Nic's cold and Julia's science homework, I was daunted. What would witnessing *itikaf*'s spiritual discipline feel like? Would tempers fray? Would people resent my *itikaf* tourism? Would I mess up somehow, or intrude on their experience?

The day was humid, my bag was heavy, and the stairs up to the women's section were steep. In the large gabled room, women sat on their bedrolls reciting the Quran, and I relied on the kindness of a stranger to help me find a free patch of wall for my stuff. A beautiful woman in her forties with a brilliant smile, she was an unofficial den mother for the women's section. She helped teenagers with their Arabic pronunciation on their Quran recitations, and she patiently explained to me the night prayer regime. The pleasure was all hers, she assured me: any good deeds during *itikaf* are multiplied seventy times, and so they are met with bonus rewards in the hereafter.

Perhaps because such incentives were at stake, the room hummed with round-the-clock graciousness: there were murmured "May Allah reward yous" when people passed plates to one another as we broke the fast. When the meal was over, there was practically a tussle over who got to vacuum up the spilled rice.

At the far end of the wall was a flat-screen TV, on which Sheikh Akram appeared twice a day, delivering his lectures. Watching him, it was hard to believe he was enduring the rigors of Ramadan: he lectured for three hours at a stretch without stumbling. His patience with the listeners felt boundless. They questioned him on subjects ranging from Allah's angels to whether good Muslims could order takeout from restaurants that sell alcohol, a banned substance in Islam. After the lecture, when the Sheikh came to greet me and I saw him up close, I detected a touch of weariness about the eyes, but listening to him, I'd never have guessed.

Maryam, resplendent in a lapis hijab, bent over her Quran, murmuring verses under her breath. Not everyone was so focused. Though *itikaf* is meant to keep the world at a distance, the world somehow found the Cambridge mosque's *itikaf*. Teenage girls at the back of the women's quarters chatted and energetically scrolled through their phone messages. A huddle of boys played Temple Run on an iPad. I needn't have worried about taking a vow of silence, either. Talk ranged freely. Beside the spigots where women gathered to wash before prayers, a young writer extolled the merits of Harry Potter. Over dinner, a recent science graduate enlightened me on the expanding boundaries of biomedical engineering. Before evening prayers, I talked to a think-tank strategist about the weirdly hermetic qualities of Sussex seaside towns.

Before evening prayers, more people streamed in from around Cambridge. "Fill every bit of floor! Not every foot, every *inch*!" came the cheerful command over the loudspeaker. Between the rows of praying women, a little girl in a golden *shalwar kameez* batted a green balloon in the air. Babies gurgled in car seats. Elderly ladies, unable to prostrate because of their knees, sat on chairs to pray. They weren't the only ones at *itikaf* worried about their joints: praying most of the night meant that even women in their twenties were taking painkillers to soothe their aching legs.

The crowd dispersed after midnight, and I found a spot on the floor and fell asleep to the giggles and whispers of the women waiting for the next prayers. I slept—and, according to one report, snored—through two prayer sessions, waking at 2:30 in the morning to find breakfast under way. On the oilcloth spread on the floor were plates of curries and rice, kebabs and cakes. Everyone stretched out around it, chatting softly and passing paper plates. "It looks like a painting of the Last Supper," said one woman sleepily, as she roused herself and served rosewater milkshakes to the group.

I dug in, blinking at the incongruity of eating mutton curry in the middle of the night. "Is this traditional food for a Ramadan breakfast?" I asked Maryam, piling my plate high with spiced fruit salad and sweetened rice.

She shrugged. "At home, we usually just have cereal."

After the meal and another rest, I woke a second time to find a different scene: the floor was a quilt of sleeping women and patches of sun. The mosque hall was quiet except for the odd dream-induced murmur and the soft rustle of sleeping bag nylon. I splashed my face, fished out my iPad, and stole out the door into a Cambridge Saturday morning. Outside, the sun and concrete felt jarring. A minute away, at the Café de Paris, Gershwin tunes played. An old man reading his tabloid pronounced loudly on last night's TV reality shows. A rumpled young couple goggled at each other over their morning cappuccinos. I gulped my own, guiltily. In the mosque, nobody but the kids would allow themselves so much as a sip of water until nine tonight. As the caffeine hit my bloodstream, I opened my iPad to write a bridge of words, trying to find ways to describe the world that lay across the street.

The Cambridge *itikaf* didn't entirely seal off ordinary life, but it did throw the everyday into relief. Like Chaucer's pilgrims on the way to Canterbury, some *itikaf* participants seemed to see it as nearly as much of a social event as a spiritual one. (Later, I'd hear that some attendees had criticized what they felt was a too-casual air, suggesting that less talking and fewer cookies might have engendered a more spiritual atmosphere.) But whether on hajj or in *itikaf*, this porous quality between a spiritual experience and ordinary life is a feature—and a strength—of Muslim life. Islam affords an infinite space for spirituality, but it also provides guidelines for society itself. It concerns itself not just with solitary souls, but with how these souls interact with the world.

12

Jesus, Mary, and the Quran

One Sunday morning I attended my first sermon on Jesus Christ. Like millions around the world that morning, I listened to a preacher clothed in white tell me that I needed Jesus in my life. The congregation sat in a spare white room with slender windows while the preacher warned them that too many had forgotten the true meaning of their religion. They had abandoned the essence of their faith in favor of going through the motions. Too often, they'd made worship more about belonging than believing, more about flaunting piety than submitting to it. To find the road to real salvation, one must follow the lessons of the prophets, the preacher said, his pate glowing with the heat and light of his message. To really live your faith, one needed to follow the stories of Jesus, Mary, and John the Baptist.

Beside him lay a copy of the scripture, containing stories of Adam and Eve, Jesus and Mary, Moses and Noah, Abraham and his son. In it, a verse commanded the faithful to

Say, "We believe in God, and in what has been revealed to us,
and in what was revealed to Abraham, Ishmael, Isaac, Jacob, and the Tribes;
and in what was given to Moses, Jesus, and the prophets from their Lord." (3:84)

So said the Quran, and so, too, said Sheikh Akram, preaching his Jesus sermon to a standing-room-only crowd at a Cambridge mosque. The white simplicity of Masjid al-Ikhlas made it feel more like a New England Congregational church than a mosque. But a mosque it was, one whose website stressed that one function of mosques was providing a place for discussions between faiths. Islam's first mosque, built by the Prophet and his Companions in Medina, was a matter of mud bricks in the sand, with a roof of palm leaves that leaked in rainstorms. When a group of Christians came from Yemen to see the Prophet Muhammad, they stayed there. It was in this spirit that Masjid al-Ikhlas had advertised the Sheikh's talk to non-Muslims and Muslims alike. The orange flyers—"Jesus Christ in Islam: The Epitome of Spirituality and Savior of Humanity"—had even drawn a few people I took to be Christians, listening intently to what the Sheikh would say about their prophet Jesus.

The pagan Arabs of seventh-century Mecca, the original audience for the Quran, probably had a better grounding in Bible stories than I do. Mecca was a multifaith city, and religious traditions being largely oral at the time, many Arabs would most likely have heard the broad outlines of New Testament and Torah stories from Christians and Jews. Into this multifaith ferment came a new prophet, bearing new words but assuming a fair bit of biblical knowledge from his listeners. As a whole, the Quran's message was much the same as the one that Abraham had brought: there is just one God. Within the Muslim faith, Muhammad is seen as continuing the biblical tradition, as the last in a line of monotheistic prophets stretching back to Adam. "God wanted to be fair with everybody," explained the Sheikh. "He's sent different messengers, but the real differences are just about language, or culture, or history. The main message is the same: to believe in God."

The Quran took care to distinguish between the pre-Islamic Arabs who were pagan polytheists, worshipping idols at the Kaaba, and the Ahl-e-Kitab, or People of the Book, possessors of the Torah and the Bible. "When it comes to Jews and Christians, we respect them, because of their scriptures," Akram once assured me. "They don't belong to the same community, but that's fine."

To reinvigorate their faith, Akram believed that Muslims must begin paying attention not just to Muhammad, but to the prophets that preceded him. Too often, Muslims skimmed over the prophetic stories in the Quran. "A big mistake," he said, peering out through his spectacles at the crowd. The five major prophets—Nuh (Noah), Ibrahim (Abraham), Musa (Moses), Isa (Jesus), and Muhammad "are the examples for the believers, at every stage of their life. If we don't know about Maryam [Mary], or Isa, we cannot live in the world as believers!"

All told, there are twenty-five major prophets in the Quran. God has sent thousands of messengers to mankind, said the Sheikh: some traditional Islamic sources say there are as many as 124,000 of them. When it comes to honoring fellow prophets, the Quran is expansive:

> Say, "We believe in God, and what was revealed to us and what was revealed to Abraham, Ishmael, Isaac, Jacob, and the Tribes, and what was given to Moses and Jesus, and what was given to the prophets from their Lord. We do not make a distinction between any of them; we acquiesce to God." (2:136)

The Sheikh had only begun thinking deeply about these earlier prophets since his arrival in Britain. At Nadwat al-Ulama, his professors had skittered over them in favor of more fashionable branches of Islamic learning, like *fiqh* and Arabic grammar. But a couple of years ago, Akram started looking at the suras on Ibrahim, or Abraham, and found his story particularly trenchant.

Both Muslims and Jews claimed Ibrahim as their ancestor: one of his sons, Ismail (Ishmael), was said to be the founding ancestor of Muhammad's tribe, the Quraysh; and the other son, Ishaq (Isaac), was the ancestor of the Israelites. Ibrahim, says the Quran, was a *hanif*, a believer who did not identify himself as a member of a religious community, only as a fervent monotheist: "Abraham was not Jewish or Christian, but he was a committed devotee, and not a polytheistic one."

The Quran says that Ibrahim and his son Ismail built the Kaaba in

Mecca. "Even the Prophet Muhammad was commanded to follow the way of Ibrahim," said Akram. When I asked the Sheikh why he admired Ibrahim so much, he said, "He showed that it is necessary to turn away from everything in the universe to God . . . all of creation, even your own family!"

When Ibrahim's father refused to abandon his many gods in favor of the true One, Ibrahim turned away from the old man. When God told Ibrahim to slaughter his son, the boy agreed. Akram told me, "He said to his father, 'Oh my father, you will find me with the patient people.'" The Quran has a voice calling out, telling Ibrahim to stop at the last minute, for "Lo! That verily was a clear test."

When we'd meet for our private lessons, the Sheikh often spoke about Ibrahim, whose stoic devotion to God greatly impressed the Sheikh. "He made submission in the full details," he said, sounding rather awed. "What he did was not only worshipping God. It was turning away from everything, sacrificing everything for the sake of God."

"It reminds me of what a famous American football coach, in the 1960s, had remarked about winners," he added. "He said, 'The difference between a successful person and others was not a lack of strength, or a lack of knowledge, but rather a lack of will.'"

"Sheikh, who was this coach?" I said, sideswiped by the sudden appearance of an NFL personality in our discussion.

"I forget the name . . . he was famous. He died in 1970 . . ."

"Vince Lombardi?" I said, producing the only name of a football coach I could remember from childhood.

"Vince Lombardi," nodded the Sheikh. "Yes."

Given my parents' casual attitude toward religion, it should come as no surprise that my first-ever Bible sermon was delivered by an Indian Muslim. Like many living far from the country of their birth, I've often engaged most fully with American culture by stepping back and looking at it from a distance. "What should they know of England, who only England know?" asked Rudyard Kipling. Not much. For me, distance has always spurred engagement, if not enchantment. I was most attentive to Western culture when I was far away from it. I'd never really listened to Bach until I discovered an LP of his flute concertos in Kabul, carefully shipped there by my parents via diplomatic pouch. The plights of Pip, Estella, and Miss Havisham felt far more urgent when read on a Turkish bus ride than they ever would have back in Missouri. The same principle held when it came to my interest in Islam: I'd never paid it much attention while we lived in Muslim countries. My curiosity grew only when I went to a college founded by Congregationalists in New England.

Such a dutiful little secularist was I that the priests I'd looked to for Bible lessons had been Renaissance painters such as Bellini and Raphael. Catholic schoolgirls are taught to follow the Virgin Mary's faith and forbearance; this schoolgirl looked to her as a fashion statement. In museums, I'd parse images of the Virgin as others do the images of models in glossy magazines: to see what she wore and how she wore it. My connection to the Virgin's image would be not through faith, but through art, and my emotional response would be not about God but about the self.

As a kid, my favorite image of the Virgin was Titian's *Presentation of Mary in the Temple*, which was the only painting I knew that showed her as a little girl. Though she was barefoot, she had a thick flaxen braid, a shiny blue dress, and, best of all, a divine spotlight. Golden rays wreathed her; all eyes were on her. I didn't know what was happening, but I wanted to be her.

That day at the mosque in Cambridge, I finally heard the story behind the Titian picture of Mary's presentation at the Temple—or rather, the Quranic version thereof. The third sura, "The Family of Imran," tells how Imran's daughter, Maryam, or Mary, was chosen to serve at the Temple despite being a girl. Imran's wife had vowed to give her firstborn to serve at the Temple, explained Akram. "But when she said 'I have delivered a female! What shall I do? How should I serve you?' Allah knew best." Maryam was presented at the Temple, and it was clear that she was exceptional—so much so that she was the only woman with a Quran sura bearing her name. Not only was she a descendent of Daoud (David), going back to Yacub (Jacob), "the purest line on the face of the earth," Akram told us, "but Allah made her to grow so nicely. Her mind is amazing! Her soul is amazing! Her wisdom is amazing!"

The angels came to her, continued Akram, saying, "Allah has chosen you. Your Lord has made you clean and pure, and has chosen you from all the women in the world." They told her she would have a baby. And this, said Akram, his voice growing in excitement, is what made Maryam an exemplar of true submission. "Believers have been known to sacrifice their lives, or their property, for Allah," he said excitedly. "You can be killed in the path of God. But to sacrifice one's honor? Who can do that? For a pure woman, honor is more important than anything. For a pure person, to be accused of *zina* [extramarital sex] is unimaginable. This poor woman is soon going to be accused that she is a sinner!"

Think, he exhorted, fixing his dark eyes on the quiet crowd, think how hard it must have been, in that community, to be regarded by society as a fallen woman. "This is something that nobody can imagine," he said. "Compare it to even how hard it is to wear a hijab in a community where nobody has headcoverings! People insult you. People laugh at you. It's not easy." Wearing a headscarf was a minor inconvenience compared to bearing a child everyone would have thought was illegitimate, in a society where unwed mothers were pariahs. And yet Maryam did it, "for the sake of Allah."

Grade school nativity plays and Tuscan paintings had left me with an image of the pregnant Mary as a pretty woman with a gently swelling tummy, perched on a donkey or reading demurely. The Quran, by contrast, gave gritty details of labor pains. Maryam withdrew to "a faraway place," all by herself: "Then labor pains impelled her to the trunk of the palm tree. She said, 'Would that I had died before this and been completely forgotten!'"

Not to worry, an angel told her. There was a stream flowing beneath her feet. "And shake the trunk of the palm toward you to let fresh ripe dates fall by you. / Then eat and drink and be of good cheer."

If the Quran evoked Jesus' birth as a bodily act of sweat and tears, its discussion of Jesus was of a flesh-and-blood man, not the Son of God. Muslims reject Christianity's concept of the Trinity: the notion of the Father–Son–Holy Ghost structure would constitute the grave sin of *shirk*, or ascribing partners to God. "The Christians somehow got confused," Akram said. "They made Jesus Christ divine, and his mother divine. But Allah is not the father, and Jesus is not the son. If God had wanted to create a son, why did that son not come in the beginning of creation?"

No, Akram continued, Jesus could not be the son of God, because God could never have partners. "The Quran is uncompromising: nobody is to be worshipped other than Allah. Allah can forgive any other sin, other than *shirk*. There is no softness there: the only people who are never forgiven are the people of the *shirk*."

For Akram, Jesus was a "man without a father," whose extraordinary life served to remind lapsed believers of God's power: "God made every single thing in Jesus' life against the norm. His entrance in this world—against the norm." His exit, too. He did not die upon the Cross, as the Bible says, but was raised to heaven alive. As Akram explained it, Christ's would-be killers "were confused." The Quran's language is more formal: "They did not crucify him, although it was made to seem thus to them."

Prophets served to remind humankind of God, observed Akram. The really important ones arrived when God's people were just going through their religion by rote, assuming that being part of a particular community made you one of the faithful. "Whenever things become habit, the way of God is to break the norm," he said. "Look at Ibrahim. He got a child when he was barren and old, to remind everyone that God is not the slave of norms, but that the norm is created by him. Zakariah has no child; his wife is barren. But he gets a son, Yahya [John the Baptist], who is born by breaking that norm."

With the coming of Jesus, or Isa, "God wanted to make a bigger point," said Akram. "He wanted people to be guided, so he created a man without a father."

The belief that Jesus was "without a father" was also a rebuke to those Jewish people who cared more about identity than faith. "God is saying, 'I am creating a prophet, but he is not connected with the family,'" said Akram. "This is to remind them that connection through genealogy is not so important. What is important is faith and action."

Jesus appears not just in the Quran, but in the *sira*, the Prophet's biography. According to Muhammad's early biographers, the Angel Gabriel whisked Muhammad from Mecca to Jerusalem on Buraq, a winged creature with the body somewhere between a horse and a mule, "whose every stride carried it as far as its eye could reach." In Jerusalem, Muhammad met and prayed with Abraham, Moses, Jesus, and other prophets. Later that night, during his ascension to heaven, Muhammad stopped off to visit them again, each in a different level of the seven heavens. On his return to Arabia, he would describe them vividly to his companions. Of Ibrahim, Muhammad said, "I have never seen a man more like myself."

Moses—tall, thin, with curly hair and a hooked nose—offered the newest monotheistic prophet a bit of advice. As Muhammad descended back to earth from his audience with God, Moses asked him how many daily prayers were required of his followers. "When I told him fifty, [Musa] said: 'Prayer is a weighty matter, and your people are weak, so go back to your Lord and ask him to reduce the number.'" So Muhammad went back to God, who took off ten prayers. When he passed Musa again on the way down, the older prophet asked the same question, and again advised asking for a reduction. "So it went on until only five prayers for the whole of the day and night were left," said Muhammad. At this point, Muhammad had to tell Musa that he was too "ashamed" to go back for any further negotiations. The agreement for five daily prayers continues to be observed to this day.

When Muhammad met Jesus, he was struck by the sight of a man "as handsome as you can imagine anyone being," the Sheikh said casually, as though he were recounting a celebrity sighting. Medium height, with a reddish complexion—"like the people from Syria or Lebanon"—Jesus had shiny, shoulder-length hair, which shook with "pearls of water, as though he was just coming from the bath," said the Sheikh.

Over and over, Akram spoke not of Jesus' teachings, but of his importance as a prophet for today's Muslims. Like the Jews of the Roman Empire, contemporary Muslims needed to heed Jesus Christ's message, since so many today were spiritually lost: "Religion comes with a body and a soul," the Sheikh explained. "But after a few generations, etiquette and manners become more important in a religion, which means the spirit of the religion disappears." Such was the situation among the Jewish people, he said, when Jesus began preaching: they had forgotten Abraham's covenant with God. Over time, their religion had settled into a matter of habit. They began to treat Judaism as a matter of belonging to a people rather than believing in a God, he argued. Such was the case for many Muslims today: "When Jesus came, the Jews really wanted to be treated as believers without being believers," he said. "We Muslims, at this moment, want to be treated as believers without being believers."

Modern Muslims often simply cling to the external signs of their faith: "People are busy worrying about their beards, or their headscarves," he observed. "So the faith becomes like their identity. It happens like this in every culture, every faith. The outer aspects become more important, while the soul inside is forgotten." He paused, shook his head, and gazed mournfully out at the crowd. "At the end of the day, people are carrying around a dead body, with no soul."

"Why do we Muslims have so much suffering, all over the world?" he demanded. "We are carrying the body of Islam! We don't have submission. We have got the law, but without the *hikma*—the wisdom— behind it. Religion hasn't come to give people an identity! Its purpose is not so you can say, 'We belong to this group.' But at this moment ninety-nine percent of Muslims treat religion as identity! But God does not like identity. He does not want people to be proud of belonging. He wants faith, and he wants action."

I wasn't surprised to hear Akram discussing the connections between Jews, Christians, and Muslims and their prophets; I knew that the

Sheikh was tolerant of differences: I'd known that since the day I bounced into our shared office in a miniskirt. I'd watched him talk politely to pierced and dreadlocked hippies. And when, just a few years ago, I finally had the guts to tell him that my mother was Jewish, he nodded, smiled, and was as warm as before. Differences weren't just to be tolerated, he once wrote, but were God's design: "If Allah had pleased, He would have created all people alike, yet Allah has bestowed on man the potential for intellect and will, hence people have diverse beliefs, thoughts, and tendencies."

But just how diverse could these beliefs be? One day the Sheikh and I were on a bad mobile phone connection, fixing a date for our next lesson, when I found the courage to ask whether Christians and Jews would be saved.

"Oh, Sheikh, before we hang up—one last question. It's about Christians and Jews. So, I understand that Muslims embrace earlier prophets," I began. "But those who worship the earlier prophets, what of them? If you're an observant Christian or Jew, and you submit to God, are you considered a true believer?"

The cell phone connection was crackly, but the Sheikh's answer was unequivocal. The Quran revered the prophets of the Jews and Christians—but the Jews and Christians, in turn, needed to believe in the message of the Prophet Muhammad: "You cannot deny any of the Prophets. They believe in their own Prophets, just as we do, but they cannot deny Muhammad and his Message. Otherwise, it is just holding on to the religion of their ancestors."

Clinging blindly to the faith of your forefathers, the Quran asserts, is arrogant. Noah's 950 years of warning didn't persuade pagans to forsake their idols, and so they were drowned. Moses warned the Pharaoh and his cronies, but they didn't listen: on the Day of Resurrection, they will head to hell. To hold on to your ancestral faith without acknowledging the new signs that God sent you was to turn away from Him, said the Sheikh. Jews and Christians who wanted salvation must acknowledge Muhammad as a prophet.

I hung up, deflated. His answer was far less encouraging than the

view of progressive Muslims, who pointed out that Islam acknowl-
edged that God allowed for a variety of ways of worshipping Him:

> For each of them We have established a law, and a revealed way.
> And if God wished, God would have made you a single nation;
> but the intent is to test you in what God has given you.
> So let your goals be everything good. (5:48)

I counted this among the Quran's most comforting verses, a
resounding endorsement of my own creed: diversity and good deeds.
Different paths to God were not just tolerated, but part of the divine
design traced out by God. Religious differences were a source of
strength, polishing belief as the faithful contrasted, compared, and
competed to please God through kindness and piety. A sort of divinely
sanctioned free market of faith. "And there is a messenger for every
people," the Quran says. For those who follow these messengers well,
there was nothing to worry about.

Omid Safi, professor of Islamic studies and author of *Memories of
Muhammad*, notes that the Quran stressed that "no one group—
including Muslims—claims exclusive salvation." Indeed, the Quran
dealt sternly with any religious group claiming that their way of worship was the right one:

> And they say: None entereth paradise unless he be a Jew or a Chris-
> tian. These are their own desires. Say: Bring your proof (of what ye
> state) if ye are truthful. (2:111)

The Quran took a dim view of any one group claiming they'd
found the sole path to paradise. Along with all the careful reminders
that only Allah knew someone's ultimate fate, there seemed to be
grounds to believe that salvation didn't belong to Muslims alone.

But that wasn't what the Sheikh had said. Hoping to find comfort
in nuance, I crept around to the issue from another angle, over tea at
the Oxford Kebab House. My nervousness was compounded by the
fact that I was the only one sipping tea, since it was a Thursday. Except

when he was exercising particularly hard at the gym, the Sheikh fasted on Mondays and Thursdays, just like the Prophet Muhammad.

"Now, Sheikh, the Quran makes clear that what it brings is nothing new, right?" I said. "God has sent down revelations before, first to the Jewish people, then to the Christians. So why send new revelations, with slight details altered, if the essential message is the same?"

"It is deconditioning people," he said. "The new Messenger deconditions the people who have been following the religion and have made it into culture and identity. So when the Messenger comes with new details, the religion becomes fresh, like a still pond getting a new water supply."

When a new Messenger comes, he said, people must believe in his message.

Oh.

I was unaccustomed to such stark certainty from the Sheikh. So I asked yet again, at a Q&A session in a public lecture, raising my hand, waiting for the microphone to be passed to me, and asking whether the Quran allowed any wiggle room on various roads to salvation. Could Jews and Christians be saved, for example?

"The basic idea, really, is that when a new Messenger comes, all the people who know him must accept him, and must follow him. As Musa [Moses] says, you must believe in the new Messenger when he comes." Moreover, it is the duty of Muslims to try to connect people of other faiths with this new message, to reach out as *dais*—people who do *dawa*, or call people to the right path.

But the Sheikh, who always took care to give the most tactful answer he could find, then gently offered a bit of hope. "I suppose . . . it could be that someone, somewhere believes in one God, makes an effort, and has no other guidance . . . has no idea of the Prophet Muhammad, no idea of Islam or access to the Quran, and he dies as a true believer, there's hope for him to be forgiven. These people who are believers without being Muslims could be saved. It's up to God."

In other words, among non-Muslims, only a hermit might have a shot at salvation. In the Sheikh's estimation, if one knew about the

Prophet Muhammad's message and turned away from it, even if one turned toward another faith, one cannot be a true believer.

But still, even many Muslims seemed to be ignoring Muhammad's teachings, said the Sheikh. It was simply human nature to focus on the most recent prophet: "The Jews took Musa to be more important than the religion of Ibrahim," he noted. "The Christians ignored earlier Prophets, and now the Muslims are ignoring the teachings of the other Prophets in favor of Muhammad."

So without Muhammad, said the Sheikh, Jews and Christians wouldn't make it to paradise. It wasn't what I had wanted to hear, but I knew he believed in freedom of belief. On this, he was as emphatic as the Quran: "There is no compulsion in religion." Don't take my word for it, he always counseled: "If you disagree with my interpretation, seek out someone else's." And so I did. I turned to my bookshelf and found Muslim writers who wrote on Islam and pluralism. In the Quran itself, in the forty-sixth verse of the twenty-ninth sura, I found a succinct expression of an enlightened coexistence between Muslims, Christians, and Jews, three groups of the faithful, theologically distinct, perhaps, but believing in the same truth:

> And do not contest the people of scripture, unless with what is better, except those of them who have been unjust: say, "We believe in what was revealed to us, and what was revealed to you; for our God and your God is one, to Whom we acquiesce." (29:46)

Relief.

I was even more consoled by *No god but God*, in which Reza Aslan describes Muhammad's view of the People of the Book. In the earliest days in Medina, Aslan writes, the Christians and Jews were "spiritual cousins who, unlike the pagans and polytheists of Arabia, worshipped the same God, read the same scriptures, and shared the same moral values as his Muslim community." Aslan even floats the theory that though they were theologically distinct, they were conceived, in Muhammad's city-state of Medina, as a single community of monotheists, committed to pluralistic living. It was only later, notes Aslan, that the jurists promoted a conservative worldview, much as they had done with women's rights. It was these medieval scholars, not Muhammad, who had deemed Jews and Christians "unbelievers" rather than simply members of the *umma*, the multistranded community of believers. Just as early Christians had worked to distinguish themselves from the Jews, so, too, had medieval Muslims sharpened the divides between their own young faith and other monotheistic faiths.

Identity politics, it turns out, has a long-standing history of its own, nested within the broader sweep of religious histories. At one dinner party, I met a screenwriter who'd recently moved back to London from Tel Aviv. She was chic, smart—and unconvinced when I argued that anti-Semitism wasn't intrinsic to Islam, only to some modern extremists. "I think you'll find," she said, slowly smoothing back her long dark hair, silver bracelets jangling, "that you're choosing not to see what you don't want to see. The Quran calls Jews monkeys and pigs." There was a shocking amount of anti-Semitism among Muslims, she said, and their scripture just condoned it. She'd once had a horrific encounter with a Muslim in a British corner shop. Taking her for a Muslim, with her dark hair and olive complexion, the shop assistant had begun flirting with her. She didn't flirt back, and things got nasty. When he began yelling anti-Semitic remarks, she decided that it was time to move to Israel.

"That sounds awful," I said, meaning it. But I also despaired of this anecdotal approach to discussing civilizations. It felt like an endless ping-pong match: "You show me your Muslim, I'll show you mine." Or, "You show me your seemingly incendiary Quran verse, I'll counter with one calling for peace." Such discussions were a relentless tit-for-tat of examples, rather than exploration.

The following day, I phoned the Sheikh about the monkeys and pigs verse. "It is not about all Jews," he said. "Just some of the Jews, in a particular fishing town, Eilat. They tried to fish on the Sabbath by spreading their nets out in advance of it. They tried to get around God's laws through their cleverness, and so they broke the Sabbath. The other people in the town, the Jews who observed the Sabbath, they are fine!"

Had we not been on the phone—and had it not been wildly inappropriate—I could have hugged him. As ever, he put the words in context, both in terms of Islamic history and thematically, in the broader messages of the Quran. As we hung up, I thought, for the umpteenth time that year, how people could use reckless readings to find nearly anything they wanted in the Quran. As with the Bible and the Torah before it, it's easy to find incendiary passages if you want to. The challenge, as ever, is to step back and consider them in context. But such study remains a luxury, beyond the means of many Muslims and non-Muslims alike. Too many Muslims are left to learn with an untrained village mufti, or to explore the badlands of the Internet with only "Sheikh Google" as a guide. For Christian and Jewish readers of the Quran, proper study takes not merely time and effort, but a careful separation of their interpretations of the text from contemporary events. It's quick work to allow modern tensions between Muslims and Jews in Gaza, or between Muslims and Christians in Egypt, to infuse a reading of the Quran. But to do so is to place the self, rather than God, at the center of one's reading of the Quran. And that, the Sheikh had taught me, will never do.

13

Beyond Politics

The Sheikh's humor tended toward the arcane. For anyone weaned on Woody Allen and *Saturday Night Live*, his jokes were nearly unrecognizable as such. More gentle fables on human folly than jokes per se, they ended not so much with punch lines as with pat lines. The day the Sheikh and I discussed how different readers bring their own agendas to a text, he told me this one: A boy and his dad go to the zoo. On seeing the animals, the boy begs his father to get him one of his own to take home.

"But how would we feed it?" the fretful parent asks. "You know I can't afford another mouth to feed."

"Not a problem, not with these animals," the son counters. "Look at the sign on the fence: 'No Feeding.'"

The Sheikh waited for me to get it.

"Aha!" I said, hoping that polite appreciation, rather than mirth, might suffice.

"Do you see?" he asked. "The boy didn't understand that the sign was meant to be read from the angle of the visitors! It was not written about the animals, but written for the visitors!"

Got it. A gag built on grammatical confusion. Does "feeding" function as an adjective, describing the animals, as the boy argued? Or is it a directive, telling the zoo visitors how to act?

The joke reminded me of a rather graver case of grammatical ambiguity, one that hinged on a single letter. It appeared frequently in the Quran and revolved around the letter *i* in the word "Islam." *Islam* with a capital *I* refers to the religion itself, while *islam* with a lowercased *i* just denotes "submission" or "surrendering" to God. In this lies the difference between a specific religious group and something rather more elastic. The space between them suggests the creative tension between the Quran as a scripture reaffirming earlier Abrahamic faiths, and one setting up a community distinct from them. The Sheikh, and other scholars, read most of the allusions to "islam" in the Quran as lowercased *islam*. "In the Quranic worldview, 'Islam' is not so much the name of a new religious tradition as it is the quality of submitting oneself to God wholeheartedly," writes the professor of Islamic studies Omid Safi in *Memories of Muhammad*. "For the most part in the Quran the word 'Islam' is a verb, not a noun."

Similarly, the word "Muslim" means "one who submits," or "one who surrenders." But there's a huge difference between Muslims with a capital *M* (a faith group) and lowercased-*m* muslims (monotheists who have submitted to God). Much depends on whether one reads it as a proper noun describing who someone is, or as a verb describing what they do. When I look up English translations of bin Laden's 1996 declaration of jihad against American troops, the online translators render the opening sura he quotes thus: "O you who believe! Be careful of your duty to Allah with the proper care which is due to Him, and do not die unless you are Muslim."

But when I opened my copy of Thomas Cleary's translation of the Quran, I found that the final phrase was translated, rather less stringently, as "do not die without your having surrendered to God."

When I point out that so much of the Quranic message seemed to be about lowercased-*m* muslims, or rather, anyone who has submitted to God, the Sheikh was delighted: "Yes! Exactly! So many times in the Quran, it is not describing a group called 'the Muslims.' The word is with a small *m*, describing those who submit to the Lord!"

But it's capitalized-*M* Muslims who inevitably make the news, or feature in government debates and sternly worded op-eds. Capitalized-*M* Muslims feed the whole "clash of civilizations" myth, with its claim that Islam and the West are two airtight systems. For those who hold with such a notion, the two are mutually exclusive; for extremists on both sides, "the Islamic world" and "the West" are straining toward each other's destruction. The Swiss burgher fretting about the threat that minarets might pose to the Alpine landscape was concerned not with a faith, but with an identity group. So was the jihadi ranting about the evils of unbelievers at the mosque; and the Islamophobe congressman, intent on protecting decent, hardworking Americans from sharia law.

The journalist traded in capital-*M* Muslims, too. Lowercased-*m* muslims weren't a story, for the simple reason that they don't create conflict. As bullies and demagogues well know, pitting one group against another produces swift and lasting results. Conflict was a gift that kept on giving, bonding these identity groups ever tighter together, laying down foundations for more conflict. Bin Laden's faithful and American Crusaders. Islam and the West. Without a bracing storyline, bristling with events, small-*i* islam just can't compete.

Akram refused to sit and listen to divisive tales, and he refused to tell them, too.

He had heard them hundreds of times, sometimes from his students, sometimes when he happened to see a headline in a British paper. In recent years, a few highly excitable young men wanted to go back to the time when the world had been divided between Dar al-Islam (the Land of Islam) and Dar al-Harb (the Land of War). Anything that wasn't Islam's, they deemed to be the Land of War. But that, the Sheikh pointed out, was strictly applicable only when Muslim societies were strong. It made no sense now. "It was for when Muslims had empires," he said. "Now, the whole world is Dar al-Dawa"—the realm of calling people to Islam.

When the Sheikh's students voiced fears about Islamophobic media coverage, or Western laws that they felt discriminated against Muslims, the Sheikh would warn them to be careful not to confuse group politics with piety. "Islam is not a property," Akram once observed during a seminar. "It's not your identity. Don't think that if someone laughs at you, you have to explain yourself. We are more interested in defending our belonging, our identity, than in the Prophet. Don't think about identity! Think about good character!"

A British-Indian novelist published a story slurring the Prophet Muhammad? Ignore it. Don't issue fatwas against him, or burn books in town centers, or stage protest rallies. Turn away from this world and toward God. Pray. Do *dawa*—call people to Islam. "If people write books against your Prophet, there are many ways to solve the problem! The best way is to pray for these people. Write some books yourself." Some cartoonist in Denmark sketched some ugly little pictures insulting the Prophet? Let it go; go toward God instead. "Someone makes a cartoon, and we protest. We make protest, and we think we're doing what we're supposed to do!" They're not. "Where is it in the book of Allah that we 'protest'? Is this business of 'protest' anywhere in the Quran or the Prophet's sunna?"

Akram urged his students to look at the Prophet and his Companions. Faced with a silly sketch, or a nasty novel, would they have demonstrated? "Let's think, really," he urged. "No matter how much the Prophet had been abused by people who opposed him, did he protest? Did he burn their houses? Did he harm them? No! He went to do *dawa*. When he wanted to persuade the people in Mecca to become Muslim, he would go to someone's house seventy times! He would have patience!"

Still, in class after class, students asked how Muslims can defend Islam from slurs against it.

"Musk smells sweet on its own," Akram advised, quoting a Persian proverb. "You don't need a perfume seller to tell you of its sweetness."

One needn't defend Islam, but one should try to spread its teachings. Britain had given its Muslims so much. "We are takers here," he said. "We come to this country, and we have taken their wealth, we have taken their technologies. Everything we have we got from them." The least they could do would be to share their most precious of gifts, their faith, with the British. The least they could do would be to try to save them from the fires of hell. "The reason people hate us is they believe we have come to this country to take," he said. "But we have to give."

Dawa could never be aggressive, cautioned the Sheikh. You weren't angling to win a debate. You weren't trying to chalk up more souls to boost a community's numbers, like some Christian missionaries. Rather than protesting, the Sheikh preferred that Muslims spend their time doing what some translations of the Quran call "beautiful preaching." Think of the Prophet Muhammad, Akram said, and how he modeled the teachings of the Quran, humanizing Islam. Where the Quran could sound forbidding, Muhammad helped soften it by presenting its human face. He showed how God's message worked in the real world.

The first Muslim community grew up in a multifaith environment. Medina was home to pagans, seekers, and three Jewish tribes as well as Muslims. Indeed, for the first years of his prophethood, Muhammad stressed that his message was for Jews and Christians as well as for pagans. Upon arrival at the oasis of Medina, having fled Mecca, Muhammad's first words framed the basic laws for the first Muslim community: "Spread peace, feed the hungry, honor kinship ties, pray while people sleep, and you shall enter Paradise in peace."

In the early Medina years, notes Reza Aslan in *No god but God*, Muhammad stressed that his message was for all the People of the Book, and so he took care to promote acts that would build allegiances between the Muslim and Jewish communities. In the first Muslim state in Medina, the Prophet Muhammad guaranteed nonaggression between the Muslims and the rest of the population, including the Jewish, Christian, and pagan clans. "He who wrongs a Jew or a Christian," said Muhammad, "will have me as his accuser on the Day of Judgment." The Muslim fast was to be observed on the same day as Yom Kippur, the Jewish day of atonement. Like the Jews, Muslims were commanded to pray facing Jerusalem. Muhammad picked Friday as the day of communal prayer so as to be in concert (and not conflict) with the Jewish Sabbath.

As the Muslim roots in Medina grew, so did the distinctions

between its Jews and Muslims. Some of the town's Jewish population began showing up in the mosque to jeer at the Muslim community, and to scoff at the differences between the Quran's version of certain stories and the Torah's. After a year and a half in Medina, the Prophet received a revelation that ordained that Muslims should switch their *qibla*, or direction of prayer, from Jerusalem to Mecca. This shift of orientation to the Kaaba was a sign, notes the author Karen Armstrong, "of a proud new Muslim identity."

In the centuries that followed, the most successful Muslim states, whether the Mughals or the Ottomans or Muslim Spain, demonstrated tolerance toward other faiths. For Akram, enjoining his students to spread the word of Islam, it helped to ignore religious divisions and focus on a shared humanity. It was a bit like being a savvy businessman, he once explained: "I open a shop, I want to get every customer possible!" he said. "I don't want to tell people, 'No, you can't come here because you are a Christian, or a Jew, or a Wahhabi, or a Barelvi.' When you are working for your money, this is how you are thinking." The same principle should apply to doing *dawa*: "With everyone, be nice to him. Treat him as an individual, not as a Jew!"

The image of the shop reverberated—and not only because it was rare for Akram to cite anything as grubby as commerce. The marketplace fits with one of my own operating principles: welcoming diversity and pluralism.

Doing *dawa* may require the expansive and open qualities of a good businessman, but it wasn't a sales pitch, warned Akram in another Cambridge lecture. One couldn't sugarcoat Islam's message. By way of explanation, he cited an editor's letter from the front of *Time* magazine. It advised readers that, as the Sheikh read, "We keep our readers in mind, and select the stories that will interest them."

(Well, of course, I thought. How else would a magazine work?)

"Salespeople are not interested in what benefits you," Akram said rather sternly. "They only want to sell you something."

It was tempting to stress "how nice Islam is, so people will love us," he conceded. "But the message itself is self-sufficient. It has its own wisdom."

That said, one had to know one's audience. "Understand people's context," Akram counseled. "Messengers always have great character. So it helps to build up your own, and then people will see it. They will know the Prophet through you. If you are generous, they will know that your Prophet is generous."

Connect with the place in which you find yourself, he stressed. It was true, of course, that "people should live in this world like a traveler," mindful that what really mattered was to come after death. But that didn't mean Muslims should float, disconnected, on the surface of the society in which they lived. Too often, Western Muslims whiled away their lives dreaming of going "back home" to the Punjabi village that their parents had quit decades ago, or fantasizing about some Islamist utopia where sharia ruled the land.

Don't waste your time, counseled the Sheikh. If you live in Britain, embrace Britain. Be a good citizen. Contribute to society—and not just Muslim society. Help out the British government, if they need it! Boost the economy! Give to the needy—whether Christian, Jewish, Muslim, or Hindu!

The speech was characteristically confident. Exhorting his students to get out there and mingle with non-Muslims, the Sheikh challenged the extremist concept of al-wala wa al-bara, the doctrine of loyalty and dissociation, which holds that Muslims should not, except in circumstances of extreme need, befriend non-Muslims.

The Muslims who warn against befriending Jews or Christians often cite the fifty-first verse from the fifth sura, "The Table," which can read like a bald warning not to mix with other monotheists: "Choose not for friends such of those who received the Scripture before you." Thomas Cleary, my favorite English translator of the Quran, sees 5:51 as a warning merely against taking "Jews and Christians for patrons, for they are patrons of each other." Whether one opted for "patrons" or "friends," the phrasing seemed to encourage Muslims to keep their distance from people of other faiths. Hostile zealots—both Muslim and non-Muslim—love to brandish that line from 5:51 as proof that "we" should keep clear of "them." I'd seen 5:51 quoted on a nasty little Islamophobic website that boasted it had "the politically incorrect truth about one really messed up religion." I'd also read it invoked by a hard-line Muslim sheikh online. In response to a young man's query as to whether Muslims could "play basketball" or "hang out" with non-Muslims, he handed down fatwa number 59879: "Allah has forbidden the believers to take the [disbelievers] as friends."

When I asked the Sheikh about it, he cautioned that 5:51 wasn't a blanket statement. Rather, it applied to a very specific group of non-Muslims at a particular moment in Medina when certain Jewish tribes aligned with the pagan Quraysh against the young Muslim community. "That verse came down when they were in war conditions," he explained. "That verse is for when unbelievers have all the power, and yet still they oppose the Muslims, and persecute them, and don't give them freedom."

Reach out to people of other faiths, the Sheikh encouraged his students. Invite your non-Muslim neighbors to your daughters' weddings! (He had, though it was fortunate that "our neighbors are very nice people anyway.") If your neighbors are sick, help them out! Take them a plate of *samosas!* "The way to bring people to Islam is not the sword," he smiled. "Sometimes, food can do more than the sword. Invite them for a nice *biryani.*" Or a kebab. All were means to "interact with the people, mix with the people. People are not your enemy! If there is a barrier between you and them, break the barrier! If people just smell you cooking your *biryani*, they will hate you! If you offer it to them, they will love you!"

I laughed, along with the rest of the crowd, at the image of *biryani*-based *dawa*. He knew his audience well: most had roots in South Asia. Whenever he invoked the reign of Shah Jahan, or recited Urdu couplets, or told a joke involving a Hindu and a Muslim, it was a reminder that he wasn't anchored just by Islam, but by the subcontinent, too. Because the Sheikh had brought his love of Lucknow, his devotion to the poetry of the Pakistani poet Iqbal, and the *adab* of the traditional *alim*, he could retain a supple, accepting outlook of his new country. It was precisely his immersion in his own faith and culture that allowed him to live in another so peacefully.

Olivier Roy, a French scholar of global Islamic movements, wrote that mass Muslim migration has frequently "delinked" religion from culture. The child of the villager who chances a better life in Karachi, or the Karachi youth who gets a U.S. green card, often feels cut off from his ancestral culture. Some seek a globalized form of Islam to fill the hole, and the result can be a brittle Islamic identity, one ripped from their past. This rootless, decontextualized strain of Islam, notes Roy, mirrors the process that has produced it: globalization. Whereas one's ancestors were steeped in a local Muslim culture, with its own memory, historical character, and customs, this "delinked" Islam functioned like a mobile SIM card: a portable, fungible faith, without roots or a culture of its own.

In the mid-1990s, many American Muslims announced that they were delighted to peel off the local customs their parents had imported when they'd migrated. They wore T-shirts to youth conventions with the Quranic verse proclaiming strength in diversity:

> O mankind! Lo! We have created you male and female and have made you nations and tribes that you may know one another. Lo! the noblest of you, in the sight of Allah, is the best in conduct. (49:13)

When I met these young Americans, they frequently assured me that they would no longer be hobbled by the narrow, localized Islam that their parents brought over from Pakistan or Syria. Their Islam would be pure. Strictly religious, rather than mingled with customs. "It's a new beginning, it's a new frontier!" enthused one Muslim leader at an East Coast college. "We can get away from all the cultural baggage of the Middle East and create something new, away from the turmoil and chaos of the Muslim world."

I remember wondering, a bit wistfully, about this all-American zeal to forget the past. Whether these New World pioneers really wanted to rush in and strip back the layers that their forefathers had set down. Whether Islam, strained of culture, was going to be sustaining enough. I wondered, too, how long it would be before they built up cultures and traditions of their own. These young Americans, with their talk of fresh starts and pure origins, were some of the newest migrants to embrace the dream described in the final page of *The Great Gatsby*. In the words of these new Muslim migrants, hoping for a pure faith, free from despots, wars, and repression, I heard echoes of Fitzgerald's description of the European discovery of America, of the first sight of "a fresh, green breast of the new world," and of the fleeting hope that it would remain fresh, green, and new.

Another joke from the Sheikh, this one about the traditional Egyptian buffoon figure Joha. He wandered down to the riverside one day, where he saw a crowd of people, waiting expectantly on the other bank.

"What are you waiting for?" he cried.

"A boat," they yelled back. "To get to the other side!"

"But why would you do that?" called Joha. "You are *on* the other side."

Too often, the Sheikh said, Muslims acted like Joha on the riverbank: "We never look at problems from how other people might see them."

"I thought that was what you Muslims always said was an American problem," I teased. "An inability to see things from anybody else's point of view."

"No, really! Like when I hear Muslims complain about why America always supports Israel. They think it's not consistent with their support of democracy and human rights. But it is consistent, because they are supporting what is in their own interests. If you look at it that way, it's very consistent!"

It was the first time I'd ever heard Akram mention the Israel-Palestine dispute. It was something I'd always assumed was a core issue for Muslims. Not for Akram. Like the struggles in Kashmir and Syria and Afghanistan, he left this Middle East conflict to the capitalized-*M* crowd. For Akram, fighting over bits of earth was far less compelling than mapping out hell or paradise. Lobbying for Muslims in Parliament was fine, if one went in for that sort of thing, so long as one didn't sacrifice *taqwa* in the process. Political gains are transient, but the afterlife endures. For Akram, Muslims' real rewards lie not within the pre-1967 borders of Palestine, nor in any Muslim state. Indeed, they lie no place on the planet, but in the infinite space afforded a single soul by God.

14

The Pharaoh and His Wife

"But what," the young woman asked the Sheikh, "about struggling against unjust rulers?" Mona was just twenty-six, but she somehow seemed older. Her face was solemn, and she wore her khaki hijab tightly tucked. A PhD candidate in neuroscience at Cambridge, she tended to ask questions that hinged on theological categories or the finer points of Arabic grammar—the queries of a student taught to analyze systems. But today's question felt more urgent. How, she pressed, should one respond when there was tyranny?

"Sometimes people's space to worship is taken away," agreed the Sheikh. "But when that happens, people still have to keep doing as much as they can." Think of the Prophet Yusuf, he urged, "in the house of that woman." In prison. The God-fearing, he said, can worship Him from any space.

So said the Sheikh from a peaceful classroom in Cambridge. But earlier that summer the streets of Mona's hometown, Cairo, were convulsed with angry Egyptians, and later strewn with corpses. It was, she said, "the worst time of my life." That summer, Egypt's army toppled the nation's first democratically elected president, the Muslim Brotherhood's Mohamed Morsi.

Mona's beloved brother Khaled had been a top adviser to Morsi, serving as his secretary of foreign affairs. A few weeks after the Sheikh counseled Mona to think of the Prophet Yusuf in prison, the army imprisoned Khaled, along with other presidential advisers and Morsi himself. For weeks, Mona and her family had no idea where Khaled was. Though just six months away from completing her PhD, Mona told Cambridge she was putting her studies on hold. She threw herself into working as the Muslim Brotherhood's UK spokesperson and lobbying for Khaled's release. At the time, Western commentators were calling the army's actions an "intervention," but Mona appeared on British television and called Morsi's removal "a military coup." Doing so, she later said, meant she wouldn't be able to return to Egypt for the indefinite future.

She was willing to make that sacrifice. Her sense of injustice dated back over a decade, to when she'd been a teenager. She'd grown up in "a niche existence" of Cairo's private international schools and expensive shops, cut off from ordinary Egyptian struggles. But privilege couldn't block out the yawning inequalities and corruption she saw in Hosni Mubarak's Egypt. Nor could it shield her family from the meddling of state security services. Her father, the headmaster of a private school, was hassled by police when he didn't hang the obligatory portrait of Mubarak, Mona told me. He even had to pay a fee for the government informers assigned to the school. "It was very Big Brother," she observed.

Of her five siblings, she and Khaled were closest, getting up before dawn prayers during Ramadan to read the Quranic sura "Repentance"— their favorite, whose theme, she said, "is victory." Khaled joined the Muslim Brotherhood and Mona followed while still in her teens, deciding that the Brotherhood was Egypt's only serious opposition to Mubarak's rule. The siblings rose quickly: Mona was a gifted speaker, Khaled an efficient organizer. Under Mubarak, Mona believed, her activism hobbled her career. She graduated first in her university class but saw the teaching job she wanted go to someone else. When she won three scholarships to Cambridge, government officials said that they would let her go, but they reminded her that they could stop her anytime, should they choose. "As though they were doing me a favor," she scoffed.

Mona spent the Arab Spring in England, where she marched in solidarity with the Tahrir Square protests. Exultant as she was that Egypt was shaking off the political torpor she'd endured her whole life, the news from home was harrowing. State police beat up her uncle and cousin and teargassed her best friend. A bullet narrowly missed her brother. When Mubarak fell, Mona rejoiced, hoping that the country would finally get democracy and justice. When the Muslim Brotherhood won the elections, Mona believed her party would bring Egyptians bread and representation. A year later, she was watching the army and Brotherhood supporters fighting in Egypt's streets. If Egypt's Arab Spring was born with hopes of democracy, it had now tilted back into dictatorship. As the months went by, she heard snippets of news about her brother. He was in solitary confinement, she learned, and her sister-in-law was doing her best to get him a blanket for his cell.

When I asked Mona what had inspired her to become politically involved in the first place, she told me she was spurred by the injustice she had seen during the second Palestinian intifada in 2000. Widespread demonstrations by Palestinians had erupted across the country, triggering casualties in clashes with the Israeli army. Just fourteen at the time, she watched the famous footage of a twelve-year-old in the streets of Gaza, Mohammed al-Durrah, cowering and clutching his father while they sought shelter from the cross fire. Shocked by the image, she decided to devote herself to combating injustice, starting by addressing the poverty and corruption she saw at home, in Egypt. "Islam is about justice," she reasoned. "I want to be a good Muslim, so I need to stop the injustice in the world."

Like Mona, I'd always been taught that justice was the cornerstone virtue of Islam, occupying much the same position that love does in Christianity. Prophets were sent to bring justice to the people through their messages. Polygamists are counseled to be just with their wives, and merchants to make fair deals in the marketplace. "A just leader," the Prophet Muhammad is reported to have said, will be "the most beloved of people to God," while the "most hated" would surely be a tyrant. While Islam's Sufi mystics might stress love, it is justice that runs through the writings of twentieth-century Muslim reformers, often intertwined with cries for freedom from local despots and foreign imperialists. The Ayatollah Khomeini called for justice and the resistance to the tyranny of Iran's Shah; Islamic feminists write of finding gender justice in the Quran. "Justice" is the cry for Kashmir and Palestine, and in petitions about Iraq and Guantánamo Bay.

I called the Sheikh to ask about justice. "It's the basic tenet of Islam, right?" I asked.

A pause. There was justice, ultimately, he said, but it would not necessarily arrive in this life. Allah would provide it in the Hereafter. In Islamic political circles, rather too much can be made of it, he said, and that hurt Muslims. "Think of Palestine," he suggested. "We have no doubt that there has been wrongdoing against the Palestinians by the Jews. But one has to really think about helping what is a very weak community. The way to help is not to bring justice."

"No?"

"No. If you insist on justice, then the weak community becomes weaker, because those in power won't give it. They will just hate them more."

"But what can Muslims do without seeking justice?" I asked.

Compromise, said the Sheikh. That will bring peace, which in turn will give a battered community the time and space to heal.

"Weak people, if they don't admit they are weak, it's going to destroy them more and more," he noted. "Some people say, 'When we make peace, we accept injustice.' I'm saying, when we make peace, we buy time."

The Quran, he reminded me, says "Peace is better."

Besides, fighting for justice never gets you peace, he said: "Look at the people in Palestine and Kashmir. They need space and time to do something, to build something. They need to get education. If they keep fighting for justice, they will lose more—and not even get that."

What at first appears to be weakness might ultimately prove to be strength. Take the Treaty of Hudaybiyah, he suggested. The incident occurred in 628, when the Prophet, then based with his followers in Medina, was still at war with the Quraysh of Mecca. Despite the fact that the ruling Quraysh still controlled the Kaaba, Muhammad declared that he would go to Mecca for *umra*. Fourteen hundred followers decided to accompany him, even when he said he would not bear arms. It was a brave decision, since the Quraysh had been trying to kill the Prophet for six years. But a few miles outside the city, at a site called Hudaybiyah, Muhammad's camel sank to its knees, refusing to get up.

The pilgrims sat in the desert, waiting for the Quraysh to send an envoy to negotiate their entry into Mecca. They eventually did, but they brought with them an offer many of Muhammad's Companions thought he should refuse. On the face of it, the terms looked pretty humiliating: Muhammad had to go back to Medina without doing *umra*, and had to wait a year before returning. But this meant there would also be a peace treaty between Mecca and Medina for ten years—so long as Muhammad would send back to the Quraysh any Meccan who had emigrated with him without their consent. This condition, however, didn't apply to the Quraysh: they could keep any Muslim that joined their side.

Despite the lopsided terms, Muhammad agreed to the cease-fire.

When he did, his companion, the future Caliph Umar, approached the Prophet.

"You're a Prophet, are you not?" he asked.

The Prophet said he was.

"And aren't we on the right path? And aren't they on the wrong one?"

Indeed, responded the Prophet quietly.

Umar was incredulous at what he believed to be a capitulation to the Meccans.

To show that the Muslims had accepted the treaty, the Prophet asked his Companions to slaughter their camels and shave their heads. The two acts were symbolic recognition that they were no longer in the purified state required of the *umra* pilgrim and thus were abandoning the plans to enter Mecca. None of the men moved to slaughter their beasts or shave. Muhammad asked them again—three times. All they did was stare at him, dazed and bewildered.

Disappointed, the Prophet went into his wife Umm Salamah's

tent. The Muslims were upset, she pointed out. "Go out, and don't say anything. Slaughter your own cattle, and shave your own head," she advised. The Prophet did so, and the Prophet's Companions swiftly followed suit, shaving one another's heads with such gusto that Umm Salamah worried that she'd see a fatal shaving accident.

The following year, the community returned on hajj, as the treaty stipulated. The pilgrims' calm decorum while performing the rituals impressed ordinary Meccans, who decided to stop supporting the war against the people they'd been told were religious fanatics. A year later, the Prophet Muhammad and his Companions rode into Mecca. The city surrendered without a struggle.

To gather strength, the Prophet Muhammad had to display what looked like weakness, explained the Sheikh. "The Quran calls the Treaty of Hudaybiyah a victory," said Akram. "Even though it was not in favor of the Prophet, he gained time. He could make contact with other Arabs. Peace gave him so much of an opportunity."

Sadly, today's Muslim leaders are rarely strong and supple enough to compromise, he said. "If the Palestinians made peace, they could rebuild. Their children could get education. All this time, all this fighting and this and that. So many youths have been killed."

"So is he a radical?" non-Muslims often asked when I told them about the Sheikh. "Not at all," I'd say, assuming we were all speaking in post-9/11 code. "Of course not."

And I'd meant it. He is not a radical. Or rather, not their kind of radical.

His radicalism is of entirely another caliber. He's an extremist quietist, calling on Muslims to turn away from politics and to leave behind the frameworks of thought popularized by Islamists in recent centuries. Akram's call for an apolitical Islam unpicked the conditioning of a generation of Muslims, raised on the works of Abu l'Ala Maududi and Sayyid Qutb and their nineteenth-century forerunners. These ideologues aimed to make Islam relevant to the sociopolitical struggles facing Muslims coping with modernity. Their works helped

inspire revolutions, coups, and constitutions. But while these thinkers equated their faith with political action, the Sheikh believed that
politics was puny. He was powered by a certainty that we are just
passing through this earth and that mundane quests for land or
power miss Islam's point. Compared with the men fighting for worldly
turf, Akram was far more uncompromising: turn away from quests
for nation-states or parliamentary seats and toward God. "Allah
doesn't want people to complain to other people," he said. "People
must complain to Allah, not to anyone else."

All the time spent fulminating, organizing, protesting? It could be
saved for prayer. So unjust governments run the world? Let them.
They don't, anyway. Allah does, and besides, real believers have the
next world to worry about. So the Saudis require you to wear a hijab?
Wear it. So the French government won't let you wear one to school?
So put it on at home. Laws of the land, so long as they don't interfere
with your ability to worship, should be respected. Ultimately, you
should not be obedient to the Saudi regime, or the French government,
or even to your own desire, but to Allah: "You are a slave. A slave of
God. You are owned by Him."

With the war raging in Syria, and the Arab Spring's fallout rocking Egypt, expressing such quietism took courage. Many of his fellow
ulama felt forced to harden their lines in their Friday sermons,
fomenting resentment against the West or calling for the strict enforce-
ment of Islamic law. But that was the sort of rhetoric so many young
Muslims demanded these days, the Sheikh sighed.

It's not that he preached utter political apathy, or told people to
abstain entirely from politics. Back in India, when Muslims used to ask
him whom to vote for, he'd shrug and tell them to tick the box for
whichever party they thought would develop the country. What was
good for India was good for its Muslims; voting for parties angling for
the Muslim vote would only foment sectarian tensions.

The major problem with Islamists, said Akram, was their ten-
dency to make Islam more about political struggle than piety. Prominent twentieth-century thinkers like Egypt's Qutb and Pakistan's
Maududi had moved politics to the center of an Islamic agenda, he

said. "Politics is part of Islam, but Islam is not politics," he explained.
"Just as Marxism made money central to everything, Maududi and
Qutb made politics the center of Islam. Nobody denies the importance of money, but money is not the center of everything. Similarly,
politics is one small part of everything in Islam."

Through the turned-around telescope of Akram's piety, Islamist
politics looked tiny and frantic. All this heated talk of implementing
sharia law, the flyers calling for the return of the caliphate (Islam's
early leadership system), the burning effigies of leaders, the banners
with slogans painted in English that were held up to appear on the
BBC, all were just politics as usual.

The day of the Sheikh's lecture "Shariah Law, Islamic State, and
Jihad," the men's side of the hall was standing room only. So many
young men had filled the auditorium at Queen Mary's College, University of London, that a few even spilled over into the women's side.
The Sheikh had heard gossip that the audience was packed with members of the hard-line group Hizb-ut-Tahrir, eager to challenge him
over his political quietism. (The group later dismissed these rumors.)
The Sheikh came prepared to disarm any young firebrands with *adab*.
When it came to his analysis of Islamic movements, he said he hoped
they'd bear in mind a bit of Urdu verse: "In the garden," he translated,
"accept and bear with me when I'm a little bit aggressive, or when I'm
offensive, or hurting you, because sometimes the poison can do the
work of the cure."

"Sometimes, you cure with medical treatment," the Sheikh warned
them. "Or with poison. So some of this poison will be coming, inshallah
[Allah willing], so don't worry."

That got a big laugh, even from the leather-jacketed dudes with
slicked-back hair and splayed legs sitting in the back. The Sheikh, in
his pale pink shirt and gray V-neck, delivered his "poison" gently. To
make political power your goal, he suggested, was to follow not in the
footsteps of the Prophet, but rather in those of the kings and elites who
were the Prophet's enemies. The quest for sharia law was quixotic:

imposing sharia sapped people's piety rather than building it. A state-sanctioned sharia, he argued, "just makes you a law-abiding animal." Real piety derives from *imaan*, an individual's committed belief. "If your *imaan* is deep in your heart, the state and powers cannot take that away from you," he said. But bring in a state-imposed Islam and "hypocrisy will come."

Over the course of the day, I sensed the crowd mellowing. By tea-time, I detected a distinct sagging of will where earlier there'd been tension. My intimations turned out to be correct: at the end of the day, several men approached Akram and admitted, in low voices, that the seminar had been most enlightening. "They said that in the morning, they really were thinking very differently from me," said Akram, nodding with satisfaction, "but that by explaining properly, with logic, I'd changed their minds."

Other students managed to resist the Sheikh's persuasive powers. At one talk, a student stood up, fulminating over the need for sharia law. "We need to forget about sharia," responded the Sheikh crisply, and focus on proper worship. Later, the man complained to the seminar organizers that the Sheikh was too "pro-government." Once, when the Sheikh said the energy spent on protesting against the British government would be better channeled into prayer, a young woman raised her hand and in ringing tones called him a "defeatist."

He didn't seem to mind the criticism. On one trip back to India, the Sheikh stopped off at Nadwat al-Ulama and delivered a speech on Islam and the West. "I don't think they liked it very much," he told me cheerfully.

"How do you know?"

"I could just feel the audience," he said. "I think they wanted me to criticize America and Saudi Arabia."

"So what did you say?" I asked.

"I told them, when you criticize the West, you assume they're just a military power, so you want to try to defeat them on military grounds," he said. "But the West is not only military. It's ideas. It's culture. It's history. All are there." It was foolhardy, in this day and age, to try to fence off a pristine Islamic world, unruffled by the cross-breezes of global culture.

He sighed. "If I had more time there, I could begin to show them my way of thinking."

At least one student in the Nadwah audience understood. An undergraduate wrote to thank the Sheikh for his "tolerant and broad view." He was "tired of listening to intolerant views of ulamas about the West," the young man wrote, "especially of Jews and Americans." The Sheikh had provided "fresh air in the narrow-minded atmosphere."

At times, even I found myself yearning for Akram to tie the Quran and Prophet's sunna more tightly to worldly events. I'll admit it: I am worldly, and so I wanted him to demonstrate how his teachings played out in the world, not just in the invisible space of people's souls. I found myself perking up in seminars when someone asked a political question. I printed out the ad for a lecture by the Sheikh with the subject line reading "English Defence League in Makkah?" The blurb pointed out similarities between the Prophet's persecution by the Quraysh in Mecca and the rise of the EDL, a right-wing party with an Islamophobic bent. But at the lecture itself, the Sheikh barely touched on the EDL. They were scarcely worth a thought, he counseled. The good Muslim shouldn't allow himself to be distracted. His thoughts were with God's powers, not earthly skirmishes.

Forged in the relative freedoms of India and Britain, the Sheikh's outlook lacked the urgency of Mona's Egyptian-born activism. While he believed it premature for Muslims to venture into the political arena, Mona and her fellow Muslim Brotherhood members disagreed. "It's a duty to stand against what is wrong," Mona told me. "It's not enough to condemn it in your heart." It was one thing to keep your soul trained on *taqwa* in leafy, peaceful Oxford, and entirely another thing living under a dictatorship: "In Egypt, you cannot be a good person, because in Egypt they won't let you," she said. "I understand when he says that politics is a corrupt environment. But if we leave politics only to the corrupt, we will have corrupt politicians all the time."

A child of postpartition South Asia, the Sheikh had been raised when memories of the region's struggle for self-determination were still fresh. The high hopes for a separate utopia for Muslims? The bloodshed over a country they could call their own? All they had brought the Muslims was Pakistan. In the run-up to South Asian independence, "there was so much writing against the British, how they wanted their own countries, one for Hindus, one for Muslims," he said. "But if the real problem is the British, why do Hindus and Muslims want to come to the UK? The children of those people who fought for independence from the British, all are coming here! All are coming to live in Britain!"

These struggles to expand your space—to a country, like Pakistan, or a dream, like a new caliphate—all diverted Muslims from their real purpose: to practice *taqwa*. Remember Yusuf, the Sheikh would say, working in his master's house, ducking the advances of his master's wife? In his own space—his head, his heart—he remained as pious as possible. "We Muslims are concerned about the wider space," he mused. "But our personal space, nobody else controls us. In my heart, if I love God, no power on the face of the earth can stop me. And if this space—the space of the heart—is not being used by Muslims properly, then you have no right to criticize about the other, bigger space."

Mona had grown up in Maadi, the same suburb where my family lived while in Cairo. We'd left Kabul in a hurry in 1978, since it was clear, after the coup, that the new Marxist government wouldn't require the services of an American law professor. My father took a teaching position at Cairo University and our family moved to Maadi, which provided a quiet approximation of Western suburban life à l'Orient, with gracious villas, Nile-side cafés, and international schools. I was twelve when we lived there, high on the suburban freedoms of a bike and quiet streets. I'd ride down to the shops on Road 9 to visit Kentucky Fried Chicken or check out bell-bottoms in the local boutiques. I attended an American school, complete with cheerleaders and a swimming pool. At my middle school disco, Donna Summer's "Last Dance" throbbed in the jasmine-scented night.

My Maadi life took place in a bubble. Under Anwar Sadat's "Openness" policy, promoting investment from the West and the Gulf States, the rest of Egypt was frayed by social and economic strain. The year before our arrival, the country was traumatized by the Bread Riots, triggered when food prices shot up after Sadat canceled subsidies on oil and flour. To the annoyance of devout Muslims, he downplayed Egypt's Islamic identity in favor of the country's Pharaonic past, promoting the King Tut treasures in the United States with an eye toward tourism and closer ties with Washington.

One response to the conspicuous consumption of Sadat's Egypt lay in Islamic religiosity. Many middle-class Egyptians turned to their faith, sometimes as a spiritual embrace, other times as a way of coping with the overrapid changes of modernity, sometimes both. Most pious activism was akin to Mona's: peaceful attempts to change society through charity work or lobbying for legal changes. But for a tiny minority, this Islamic revivalism would mean more than peaceful protest. Across the rail tracks from the Maadi of riding lessons and Friday night discos lay a very different Maadi, in the *baladi*, or "native" quarter. There lay the clinic of Ayman al-Zawahiri: a brilliant young doctor, an activist in the Jama'at al-Islamiya, and the future leader of Al-Qaeda.

It was all too easy, as an American in Anwar Sadat's Cairo, to imagine one had the run of the place. My American school held its high school graduation in front of the pyramids, with the commencement speech delivered by Egypt's First Lady, Jehan Sadat. Egypt was poised to become the second-largest recipient of American aid, a reward to Sadat for signing the Camp David Peace Accords with Menachem Begin. I remember the crush of crowds near the Nile as my brother and I strained for a glimpse of the motorcade bearing the presidents the Americans were calling peacemakers: Jimmy Carter and Anwar Sadat. "Carter looks awful," my mother wrote in a letter home. "He and Sadat and their wives rode in an open car throughout Cairo. Really scary, and I think unnecessary. All they needed was one person from the PLO there." In the great tradition of Arab dictators, Sadat was everywhere; his balding head and stern military bearing loomed over us from billboards and pictures hung in every café. He even stared me down in my own bedroom. I'd bought a cheap poster in the bazaar showing Sadat's head flanked by doves with olive branches clamped in their beaks. The poster outlasted the president, yellowing on my wall in St. Louis even after his death.

The death came in 1981, in a plot by a Jama'at splinter group. A young radical named Khaled al-Islambuli, a member of a small group of conspirators called Islamic Jihad gunned down President Sadat as he reviewed troops in a military parade. "I have killed Pharaoh," he shouted.

For Egyptian Islamists, the Pharaoh was a potent symbol of oppression, tapping into both the country's own history and the Quranic story of the tyrant oppressing Moses and his people. The image of the Pharaoh was harnessed in Revolutionary Iran, too, where posters depicted the Shah as the Quranic tyrant—and the Ayatollah Khomeini as Moses.

The year Akram and I read the Quran, crowds filled the Egyptian streets, once again pitting themselves against an Egyptian leader styled as Pharaoh. Protesters hoisted signs showing an Egyptian president's face framed with the blue and gold stripes of King Tut's crown. Which president it was hardly matters: to rule in Egypt means that someone will eventually call you Pharaoh, whether you're an Islamist, a secularist, or a nationalist.

Akram wasn't particularly interested in the political imagery of the Pharaoh, or in struggling against him for justice: he was far more intent on the Quran's story of the Pharaoh's wife. Over and over, he ignored him and invoked her. Named by the Quran as "an example for those who believe," the Pharaoh's wife chose belief in God over her husband's idols and magicians. She asked her God, "Build me a house in Your presence in the Garden; rescue me from Pharaoh and his course of action, and deliver me from tyrannical people."

"She had everything," Akram marveled. "House. Jewels. Servants.

Power. But she turned away from all that, turned away from her husband, and submitted to her Lord."

The division between those who focused on the repression of the Pharaoh and those, like Akram, who ignored it spoke to an essential division between contemporary Muslim thinkers: Should Islam be used as a political tool, or simply as moral guidance? Reformist Muslims of all orientations, from jihadis to feminists, have argued that the faith—or at least its symbols—should be employed for political change. Traditionalist Sunni ulama like Akram view their role as moral stewards, offering gentle guidance to rulers but not ruling themselves.

I thought about the Pharaoh and his wife, who seemed to perfectly illustrate those stock characters we read about from the Middle East: strongmen with an iron grip over public life, and pious women who turn inward to their houses or families or faith. These were the archetypes that seemed to appear in every piece I wrote for American magazines, the strands woven into the Western narrative of the Islamic world. By and large, the dominant story of Islamic countries was to be told by and about powerful patriarchs—whether mullahs or secularized despots like the Shah or Saddam Hussein. Too often, these hulking Pharaohs have blocked out our view of the rest of society, obscuring people who might not buy arms in bulk, or attend summits in Western capitals.

The Sheikh opposed any extremes, and indeed questioned any system, Western or Islamic, that claimed to be comprehensive. Islamist thinkers like Sayyid Qutb and Maulana Maududi, who wanted Islam to provide the answer for virtually everything in a modern society, were misguided. The great irony, in the Sheikh's view, was that these great defenders of Islam were actually more Western than traditional Muslims. Qutb, with his talk of "systems" and his call for a "vanguard" to create an Islamic state, could sound awfully close to a twentieth-century Western revolutionary at times. Malise Ruthven, a scholar of Islamic movements, notes that Qutb's concept of the vanguard is a European import, with a lineage starting with the Jacobins, and developing through the Bolsheviks and more recent Marxist guerrillas like the Baader-Meinhof gang.

Akram put it more simply: the young people who looked to Islam as an answer for everything from penal codes to banking practices simply wanted a Western state with an Islamic flavor. The "Islamicization" of everything sprang from a deep envy of the West's power and geopolitical supremacy. "All they want," he said, "is what the West has."

Sayyid Qutb, the godfather of modern extremism, sailed on a steamship from his native Egypt into New York Harbor in 1948. Onboard, he'd been sexually propositioned by a "beautiful, tall, semi-naked" woman in his cabin, an encounter that Qutb would describe as a major test of his Muslim mores. Things went downhill from there. He likened New York to a "huge workshop," with traffic that "surged forward as if it were the Judgment Day" and citizens with eyes "filled with greed, desire, and lust." His stay in America, and the racism, spiritual vacuity, and licentiousness he found, provided fodder for his critique of the West, one that would go on to inspire radicals, from Sadat's assassins to Al-Qaeda's Ayman al-Zawahiri.

Akram had also stood at the edge of Manhattan looking out over New York Harbor. In 2006, when the Islamic Society at New York University invited him to speak, he stayed near Ground Zero, the site of the Twin Towers. From his hotel window, he had watched the crowds streaming off the ferries and squinted at that famous statue of a bare-armed woman holding a flame. Visiting Ground Zero, he saw a hole in the street surrounded by policemen and flags. The men who'd flown their planes into the Twin Towers had wrought havoc on America, but also on the world's Muslims. As he looked down, he thought of the World Trade Center bombers, and of the American politicians who fought back with their War on Terror. Both obsessed with external threats, they seemed as symmetrical as the Twin Towers. The jihadis blamed the West for the ills of the Muslim world, while the American hawks exaggerated the threat from the jihadis. Neither side was willing to look at what was really ailing their societies, thought Akram. In the Muslim case, it was their mistaken turn away from true piety to identity politics. In the United States, it was a moral decline and an unquenchable desire for "eating, drinking, money, and sex and all this and that," said Akram.

Too many Americans misread the meaning of the harbor's statue of the lady with the torch, he observed. "This freedom people talk about, to buy whatever they like, wear whatever they like, drink, and so on, this is not good for the people," he later told me. "True freedom means freedom from desire. True freedom means freedom of thinking. If your mind just follows your desires—how to make more money, how to eat more, drink more, have more things—it's really worse than slavery."

Americans weren't always like that, he added. "In the beginning, when American people were getting their freedom, when they wanted to build their nation, they were willing to make sacrifices. But now, too many people are slaves of desire, and that's not good for people. These things are more likely to bring death to America than any Al-Qaeda, any destruction of towers. If people have the right ideas, then people can't destroy the nation."

"Anyone can make anything comprehensive," he said one day as we sat in the Oxford Kebab House. "Maududi wanted to do that. But he came at a time when Muslims lost power. Young people want something like power through Islam, because when Western people talk about power, they feel inferior."

He leaned forward as though about to share a confidence. "You know what these Islamic reform movements are really for?"

"What?" I smiled.

"They're for Western-educated Muslims, to convince them that Islam can also deliver what the West has. It's to tell them, 'Oh, they laugh at you? Well, you have the power to laugh at them.' But Islam is not like that.

"Islamic movements, they think they can get a reward in this world," he sighed. "If the state and power are so important, why are the Prophets so important? Ninety-nine percent of them didn't have any power. Ibrahim didn't have a state. Jesus Christ didn't!"

As for political Muslims, fond of talking about Medina as the first Islamic State, and the Constitution of Medina as the ideal basis for contemporary politics? Misguided, to his mind. The Prophet hadn't wanted to leave Mecca in the first place: he was forced to leave, since he was unable to practice his faith. And when he got to what would become Medina, it was in search of freedom of religious worship, not power. Power was thrust upon him. "He did not especially want to run a state," explained the Sheikh. "But when he got to Medina, he had to organize it properly."

One website proclaims the Constitution of Medina "the first written constitution in human history" and claims it laid the "practical foundation of democracy." Such parallels suggest a profound insecurity, he suggested. "Many Muslims became influenced by Western ideas of the state, and they want to find it in their own history," he said, shaking his head. "They want to show that 'what you Westerners are doing now, we have done already.'"

That naked envy of Western power, and of worldly riches, informed so much of the Islamist project, the vogue for "Islamicizing" everything from war to elections. Too often, Islamic leaders bought into it, since talk of politics and war often filled their mosques faster than spiritual ruminations. "You know, Carla, there's been a Saudi preacher, very famous. He's been telling people to go on jihad in Syria. And there he sits in London! Really, this is rubbish. If jihad is true, you should go, too!"

He wasn't finished. "Oh! And he has sons, too! But when people asked him why he didn't send his sons, he said they are doing something more important. Well, other people's sons are doing something important, too!"

In matters of war, the Prophet Muhammad never asked his Companions to do what he himself wouldn't do, the Sheikh observed.

He drew his palm over his face, weary. "All this about Caliphate and sharia and jihad," he sighed. "So leave the power in this world to the Americans! At the end of the day, the world is not ruled by the Americans, but by God."

We laughed, and he slapped his thigh. But he wasn't kidding. "You know, Carla, if Muslims just stop and don't do anything, Islam would have much more attraction. Many more people would come."

I whinnied with laughter.

"No, really! You can quote me on this! It would be better if we didn't do anything. All this fighting, this jihad, this sharia, it would be better if Muslims just stop and do nothing. Don't work. Don't pray. Nothing. If you don't do anything, then it would be better."

Every modern political struggle undertaken under the mantle of Islam, he argued, had failed. Islamist political programs were overwhelmingly negative, he said, far more focused on getting power than governing effectively. When they did get into office, their governance was often disastrous: "It's like when someone says 'I'm such a good cook,' and then they cook for you, and then . . ." he turned his hands skyward and grimaced.

"Look at the Muslim Brotherhood," he said. "Is Egypt better now than before the Revolution?"

At the moment, it looked a lot worse.

He shrugged. "If you don't do anything, then it's better."

A few months after I'd first interviewed her, I spoke with Mona, who appeared on my computer screen via Skype from a café in Cambridge. She had lost weight, and she seemed both calm and animated, charged with some new strength. The evening we spoke, it had been 195 days since her brother had been arrested. A few months after his arrest, the police burst into her parents' Cairo apartment at dawn. "They trashed the place" and arrested her father, too, she said. Then they froze the family's bank accounts. Faced with these hardships, Mona was accepting, even grateful. They provided, she believed, "an opportunity from Allah to learn more about myself. I am learning what I am capable of." With very little money now, and no way to return home, she had learned "how to be fully dependent on Allah." Back in Cambridge, she was trying to finish her PhD, and Allah gave her the strength to endure. One's anchor, she told me, "is not family, it's not money, it's not a place. It's Allah."

And yet there were moments, I could see, when even Mona wavered, finding the Sheikh's faith in stoicism hard to bear. "What should I do?" she once asked him. "Just stand here, and let my brother hang?" The Sheikh smiled gently and said that life was a test. Political action should never take the place of a Muslim's true work, which was practicing *taqwa*. Rather than agitating for change, one should be still and resolute while facing it. The rise and fall of presidents and world powers was inevitable, but faith outlasted them all.

15

War Stories

Every war has countless beginnings, hundreds of moments pushing toward that first shot fired, the first pulse stilled. For many Americans, the modern conflicts between Islam and the West began on a September day when horrors fell from a blue sky over Manhattan. An Al-Qaeda combatant might date their start back to 1991, when American troops flooded onto Saudi Arabian soil after Saddam Hussein's invasion of Kuwait. An Iranian government cleric may point to 1953, when a CIA-backed coup toppled the democratically elected prime minister and installed the Shah. A Pakistani jihadi might set the conflict's origins back to 1947, to a summer when a London barrister created India and Pakistan, carving up the subcontinent like a Sunday roast. Others would cite 1933, when the Saudis granted a concession to a California oil company. As always with history, there are scores of beginnings to choose from, leading back as far as the day in 1600 when Queen Elizabeth gave the East India Company their royal charter.

For me, the great geopolitical struggle of the twenty-first century began one Saturday afternoon in 1978, a couple of hours into Little League practice. Eyes squeezed tight, mitt stuck up, I caught my first pop fly by dumb luck out of the clear blue sky. Leaving Newman Field, still wreathed in the glow of all-American victories, we turned—right

into a convoy of tanks, their khaki treads gnashing up the road leading toward the presidential palace.

"Mom, is it a coup?" I asked. At eleven, I hadn't yet learned to leave
unspoken fears unspoken.

Ever since we'd arrived in Afghanistan, I'd heard about coups,
which seemed the standard regional practice for changing governments. A month before we'd arrived, there'd been one down the Khyber Pass in Pakistan, when General Zia ul-Haq had staged a military
takeover from his predecessor, Zulfiqar Ali Bhutto. Four years before
that, Kabul had seen its own coup, when President Daoud had seized
power from his cousin, King Zahid. It had been a "white" coup, my
parents assured me, every time I'd asked—a peaceful one, with no
bloodshed. Since we'd arrived in Kabul, I'd worried about coups, particularly "red" ones.

"A coup? Oh, gosh, no," said my mother, in a voice varnished into
certainty. "It's a parade of sorts. They're probably getting ready for the
Non-Aligned Nations meeting here next month." She looked out the
car window. In the tank behind us, the soldier had a pistol out, pointed
skyward, and a fierce sense of purpose not commonly associated with
parades.

That afternoon, safe inside our friends' compound, we played tag
in the yard until a call came from the embassy and the grown-ups
called us inside. "Let's play indoors this afternoon," my mother suggested brightly. A fighter jet ripped the sky wide open, leaving a white
scratch in the bright blue. We edged away from the windows and bed-
ded down in the windowless back hall.

My father tried to jolly us along, putting on a plummy English
accent and pretending to be a BBC announcer during the London Blitz.
From the direction of the palace, less than a mile away, came loud
popping, like the crack of baseball bats on balls. Sometime amid the
noise that night, bullets killed President Daoud and nineteen members of his family. By 8:00 p.m., the radio announced that resistance
had been crushed, and the new People's Republic was proclaimed.

When we woke the next morning, the sky was quiet, the same
blameless blue as the morning before. We arrived home to find that

our guard, Mir Ali, had patrolled our compound all night. He'd paced up and down in the yard as the skies over Kabul reddened with explosions from Russian-built shells. His only weapons had been the ax he used to chop wood—and my brother's plastic baseball bat.

If there'd been signs that the coup was coming, we'd missed them. Two nights before the tanks rolled in, the American center in Kabul had held a Soviet-U.S. friendship night. Whether or not the rumors were true about the local CIA station chief having been in the stands watching our Little League game while the tanks rolled into Kabul, it's clear the coup surprised pretty much everyone, Afghans and foreigners alike. Within days, the new government made their Marxist ideology clear. The tanks parked at intersections were decked in paper flowers—"no doubt following the prescription of some revolutionary handbook," my father wrote. The radio beamed reports of the people's joy at the overthrow of the feudal Daoud regime and vilified the enemies of the glorious April Revolution as "foreign agents." Across the street from our house, the portrait painter swiftly replaced his painting of President Daoud in his window with one of Nur Mohammed Taraki, chairman of Afghanistan's new revolutionary council. The regime spoke of vigorous new efforts to help women and workers. At first, my parents greeted these promises with cautious optimism. "Maybe," my mother said, "a little socialism is just what Afghanistan needs."

Twenty-three years later, in the weeks after watching the Twin Towers fall, as the United States prepared to rain missiles down on Afghanistan, I often thought back to that spring. The 1978 coup that toppled President Daoud began to weave American and Afghan histories together, first into the loose braid of "aid" to the mujahidin groups fighting the Soviets, then later into the tight, then tangled knot of direct conflict. The events unfolding after that first coup, ones that would eventually lead to 9/11 and the wars that followed, are covered in other books. But for me, looking back from the twenty-first century, the coup marked the end of my father's Islamic world and the beginning of my own. With the Russian invasion of Afghanistan and the revolution in Iran the following year, Islam could no longer

be dismissed as a faith for old ladies or village elders. For my generation, it was to become an engine for rebellion against old political
orders and for fighting the Western powers who supported them.

Twenty years after the 1978 coup, I found myself sitting in the
home of a major from the Pakistani army, hearing how the Afghan
war had made him into a jihadi mastermind. A short man in a hound-
stooth blazer and loafers, he wore his salt-and-pepper beard neatly
clipped and lived in a large white house in a Lahore suburb favored by
army elites. In his high-ceilinged hallway hung framed pictures of
him shaking hands with other heavily decorated men. By the time I
interviewed him for *Newsweek* in 1998, Major Ehsan ul-Haq had
retired from Pakistan's army, but not from war. For ten days every
month, he managed a textile factory, a job that funded his true calling: running a jihadi training camp in the mountains of Kashmir to
send guerrillas to fight the Indian Army.

Stony-faced, he ushered me into his salon, with its marble floors,
comfortable couches, and cut glass bowls of flowers. A servant poured
tea, which the Major took in three sips, in the manner of the Prophet.

American Green Berets had helped train him, he said, back in the
1960s, in the same elite corps as Pervez Musharraf, later to become
Pakistan's president. "A brilliant strategist," he conceded. But ultimately weak, since his tactics were based on what he could see rather
than the otherworldly. The Americans he trained with were also hobbled by secularism: "When you are fighting for Allah, you believe in
the unseen." What really made a truly good fighting man, he told me,
were "the techniques of Allah." One needed to marry a Green Beret's
discipline and professionalism with piety. Firing a bullet, for example,
should be followed by a submission to God. "You say, 'Oh, Allah, I'm
firing with your power, kindly make this bullet reach the enemy,'"
explained the major.

The command to fight the oppressors of Muslims, he said, lay in
the Quran. He turned to the large copy on the table in front of him.
"All the directions to human beings are here," he said. He opened it to
the fourth chapter and quoted verse 76: "Believers fight for the sake of

God, while atheists fight for the sake of idols; / so fight the friends of Satan, for the strategy of Satan is weak."

"One has to fight the friends of Satan," the Major said.

Looking around his white suburban palace, I wondered what had curdled his outlook. Was it a slow drip-drip of frustration? A snide comment from a superior? Millions were angered by the unresolved conflict in Kashmir; millions more were incandescent over Western powers' meddling in the affairs of Muslim countries. But what had made the Major a jihadi?

When I asked him, he cited not anger, but angels. Specifically, the white-gowned angels on horseback that helped him one day on an Afghan field when he was a young commander, fighting alongside the mujahidin. Between his 125 men and the ridge they needed to take was a plateau sown with mines. A thousand soldiers loyal to the Soviet Union lay in wait for them, he claimed. But his men charged across the field, coming under fire from antiaircraft guns and long-range mortars. Armed with Kalashnikovs and Allah's help, his men made it through without any casualties. Protecting them, he claimed, was "a huge fighting force, with horses and white dresses." Angels on horseback guided and protected them, he said, just as they did throughout his Afghan campaigns: "I have seen corpses where the heads were chopped off," he told me, reaching for his teacup. "Not by men, but by angels."

The Major showed me a sheaf of pictures from his training program. If you ignored the shots of soldiers crouching behind rocks with rifles, they could have been publicity stills from a summer camp in Wisconsin. A cook in his mess bent over pots. Fir trees. Tents. Young men working out in a sun-dappled clearing.

He invited me upstairs to meet his wife and teenage daughter and suggested we all watch a video. The daughter was studying for her master's in English literature. We exchanged pleasantries about Shakespeare as her father lowered the lights and popped a VHS cassette into the machine.

"Bosnia," the Major said, nodding at the screen.

The tape spat out a montage of howling, wounded machismo. Corpses, eyes staring. Crying women. Fierce fighters leaping, running. Fallen fighters, borne on stretchers. God is great, intoned the voice-over.

Afterward, the Major escorted me downstairs. When he was done with jihad in Kashmir, he said, he and his men would move on. Perhaps to India. Perhaps beyond. Wherever they were needed, they would keep fighting, forever, until the whole earth became Muslim. "We want to convey the message to the whole of the world," he said as we stood in his doorway. "The whole of the globe belongs to Allah, and the whole of His Law has to be executed on the globe. Wherever the United States and Europe stop the expansion of Islam, there will be war."

I left the house queasy-spirited. His jihad wasn't inspired just by angels, but by foreign powers' involvement in the region. Specifically, American power. Everyone knew that the men Washington trained and armed during the 1980s to fight the Soviets in Afghanistan had helped produce future jihadis. It was a commonplace, even before September 11, that global jihadis were "blowback" from the Afghan war, the unintended consequences of a covert military operation. The Major was blowback's human face. That this face spoke perfect English, polished by training with Americans, made it all the more chilling.

In the roughest of sketches, the Major and the Sheikh would seem to have similar worldviews. Both are devout Muslims in the scriptural tradition who take the Quran as the central text in their lives. Both are educated South Asians who have achieved professional success. Both worked in prestigious institutions, for a time, alongside Western elites—the Major with the Green Berets, the Sheikh at Oxford. Both despair of the spiritual drift and materialism they see in contemporary life. And both men hope to see strong Islamic societies emerge one day.

From that point, their visions diverge dramatically. The two men differ markedly on what those societies would look like and how they'd be achieved. While the Major calls for armed struggle against unbelievers and an imposition of Islamic law, the Sheikh sees the need for personal piety and peace. While the Major is trapped in an agonistic struggle against everyone he thinks thwarts Islam, Akram's vision of *taqwa* frees him. Rooted in the Islamic classical tradition, Akram can transcend the static categories that have come to define modernity. Since the East India Company set up shop in Surat, since Napoleon stepped onto the banks of the Nile, the colonial experience and its aftermath have too often been cast in terms of opposing categories. Western and Islamic. Modern and traditional. Indian and Pakistani. Such labels don't distract the Sheikh much, steeped as he is in an altogether different world order. His own attentions are trained on the details of religious texts. While the Major reads 4:76 as a general directive to "fight the friends of Satan," the Sheikh reads it as an account of a specific moment in Islamic history, when the young Muslim community was at war with the far more powerful forces of the Quraysh and their allies.

Attention to context, both textual and historical, is all too often overlooked by jihadis and Islamophobes alike. Take the case of the so-called "Verse of the Sword":

> But when the sacred months are past,
> then kill the idolaters wherever you find them,
> and capture them, and blockade them,
> and watch for them at every lookout. (9:5)

Court scholars during the Muslim Empires cited this verse in fatwas supporting rulers' foreign wars. Bin Laden used it in his famous 1996 fatwa declaring jihad on the Americans. The scholar Bruce Lawrence has described the sword verse as the "shibboleth, the battle cry" for jihadis.

What the jihadis tend to leave out, however, is the verse's second half: "But if they repent and practice prayer and give alms, then let them go their way; for God is most forgiving, most merciful."

Equally crucial is the historical moment the verse was revealed. The Quraysh in Mecca had broken a treaty with the Muslims and, along with their allies, continued to attack them repeatedly. It came down when the Prophet "had done everything possible to preach to the people of the Quraysh," the ruling Meccan tribe, and to their allies, said Akram. "They started fighting him, and making things very difficult for the Prophet." Earlier verses of the Quran had entreated the Prophet to hold back, to be patient, not to fight. Finally, when the tiny Muslim army—a few hundred men—faced the larger, better-equipped army of the Quraysh, the Quranic verse came down that "allowed him to become tough" against his community's enemies, said the Sheikh. Even then, "he only killed a few people, and then forgave all his opponents."

Contemporary jihads were worldly, not spiritual, said the Sheikh. The men waging them operated not from an excess of piety, but a lack of it: "It is just the Islamicization of violence," he said. "People think they can use Islam to fight for land, or honor, or respect, or money. But these are not religious people. They are just following non-Islamic examples."

The jihadis tended to be far more Westernized, in a superficial sense, than the Sheikh and his fellow ulama. Contrary to popular belief, most of the jihadi extremists weren't trained in madrasas. Rather than studying the nuances of classical Islamic thought, their training tended to be secular and technical, in subjects like engineering, computer programming, or medicine. An influential study examined the backgrounds of four hundred violent extremists and found that only 13 percent were from madrasas or Islamic boarding schools.

The Sheikh hadn't heard of the study, but its profile of extremists with day jobs as engineers and doctors didn't surprise him. It was "Western-educated types," not madrasa graduates, he said, who harbored the biggest grudges against the West. "They want what the West has," he said. "They want power."

If the Sheikh thought little of jihadis' Islamic credentials, jihad's ideologues were similarly dismissive of madrasa scholars. It was the ulama, they charged, who wanted what the West had: a religion as privatized and part-time as Christianity had been ever since the

Enlightenment. Traditional Islamic scholars were simply "defeated people," charged Sayyid Qutb. "They have adopted the Western concept of 'religion,' which is merely a name for 'belief in the heart,' having no relation to the practical affairs of life." In his influential book *Milestones*, he called for a movement to free the world from the state of *jahiliyya*, or pre-Islamic alienation and ignorance. The goal was "to establish the reign of God on earth and eliminate the reign of man, to take power out of the hands of those of His worshippers who have usurped it and to return it to God alone."

For centuries, traditional Islamic scholarship had shriveled, and the prestige of the ulama along with it. European colonizers had left madrasas to languish, favoring modern education as a means of producing able administrators with Westernized outlooks. A widespread perception of the ulama's overcozy relationships with unpopular regimes didn't help; in many Muslim states, governments put scholars on their payrolls, undermining the ulama's traditional political independence.

With the advent of modernity, many people simply stopped consulting traditional scholars. Rising literacy rates and new technologies allowed ordinary Muslims to begin interpreting texts for themselves. Today, anybody with an Internet connection can consult what some wag called "Sheikh Google" instead of a trained scholar. This democratization of Islamic knowledge—though not of its more rigorous disciplines—allowed self-styled sheikhs to flourish. One didn't need a madrasa degree to declare oneself an authority. Indeed, the newly minted authorities wore their scorn for the old guard as a badge of honor. Osama bin Laden loudly disdained the ulama and began issuing fatwas of his own. Abu Hamza al-Masri, a former nightclub bouncer and civil engineer turned radical preacher, felt free to dismiss traditional religious authorities while claiming his own right to be one. In medieval times, people had to rely on sheikhs, but "today, information is available in books and computers," he said in 2002. "All one has to do these days is to read. You can even phone a scholar for an opinion. We have direct access to Islamic information these days."

At their worst, these new challenges to traditional religious authority have resulted in rampant textual looting, a free-for-all trawl through the Quran to find verses to legitimize violence in the name of God. To make jihad the center of Islamic life, as many extremists have done, is to do real violence to the text of the Quran, said the Sheikh.

In the West, the word "jihad"—literally, striving or struggle—has become synonymous with wars like the Major's. But *jihad al-nafs*, the struggle of the individual against his lesser self, means a person's effort to quell negative impulses and to lead a pious life. The twin meanings of "jihad" are threaded through a story the Sheikh liked to tell. A group of mujahidin on their way to battle stayed overnight at the lodge of some Islamic mystics, or Sufis. In the morning, one young Sufi disciple, awed by the warriors' steeds and swords, went to his sheikh and told him that he was joining the mujahidin. Armed jihad was the easy route, his sheikh warned. Far harder was the struggle to maintain a lifetime of submission to Allah. "It is easy for me to have my neck cut once," the elder explained. "It is hard for me to bow my head all the time, day after day."

I experienced a contemporary version of the tale in the British city of Bradford, shortly after 9/11. On assignment for a magazine story, I encountered two young men, Zubair and Muhammad, who were passing the time before Friday prayers. They sat in the front seat of their car, fiddling with their hand-rolled cigarettes and watching the rain spit down outside. They had rolled down their window so we could chat. Zubair had a broad Yorkshire accent, Bradford-raised as he was, but he told me he identified as an Afghan Pathan, and as a Muslim. They were not the best of Muslims, admittedly: "We smoke this and that," said Zubair. "We look at women we shouldn't. We're weak, the lowest of the low." Nothing, in fact, compared to the mujahidin, the warriors who were defending the Muslim cause in Afghanistan and Iraq. It was these jihadis "who are the real serious Muslims, man."

But the more the two friends described their lives, the more they sounded like the old Sufi sage in Akram's fable rather than the young firebrand. It was tough, they told me, trying to be pious surrounded by temptation. Tougher, perhaps, than actual battle: "The real jihad is when you grow up in a place like this," Zubair said. "You want to be a real man and fight the real fight? You try being a good Muslim when you're in a place with naked women, with miniskirts, with casinos and guns."

"So what would the conditions for a just jihad be?" I asked the Sheikh one day over tea at the Oxford Kebab House.

Jihad had very specific parameters, he said, sternly. One couldn't harm women, children, or other noncombatants. The enemy's crops and fields must be respected: "You can't harm even a tree." A jihad can be waged only by legitimate Islamic leaders operating openly, not by self-appointed guerrillas striking covertly. And jihad must not target fellow Muslims. "Those who raise their weapons against us," said the Prophet Muhammad, "are not from us." Today, the vast majority of the people dying in the name of jihad are Muslims.

"So what would you need in place to make a jihad legitimate?" I asked the Sheikh.

"First, believers must make *dawa*—call people to Islam. Once they have done this properly, and have found a place where they can live as a community . . ."

"Then they are allowed . . . ?"

"When they have a community—not a state, but a Muslim society," he said, reluctant, as always, to graft modern political terms onto Islamic concepts. "If you have one, and there are people who are preventing you from preaching, or from worshipping—then Islam allows you to fight back."

Then and only then: one could wage jihad only if one was being prevented from worshipping freely. While Qutb and his ideological grandchildren had cast jihad as an offensive war, the Sheikh saw jihad solely as a matter of self-defense.

"And then," he continued, "there are two more conditions."

First, the Muslims need a safe place from which to launch the jihad. Second, Muslims needed enough troops and weapons so that victory looked likely. Today, Muslims had neither: "Muslims have no safe places in our time, so when they try to wage jihad, many of them are killed." Contemporary Muslims lacked the causes or the conditions for armed struggle. "If you do things in the wrong order, it can never work," said the Sheikh. "Are you going to give *biryani* to a newborn? No! You must wait until his teeth are grown!"

Context, he counseled. Always context. Muslims needed to know the context of these verses, and the only way to acquire it was through education. After 9/11, it was fashionable to dismiss madrasas as the problem. In truth, one needed more Islamic education, not less. The term that appears most frequently in the Quran, after "Allah," is *ilm*, or knowledge. Islam began with the command, "Read." And the Sheikh's own message was not a call to arms, but a plea to his students: "Think!"

During my studies with the Sheikh, I often thought of a mother I'd once met in Cairo. With a colleague from *Newsweek,* I'd gone to report on the neighborhood where the World Trade Center bomber Mohammed Atta had grown up. The Attas were long gone, but the family who'd moved in after them remained. We sat and sipped tea in a pin-neat living room, where a poster of an Alpine scene brightened the peeling yellow wall and lace doilies dotted small tables. Anhar Sayyad Mursi, the mother of two sons in their twenties, was surprisingly eager to talk. Atta's story—of a boy who went abroad and went astray—had made Anhar more protective than ever of her two boys. "September 11 put me on a heightened state of alert," she said. "It was a good lesson to me as a mother." She ushered us into the boys' bedroom, the same room in which Atta had done his engineering homework. Even now, she said, there might be extremists in the neighborhood, keen to lure her boys toward misadventure. "In my house, I'm a microscope," she said. "I know what my sons are thinking about. I try to protect them with my belief in God."

Her battle had two fronts, one against Western-style corruption, the other against the Islamists. While dusting their room, Mursi admitted, she'd sometimes "accidentally" rip down one of the Michael Jackson or Spice Girls posters. When the boys came home, she sniffed their breath for alcohol and peered into their eyes to make sure the pupils weren't dilated from hashish. But her main weapons against extremists, she said, were the Quran and the sunna of the Prophet. "I try to fill their heads with them," she said, so they would have no space for any radical thoughts. And when her boys claim to have prayed, she checked their prayer mats to make sure they were warm.

I often think of Mursi, battling Spice Girls poster by Spice Girls poster and verse by verse to protect her sons from suffering a similar fate as the apartment's previous occupant. Over the last generation, millions of mothers have doubtless done much the same. But as the sage in the old story suggested, it's far easier to ride off on a plane or a horse to jihad than it is to submit day after day. Part of that submission is the patient labor of setting individual verses in context and seeing how they might fit into larger Quranic themes of peace and preparation for the world to come.

16

The Last Lesson

I'd never attended a hellfire sermon, not a real one. I'd seen them, of course, in movies set in Puritan New England or the Depression-era Ozarks, with shaggy-browed actors, filmed from below, leaning over pulpits and issuing spittle-flecked certainties. Their voices and chins vibrated with righteousness as they spoke of flames and the Day of Judgment. I'd not imagined I'd see my first such talk in Cambridge, a town twinned with English refinement and Anglican reserve. But it was there that I first heard Akram's description of the afterlife, in his Magnificent Journey seminars, which covered the last two sections of the Quran.

The intensity of these eight-hour lectures—and their frequent mentions of death—made the morning walk from the Cambridge train station feel elegiac. Except for a lone student slinking home, or tourists huddled over damp maps, the streets would always be empty. Crossing a college town on a Saturday morning meant tiptoeing through a certain amount of Friday night debris, stepping over squashed burgers and beer bottles, dodging the odd slick of orange vomit. With the air of someone going abroad, I'd stock up on provisions, buying a cappuccino and a croissant before reaching the River Cam. It was silent at that hour, the empty punts moored, waiting for the day's passengers. The bridge, flanked by willows, marked a frontier between my world and Akram's. At Cambridge's King's College, on the west side of the Cam, Salman Rushdie had studied Islamic history, which he later used, to infamous effect, in *The Satanic Verses*. To cross the bridge to the east bank, and to "The Magnificent Journey," was to scramble away from relativism and into a world of certainty, for a day discussing what the Quran called "the Scripture whereof there is no doubt."

The town seemed to recede. Gone were the stately colleges, the chic boutiques, and the sleek glass offices, monuments to Cambridge's high-tech boom. The world burned off as I walked along a quiet road, through a parking lot, and into a squat, modern university building. For hours, the world was stripped back to a bare auditorium and Akram's stark message: that this life is but a sideshow compared to the next. "Your life is governed by death," he said. "The next world is our destination. This one is for travel."

That fall, we kept returning to what was lying in wait for all of us: death. "Whether we like it or not, every single moment, people are moving toward their death, whether walking or sitting, whether happy or not," the Sheikh said.

In this life, there are certain things one had to do: "You need to eat and drink, you need a house, you need to get married. These are only needed to help you worship Allah. But they all end with death." To become too attached to this life, he insisted, was akin to being a traveler who decided to build a house in a train station rather than passing through it.

For those who submitted, there was the promise—though not the guarantee—of paradise. It was a garden, whose cool lushness would have been particularly dazzling to the desert dwellers who first heard the Quran. Rivers flowed beneath it. Trees shaded it, heavy with low-hanging fruits. Believers would sit on couches, dressed in silk, sipping a gingery drink from shiny goblets. When they wanted more, their cups would be refilled by young boys, all "so nice-looking, you will think they're sprinkled with pearls!" said Akram.

Those who did not submit to God's commands, however, were destined for another place, described vividly in a sura called "Dominion":

> And for those who reject their Lord, there is the agony of hell, a
>   miserable destination:
> when they are thrown into it, they will hear its gasp as it flares,
>   nearly exploding with fury. (67:7–8)

Akram parsed the Arabic words describing the fire. The Arabic evoked the fire's sound and fury. Its hunger was like a lion in the forest, he said: "When the fire receives the people, it's so hungry, so angry," he explained. "It wants to eat them as soon as possible."

At question time, I raised my hand and then stretched it out for the microphone.

"Um . . . that bit about the fire. Are we to read it as a metaphor? Are these really flames we are talking about, or is it just to suggest that bad things happen to sinners?"

"The fire is fire," Akram responded. "It is really very real." He had read the philosopher Bertrand Russell, who questioned Christianity's emphasis on the flames of hell as a doctrine of cruelty at odds with the faith's central message of compassion. Over the past century or so, fewer Christian preachers talked about hellfire, for fear of scaring their flocks, he said, clearly disapproving: "They felt it was very frightening for the people."

Soft-pedaling the threat of hell, continued the Sheikh, was a mistake. He recalled the day when he'd answered his front doorbell to find a Christian there with a Bible. The Sheikh listened to his pitch, then asked the man, "What will happen to me if I don't believe you?"

The man was silent, clearly not wanting to scare off a potential convert. What about hell? Akram asked him. Oh, no, the man assured him. There was no mention of any hellfire in the Bible. "I had a Bible in my house," the Sheikh said. "I'd underlined it, and I went and got it, and showed him." Here, and here, and here, he'd showed the missionary, the Christian scripture spoke of the flames of hell.

"Never feel shyness to mention the fire of hell," he assured his listeners. "You either believe, or if you don't believe, then it's the fire of hell."

The discussion of hell was a rare moment of literalism for the Sheikh. Other Muslim thinkers had ventured that the descriptions of the afterlife were allegorical, not least because, as the Sheikh often reminded us, so much of the language of the Quran was suggestive of realities beyond human apprehension. But the Sheikh's fear was very real, just as real as he believed the flames to be.

My father had died when I was twenty-six years old. At the time, my sense of where he went afterward was thin and tinny. While grieving, my mother and I told each other rather feeble stories of Dad being pulled around on a cloud, hanging out with Billie Holiday, Tennessee Williams, and other luminaries he'd always wanted to meet. We comforted ourselves that he lived on, in my love of wandering the world, in my brother's talent for wheeling and dealing and his suspicion of authorities. Splitting the difference between belief and skepticism, I'd indulge myself in childish and soothing fantasies, pretending that he'd simply gone on a long trip somewhere.

The last time I saw him he was in fact embarking on a trip, one that took a sudden, tragic turn. He'd waved at me from a London bus stop, heading to the airport, on his way home to St. Louis and, a few weeks later, to Mexico. We had a rental property in San Miguel de Allende, and he was going to fix it up for new tenants. While there, he was approached by men who believed he owed them money, and they beat him. A few days later, he died from his injuries.

The phone call telling me of his death had come at dusk, on the first day of October 1993. I was alone at home, in London. I remember the vague smell of mold in the flat, the warm, rough pine table with the phone on it. I remember picking up the receiver and hearing the words. "Daddy's died," said my mother, in a voice carefully steadied for the purposes of the call.

There'd been an earlier phone call, six days before, bringing bad news, but not as bad as this. Three men had broken into the house in San Miguel, on the day of the annual celebration of St. Michael Archangel. When crowds clogged the streets, and music and confusion would have drowned out my father's cries, they forced their way into the house and tied up my father, the gardener, and the maid with ropes. Then they beat him, calling him *el abogado*—the lawyer—and demanding "the money," over and over. My father had no idea what they were talking about, and told them so. That only brought more beatings. Somewhere there was a blow that would dislodge the clot of blood that would stop up his lung a week later.

Just after the attack, my father had told my mother she didn't need to fly down. Not to worry, he had said. He was fine. Somewhat shaken, a bit sore, but fine. Lucky, really, not to have been hurt worse. Two days afterward, our tenant in the casita, the little house next door, had found him lying on the floor, unable to get up. She called an ambulance, which took him to the hospital, where the doctors noted internal bleeding from a tear in the liver and operated immediately. As he lay in a hospital bed, my mother flew down from St. Louis. She arrived off the bus from Mexico City to find him so thin that "his little cheeks stuck out like a cherub's," she said. "He'd been so glad I had come down." She'd read aloud to him from the *New Yorker*, and that night, he hadn't wanted her to leave. His delight on seeing her, his naked neediness, shocked me most. We were raised to make journeys, but not sentimental ones. I had not traveled back to my grandfather's funeral from Italy, and I had not come back from Britain to help bury my grandmother. As a family, we were trained to be hardy, to stand our ground, even if it was foreign. It was a sign of how scared my father was feeling that when my mother had flown down to see him, he hadn't forbidden her to do so.

"They wore good shoes," Maria Elena, our placid, moon-faced maid had told the police of the attackers. The shoes were all she'd managed to see of them, having kept her head down during the ordeal. They were the only clue that this was a professional call by men who'd done well in the drug trade. My father's death had been a case of mistaken identity: the *abogado* who owed the men money must have been a former tenant, an American lawyer. That night, I filled in the gaps of

Maria Elena's description with cartoon images. I imagined my father's killers as banditos with flaccid mustachios, flashing teeth and eyes, and sombreros hung with tassels that jiggled as they kicked him.

The next morning I went into the office to get some books and papers I'd need for my trip back home. The place was empty, except for the Sheikh. Back then, without a family in Oxford to draw him home, he'd often work late and early. I found him sitting in the office we shared with other researchers, hunched over an Urdu text. "My father died," I blurted. Akram stood up and pressed his hand to his heart. "Losing a parent is very hard," he said.

Then, standing straight, his hands resting on the back of his plastic chair, he began, in a loud, clear voice, to recite a poem. He made no concession to its being midweek or to our being at work. With the burnt-gold of an Oxford autumn behind him, he recited without pause or embarrassment. It didn't matter that I didn't understand the words: for a minute or two, the tiny office blazed with Urdu verse and the late afternoon light.

When he finished, I asked what it was. An elegy the Pakistani poet Iqbal had written when his mother died, Akram replied. "He is asking, 'Who will wait for my letters now?'" he translated. "He is asking, 'Who will welcome me home, now that she is gone?'"

Later, I would find a translation of the elegy Akram had recited. Verses from a poem written after Iqbal's mother's death capture the gray disorientation of grieving for a parent:

Who would wait for me anxiously in my native place?
Who would display restlessness if my letter fails to arrive?
I will visit thy grave with this complaint:
Who will now think of me in midnight prayers?

The Sheikh and I didn't yet know each other well, that day. His words, and Iqbal's, were the first hint I'd had that our collegiality might break through to friendship. Of all the condolences offered after my father died, the Sheikh's comforted me the most. He hadn't known my father; he barely knew me. But the Sheikh's recitation was a balm because of its foreign qualities, not despite them. His recitation was a reminder that death was a universal occurrence, as common as life itself.

"Ah, you've been reading *The Road to Mecca*," said the Sheikh as I unloaded my book bag onto our table at the Oxford Kebab House.

"Yes, you kept talking about Muhammad Asad, so I picked up a copy. Whenever you say that the Quran urges people to think, you tend to mention him."

"Do I?" said the Sheikh, allowing himself a tiny, pleased smile.

He did. Muhammad Asad was among the most eloquent proponents of Islam in the twentieth century. He began life in 1900 as Leopold Weiss, born into a family of bankers, lawyers, and rabbis in what was then the Austro-Hungarian Empire. Raised in Vienna by parents whose Judaism was practiced as, he later wrote, "the wooden ritual of those who clung by habit," he became a foreign correspondent in the Middle East, then a sometime screenwriter and bohemian in Weimar-era Berlin. In Islam he found an antidote to the "complicated, mechanized, phantom-ridden age" of interwar Europe. He moved, first to Arabia, then to India, where during the 1930s he collaborated with the poet-philosopher Iqbal, laying the intellectual foundations for the future state of Pakistan. For a time, he represented Pakistan at the United Nations, before turning to translation and writing. He dedicated some of his works to "People Who Think."

Asad's defense of Islam as a religion based on reason rather than blind faith particularly impressed Akram. The story the Sheikh loved to tell was of the debate Asad once had with a group of Jesuit priests. During World War II, Asad had been held in an internment camp in India as an "enemy alien." His fellow inmates included a group of German Jesuit priests, who delighted in debating religion with the brilliant young Muslim. One day, their leader, an aristocratic and erudite Bavarian, asked Asad why someone born an Austro-Hungarian Jew would choose Islam over Christianity. Asad said he'd willingly convert to Christianity, provided the Jesuit could just clear up one question. "If you do, you can take me next Sunday to the chapel tent and baptize me," said Asad.

Done, said the Bavarian.

Asad's question concerned the Trinity: How could God be One, and yet Three?

The Trinity, responded the Jesuit, is a great and mysterious truth, a "mysterium." "When you achieve faith," he assured Asad, "then your heart will make you understand it."

That, Asad told him, is why he became a Muslim. "You tell me, 'Believe in faith, and then you will understand it.' My religion tells me 'Use your reason, then you will gain faith.'"

The Jesuit gave up.

When Muhammad Asad's own son Talal was growing up, he impressed on him that one should always try to approach non-Muslims using reason and tolerance. "There is no compulsion in religion," he'd remind the boy, citing the Quran.

I knew Akram felt the same, which was why I was only slightly nervous at this, our last lesson. Because I'd saved until now the question that I'd been wanting to ask him ever since he'd first started talking to me about hellfire: What did he think was ultimately going to happen to me, somebody who believed in some sort of God but was nowhere near ready to submit to a faith?

After a year of classes, I knew his worldview was broad enough to encompass mine—broad enough, indeed, to respect it. But though he'd never said so, I'd often wondered whether Akram had embarked on our lessons in the spirit of *dawa*, or calling me to Islam. I was a friend who had asked for the favor of his time and learning. But I was also a non-Muslim. For me, our Quran lessons had been a listening exercise; I wondered whether he'd hoped that through that listening I'd embrace Islam. Others had hinted that I might convert. The day I went to see the Sheikh and his group off on *umra*, one man had turned and, with a conspiratorial grin, said, "Who knows, maybe you'll be going next year . . . ?"

"Do you know something I don't?" I asked.

He just smiled.

On the bus up to Oxford, I'd read Asad's description of his conversion to Islam. As a young man traveling in Arabia and Afghanistan, he'd been drawn to the faith's spare self-sufficiency, but he couldn't yet bring himself to submit. Becoming a Muslim seemed "like the prospect of venturing out onto a bridge that spanned an abyss between two different worlds: a bridge so long that one would have to reach the point of no return before the other end became visible."

Just reading the description gave me vertigo. The mental bridge I'd built between Akram's worldview and mine was miles shorter. So much of the Sheikh's worldview appealed. A genuine belief in people's equality before God. Humility. Kindness. What I took to be certainty. At *itikaf*, watching rows of Muslims, shoulder to shoulder, praying together, I couldn't remember having seen a similar soulful solidarity. Cathedral choirs, Catholic masses, Quaker meetings: none had the simple power of a roomful of women prostrating. But I couldn't make the leap. I kept thinking, with a smile, of my father's take on faith: "I would love to believe," he'd say, stretching out his arms as though waiting for some deity's embrace. As for me, I still remained an appreciator of Islam. Like my father before me, I was a collector of its treasures, peering through glass cases at the museum instead of prostrating at the mosque.

What finally drove Asad out onto that long bridge was the moral bankruptcy of interwar Berlin. It was 1926, an era of go-go economics and tinselly values. Germany was gripped by vast, screaming inequalities and a frantic materialism that would soon come crashing down. One day on the Berlin subway he looked around his carriage, at the prosperous passengers, at a man with a glittering diamond ring, at a woman with a mouth "fixed in a stiff semblance of a smile." To Asad, they all seemed miserable. They were "without any faith in binding truths, without any goal beyond the desire to raise their own 'standard of living,' without any hopes other than having more material amenities, more gadgets, and perhaps more power."

Asad responded by going home and opening his Quran, seemingly at random. His eye alighted on a verse:

You are obsessed by greed for more and more
Until you go down to your graves.
Nay but you will come to know! (102: 1–3)

For Asad, this was the answer, one that proved "beyond any doubt, that it was a God-inspired book I was holding in my hand."

The tea arrived, and prayer time was in an hour, so I decided to seize the moment. "Sheikh, so what do you think is going to happen to me? Do you think I can be a good person but still not submit? Am I still going to hell?"

Never had a fire-and-brimstone message been delivered more gently.

"The thing basically is," the Sheikh said evenly, "in the way of the Quran, people have no salvation until they believe there is no one to worship except Allah. If people are good without that, there could be some reward for them in this world, but it's not real salvation."

His kindness prevented him from saying "you," or from mentioning the manacles and flames. He smiled and observed that it was difficult to accept when one has been on the wrong path. "The problem actually is, Carla, we don't want it, but it's always better for people to correct themselves before it is too late. Even people who correct themselves one hour before death, it's fine." He continued, "Belief in God—every good starts from that. Then after that, people can get better and better. The basic level is to believe properly."

We sat for a second in silence.

"And you've never had any doubts?" I ventured.

"Sometimes, I really feel very frightened." The Sheikh hesitated. "For myself. There is no guarantee that you will die a believer. It could be that someone who thinks they are a believer is actually an unbeliever. Everything depends on God. Nothing is certain."

This uncertainty, not of God but of himself, felt reassuringly familiar. Secularists often assume that the faithful have the comfort of certainty. But the Sheikh's humility wouldn't allow him to trust in his own piety. Every time he prays, he adds a prayer asking God, once again, to let him die a believer.

If nothing is certain, I asked, then "how can you prove that God actually exists?"

"You can't, not one hundred percent, offer a proof of God," said Akram. "Just as you can't offer one hundred percent proof that He doesn't exist."

For Akram, the signs were all there. That we were here talking about it at all was proof. So were sunsets and skin cells, gnats and Niagara Falls. "Allah has created enough signs for all the arguments," he said. Believers are meant to be readers of these signs: the Angel Gabriel's first word to Muhammad had been "Read."

"If Allah had wanted to make all people Muslim, he could have," explained the Sheikh. "But instead, he sent guidance. He wants people to think."

"I do think," I began. "But it seems to me that believing still requires a leap."

"You know, in the English language, when people say they 'believe,' it means 'I doubt.' Like if I ask you if you're coming to see me, and you say, 'Oh, I believe so,' it means you are doubtful. But belief in Islam is not like that. Belief in Islam means that you are certain it must be true."

"Exactly. A leap."

Less a leap, more a dawning sense of certainty, said the Sheikh. "Coming to belief is a bit like understanding a mother's love," he said. "It grows. She is kind to you, so you believe five percent. Then as you grow, she keeps on showing her love. Feeding you, teaching you, and so on. So it grows to ten percent, and the more you notice, the more you believe."

"Well, have you ever had any doubts?" I asked again.

"I don't remember ever having any doubts. I really have no doubt that the world is created by God. In fact, it's not a matter of proof. It's just that people don't want to see."

Two teenage girls clattered into the restaurant. In the distance, the sound of an ambulance. A motorcycle tore down the road. The Sheikh's focus didn't falter.

"I'll give you an example. Everyone knows that death is coming. So why don't people mention it? All you have to do is think! It's certain. But people don't. Because if people think, they can't enjoy life. If I am told by a doctor that after ten days I am going to die, do you think I have time to go to the party and enjoy the roses?"

"Well, lots of people think that the certainty of death is precisely the reason to smell the roses," I said.

But the carpe diem attitude denies reality, said the Sheikh. "In this society, old people, sick people, they've all been put aside. People only see young faces, shining faces. Look at how they portray the movie stars. They don't advertise what happens to that person after their twenties! You only see them when they're young."

Western culture doesn't give life's full arc its due, he argued: "Everybody says, 'If you want to understand something properly, look at all the different aspects of it, put them together, and then you can understand.' In the West, people only know one part of life."

"Which is?"

"You see youth shining, but you never include death. Okay, so maybe not everyone will believe in the Day Hereafter, but at least death should be mentioned properly! It should be seen by the people: people should know what death means! Old age, sickness—these should be part of society! People who are poor, they should be part of society!"

I nodded. "It's a relief when a culture can admit to death."

I told him how, when my father died, I had gone to Pakistan for a few months. Officially, the trip was meant to get me started as a journalist, but really I went to grieve. I chose Pakistan because I'd wanted to mourn in a part of the world where my family had once been happy, but I also wanted to be where death was viewed as part of life, not as a fluke or a failure of medical science.

Many people mourn every day in America, but it is often a lonely place to do so. There's a heavy pressure to heal, to get back in shape to pursue happiness. Death is forced underground, or into encounter sessions with grief counselors or priests. Death felt too irrevocable, too unfixable, for the land of the people who tend to look on the bright side, home of the self-helped and self-made.

In Pakistan, death was allowed out of the closet. Because I was looking for it, I found it everywhere. In grisly newspaper headlines about tribal wars and honor killings. At the cocktail party, where a socialite told me how her fiancé had gone out for cigarettes and never returned, killed in a car crash. At the Lahore Museum, in a statue of Buddha, rendered so skinny that the stone carver had seemed to place the bones outside the flesh. At night, I found myself telling a casual dinner companion about my father's death—and even as I did so, I knew that such talk from a near-stranger was as irrelevant, intimate, and unappetizing as finding a hair in your soup. Yet my date was polite, dipped his bread into yogurt, nodded, chewed, swallowed: "Ah, yes. My own father was killed in a tribal war when I was six. Luckily, my uncle raised me." And then he craned his neck to find the waiter, as though being an orphan was as minor an inconvenience as a dish without salt.

When I pressed the Sheikh about whether he'd hoped I would convert over the course of our lessons, his answer, as ever, came back to death. I was free to make up my own mind, he said, but he wanted to tell me of what lay ahead. "When I stand on the Day of Judgment, and I am asked whether I warned the people about the Fires of Hell, I want to be able to say that I had. Those who are my friends, like you, I should certainly try to save them." After all, would I not do the same for him? "If there was something in this country that would put me in prison, or cause me pain, wouldn't you warn me?"

A week after my last lesson with the Sheikh, my brother called me to tell me that our mother had died. The twenty years since my father's death had tested her. Three weeks after his death, she'd had a heart attack so severe that when she survived, her doctors called her "the

Save of '93." Survive she did, and for the following years she forged a plausible, if lonely, life. She taught feminist studies at the university, and visited Egypt and Italy, where she and my father had lived, and returned to the house where he died, in Mexico. At times she could project a semblance of her younger self, a woman who had road-tripped with a friend from Tehran to Herat, who could whip up a five-course French meal with barely a glance at her copy of Julia Child. But my father's death and her own depression wore her out. "What to make of a diminished thing," she'd say, quoting Robert Frost. Her last seven years were spent with Lewy body disease in a St. Louis nursing home. Cruel little chips of calcium lodged in her brain, so that her old self would wax and wane.

During her life, my mother had worn her Judaism lightly. But it's a truism that ritual and belonging provide comfort for those left behind after death. I boarded the plane from London steeped in my Quran, but when I got off in St. Louis, I fell gratefully into the embrace of my mother's circle of friends, most of whom were Jewish. "Getting more Jewish by the minute!" I texted my husband. My mother's real tribe was largely drawn from the university, so the service, held down the hall from the English department, had speeches quoting Shake-speare and Adrienne Rich. Though we didn't have a rabbi, we did have my mother's friend, a Hebrew professor, lead us in saying the kaddish, the Jewish prayer for the dead. My brother Nicholas and I had managed to misspell it as "kadish" on the program, and when we recited it, everyone seemed to know it but us. Still, I found comfort in stumbling through the unfamiliar words: "In seeking peace and under-standing for ourselves, we promise our own understanding to bring peace to all we meet."

When I returned from St. Louis, I called the Sheikh and told him my news.

"I keep thinking of that Iqbal poem you recited when my father died, about 'Who will wait up for me? Who will wait for my letters?'"

"I'm really very sorry, Carla," he said simply. "There is nothing in this universe like a mother."

I knew he believed it. It was always a mother's love, not a father's, that he invoked to illustrate Allah's benevolence toward the universe. I hung up, and once again looked up Iqbal's elegy. I realized why the poem had moved me so deeply, that day Akram had recited it. Iqbal captures not just loss through death, but the pain of separation during life. As any migrant will tell you, a death at long distance has its own rhythms. Time zones and logistics give the pain sharp new twists. Only two weeks before, with Julia and Nic watching wide-eyed, I made long-distance phone calls in the early morning dawn. Many deaths feel unreal, but for the migrant in mourning, they're doubly so. Having lost the presence of your loved one in daily life, you've only had them as a ghostly presence to begin with. Visits home and phone calls can bring them to life, but only temporarily. So after the call with the news comes, the long-distance griever has to resummon the love object in her mind, then lose the beloved again. The gears of the imagination grind through a painful game of found-and-lost, lost-and-found.

At my mother's memorial, a friend, reflecting on her last years, quoted Shakespeare: "When sorrows come, they come not single spies / But in battalions." A few days after the service, the Sheikh's student Arzoo texted me. The Sheikh's own mother had died unexpectedly, earlier that day. It felt as though we were in the grip of some mad transnational epidemic of maternal loss.

Stunned, I texted condolences, not wanting to intrude so soon.

A few minutes later, my phone registered a missed call. It was the Sheikh.

I phoned back.

"You saw her last when I saw her last," he said quietly.

"It was a privilege," I said. I knew only too well the importance of the last time. Of replaying memories of the last backward glance—or worse, the lack of such a glance. Everyone who's lost anyone has them, but they're particularly vivid for migrants like Akram and me. I had my own two stretches of film that played on loop: My father, with a yellow backpack, getting on a London bus to catch his plane. My mother, waving gamely from her wheelchair, telling me to kiss my kiddies back in England for her.

I'd gone home with Akram the last time he saw his mother, perched on her charpoy. Tonight, I was a bridge back to Jamdahan.

He was quiet on the phone, murmuring low and speaking little. Such was his natural reserve, of course, but he was also following the sunna: the Prophet had spoken out against loud wailing over the dead. Quiet tears are acceptable, Muhammad had said, but loudly crying was not, as it was too much like the extravagant mourning of pre-Islamic Arabia.

The call was short, which was a good thing, because I was on the verge of some loud and un-Islamic lamentation myself.

"You are very close to our hearts," the Sheikh said, before hanging up.

The family would be receiving condolence calls on Sunday, Sumaiya told me. As in Judaism, it is a Muslim tradition that friends and family come to pay their respects to the dead and to comfort the living. Back in St. Louis, friends and I had asked whether my brother and I would sit shiva, the week-long Jewish condolence period after burial. We hadn't. At the time, the practice had felt rather more formal than our diluted Judaism called for. Besides, sitting shiva wasn't practical for scattered families like ours. Since both of us were sleeping in friends' spare rooms, there'd been no obvious place to sit.

Returning to England, I regretted not having done it. I spent a weekend at the house of my English mother-in-law. An old-fashioned Briton, she's not one for grief's messiness. Her generation prided itself on making it through the war without a fuss. She doubtless hoped that her chat about her book club and crossword puzzle clues would be welcome distractions from thoughts of death. It just made me want to shove wads of raw pain into every conversational pause and to hurl every teacup meekly passed.

After a weekend of Anglo-Saxon stoicism, the Sheikh's house felt reassuringly familiar. I found relief in the signs of wakeful sadness—the unmade bed set up in the front room, the Sheikh's reddened, half-shuttered eyes. The chaos of loss was comforting: the fretful children, the stuttered attempts at conversation, the scramble for travel arrangements.

The Sheikh was having trouble getting a visa to return to India. To get fast-tracked at the Indian consulate, he needed a death certificate, something his mother didn't receive, dying as she did in a remote village. The Sheikh had already missed the burial, which Muslim tradition dictates should take place within three days. In Jamdahan, where there was no electricity, the September heat meant the funeral rites were concluded even sooner. Akram's mother had been buried the day after she died, with Akram's sisters washing the body in accordance with Islamic custom and wrapping it in the customary five white shrouds. The day after, his eldest sister had fainted and had been rushed to the hospital, to be put on a drip for exhaustion.

The afternoon I paid my condolence call, the Sheikh was nowhere to be seen. I was ushered into the living room, where I sat with Farhana and the children. The Sheikh, they told me, was receiving male callers in another room. When the men were just about to file out the front door, I heard him call softly for the door to our room to be closed, so we could observe purdah as they left.

Then the Sheikh came in, wearing white, the color for Muslim mourners. "Thank you so much for coming, Carla," he said, lowering his head. "We were going to come to Brighton to see you, when . . ."

"We should just meet midway," I joked, envisioning the two of us perched on the shoulder of some British highway, two foreign-born orphans condoling each other for our lost mothers.

He sat briefly but then excused himself: there were more men waiting in the other room to pay their respects.

Unsure what to bring, I'd settled on flowers. Later, I found out that Muslim condolence callers traditionally brought food. As in Judaism, custom called on the community to feed the grieving.

"Food!" I cried, gratefully devouring a plate of spiced potatoes and spinach. "Food for the bereaved! That's exactly what we Jews do!"

"I can't see why there's so much fighting," smiled Sumaiya, as she ladled out more. "So much is the same."

"Will your father be able to say prayers for your grandmother?" I asked.

"The custom is to get as many people to pray at the grave as possible, so he's missed that. But we've all been keeping her in our prayers from here."

Akram's parents had always hoped to move to join their son's life in England. "My father always said he'd bring them over," said Sumaiya. "But it would have meant so many arrangements. We'd have had to build an Eastern-style toilet for them. We'd have had to find people to care for them who spoke Urdu. And there would have been the matter of the weather. After Jamdahan, they'd have felt cold, even in the summers."

Akram's piety connected him to the life to come. He carried an awareness of death the way other men carry their car keys. But even with his honed sense of impending death, he could not block grief. The force of faith might weaken the lesser emotions that beset humans, like lust or covetousness. But piety can't fill the hole a mother leaves when she dies.

Everlasting Return

When the call came telling the Sheikh that his mother had died, his first words were those that Muslims traditionally use on news of death or hardship: *Inna lillahi wa inna ilayhi rajioon.* "We belong to God, and to God we return." Taken from the second chapter of the Quran, the phrase cradles the speaker, the listener, and the deceased together in a common destiny. Its power derives from its symmetry: our origin is our destination, in our end is our beginning.

There's a story the prominent British sheikh Abdalhaqq Bewley tells about how those six words changed his life. Born a Christian, he indulged in the excesses of the Swinging Sixties in London before he embraced Islam. His conversion came when, as a young man, he was traveling through Morocco. One evening in Fez, he and two companions hiked to a hill above the city to watch the sunset. Since it was time for evening prayers, the sky was crisscrossed with calls to prayer, the muezzins calling the faithful from minarets. The three men met a shepherd passing with his flock. One of his companions, who spoke excellent Arabic, greeted the old man, asking, by way of conversation, where he was going. "We belong to God," the shepherd replied, "and to God we return."

On hearing this, Bewley decided to convert, and did so the following day.

It's a powerful story, with a satisfying "Reader, I married him" sense of closure. Boy meets Truth. Boy embraces Truth. As I imagined it, the scene on the hill above Fez was something straight from a scripture—or the Hollywood version thereof: The bowl of the ancient city stretching out below the men. The sun burnishing the dun buildings to orange. The shepherd's craggy face, calm as he watched his goats pick over ruddy, crumbling rocks. Then the words of the Quran, piercing through the atmospherics, promising reunion with the Creator.

Unlike the man who became Sheikh Abdalhaqq Bewley, I didn't convert. But my year with my own sheikh and the Quran provided me with many moments of grace. I found comfort in how small I felt reading the text, as when I considered the images of the "Lord of the heavens and the earth and everything in between, and Lord of all points of the sunrise." Even as a nonbeliever, I still found myself taking refuge in the Quran classes as a calm inlet from daily life. The Sheikh's disregard for all the measurements of getting and spending was soothing. Yesterday's close on Wall Street, the exam score or dress size, even happiness itself; all were nothing next to the fact that from God we come and to God we return. The constant reminders of one's own puniness and powerlessness were strangely bracing. When my mother died, I remember thinking how sensible it was, the Muslim practice of saying "Inshallah," or "God willing," after every plan, every promise, no matter how minor, since only God can be sure whether next Wednesday's lunch date will indeed be kept. It was a comfort, in a season of grief, to hang out with a community that honored this world's uncertainties.

The shepherd's quote from the Quran still haunts me, not least because the circle it describes gives Akram's life shape and meaning. To study with Akram was to learn how his life runs on an awareness of this return. For the Sheikh, existence was a circle with God at its end, beginning, and every point in between. From Allah he has come, and to Allah he will return. Those drawings of a circle and a line on the board, that day he'd lectured on the story of Yusuf, were a sketch of a pious Islamic life. The circle: a cycle of days, a Muslim's constant turn toward God. The line: the space in which the Muslims found themselves. The line was not your problem, he said. The circle was: "Observe it, always, in the fear of Allah." So it is that for Akram, the high point of every hajj was a circling: the ritual circumambulation of the Kaaba. Walking seven times around the black stone "is always the most beloved thing in my heart," he said. Every day circled back to his God. Thirty-five times a week—and often many more—he returns to prayer. In standing, kneeling, bringing his forehead to the earth, then standing again, his attention returns to his origins and destination, which are one and the same. On good days, prayer could feel like returning to "the arms of your mother, when you are a child," he said.

I continue to envy him that feeling, even though I still don't understand the Quran as a unified whole. While many passages move me, none has moved me to tears. To be fair to my teacher, it's a truism that the Quran cannot be translated. Anyone who can't read it in the classical Arabic, we are repeatedly warned, misses much of its poetry and power. I began my year feeling really bad that I couldn't read it in the original. Over the year, I've grown to feel less so, even though I now have accumulated even more copies of the Quran than I had when we began studying. Next to my college paperback of Muhammad Marmaduke Pickthall's translation, with his florid verbal flights, and my Saudi Arabian–issued tome, I now have four more translations. To the purist, each new effort at interpretation might signal the impossibility of translation, a reminder of the receding of a Single Truth. But there is another way to look at the impossibility of translation, a way that chimes with my own secular humanist creed: each new translator embarking on a fresh foray to understand the Quran suggests not its untranslatability, but its richness.

When I began my Quran lessons, I assumed, with pert certainty, that I would read a book through and learn what was inside it. The first clue that I couldn't had arrived during that first lesson, back at the Nosebag. "Ah, but is it a book?" the Sheikh had asked. I'd patted my paperback, clueless as to what he meant. I'd come a long way from my earliest encounter with the Quran, making it a Brontë novel for my doll, but I still hadn't understood that it was far more than a much-revered book. Over the course of the year, I began to see that the Quran was not merely a set of pages between two covers. Calling it a book, something one can read from beginning to end, embalms it in expectations. It was just another way of limiting it into something small: an amulet, a manifesto, an instruction guide, a political tool. In the life of a Muslim like Akram, its meaning is much more diffuse. So, too, is the Quran's reach in Muslim societies, where its words blare from mosque loudspeakers, issue from radios and CDs, or hang on necks or walls. Grasping at what the Quran might be, I can only settle on the metaphor of return. It is a place to which the faithful return, again and again.

Much as they do to prayer. Scientists who have studied the postures of Muslim prayer have found they encourage calm and flexibility. Standing straight in the opening stance, they discovered, strengthens musculature. Bowing stretches out the lower back and hamstrings. The pose of sitting after prostration keeps joints mobile. Akram's prayers have rendered him culturally supple, too, stretching his humanity in surprising ways. The act of return—to his prayer mat, to his Quran and his classical texts—has often afforded an expansion of his worldview, not a restriction of it. Going back to primary sources of hadith scholarship has allowed him to see a pattern that others had missed, or had chosen to ignore. In piecing together a history of thousands of learned women, he's found a past that argues for a liberated present. Unlike the traditions invoked by the men who would confine women to the home, he's discovered a past that propels women forward.

The Sheikh's beloved prophet Ibrahim had warned against worshipping in a certain way simply because one's forefathers had done so. Akram's counsel to contemporary Muslims echoes Ibrahim's warnings of spiritual sclerosis: "When a culture focuses on the outer aspects of a faith—like a headscarf—their religion just becomes about identity," Akram cautions. "At the end of the day, people are carrying a dead body, with no soul." Go back to the sources, back to your prayer mats, and make your faith your own, he counseled. Don't do what everyone else does. Read. Think. Brush off the dust of tradition, and with it the certainties of your ancestors. True worship requires one to look past burqas, beards, and sharia laws, which too often are just the props, not piety itself. True worship was *taqwa*, consciousness of the Return. And this ever-present sense of the Return gave Akram the grace to set out in the world. With it he moved nimbly from the village of Jamdahan to the city of Lucknow to the West, unburdened by bitterness and without feeling conflicted, or crippled by loss.

Migrants, particularly Muslim ones, are often cast as people whose lives are broken in two by moving to the West. In the United States and Europe, the post-9/11 focus on security and integration among Muslim minorities has meant that hyphens, such as those in "Muslim-American" or "British-Pakistani," are read as breaks, not bridges. But migration can double a self as well as halve it. Salman Rushdie has called migrants "translated men." Too often, it's assumed "that something always gets lost in translation," Rushdie wrote. "I cling, obstinately, to the notion that something can also be gained."

Much has been gained through Akram's translation from India to England. His migration has meant a layering of cultures rather than a break with them. Life in the West provided perspective, allowing him to see which parts of the faith were Islamic and which were simply ancestral traditions. Akram's Oxford life gave him the money to return to Jamdahan and to set up a girls' madrasa. It meant he returned to Nadwah to deliver a lecture widely perceived as daring, in the community of ulama, in its suggestion that Muslims must share the blame for their contemporary ills. In Britain, he could seem like a translated man. But step back far enough from the globe to hold both India and Britain in a single gaze, and you'll see him not as translated, but as translator.

The writer Mustafa Akyol pointed out that Muslim cultures often clung to rigid, unchanging precepts and created traditions when they felt threatened by the West. Like every other culture, Muslim societies have shown the greatest flexibility in times of confidence. The powerful Ottoman Empire, noted Akyol, never lost its Islamic identity even as it gave Jews and Christians equal rights as citizens and abolished apostasy laws. There was a show of similar confidence, too, in a 2011

Pew survey of Muslim Americans. Most agreed that there was more than one true interpretation to Islamic teachings, and that different religions can lead to eternal life. When I asked the Sheikh how I could deepen my understanding, his answer invariably echoed the command that Muhammad heard: "Read." Keep reading the Quran, he told me at our last lesson. Read it, and read it again. Return.

As I talked to Akram, my own fundamentalist beliefs frequently collapsed. My assumption that literalist readers of scripture like the Sheikh saw their faith as something in opposition to science? It crumbled. Akram simply saw science as another way of understanding God's creations. The universe was big enough for both approaches. ("Never," said Arzoo, "when I was doing my physics degree at Oxford, did he ever say I shouldn't do the course." Just the opposite. "He kept telling me that I must finish it.") My belief that the devout were spared doubt? Groundless. Flattened the day Akram confessed that he worried, often, that he was being faithful in the wrong way, and that on the Day of Judgment, his devotion would be found wanting.

My neat opposition between my own post-Enlightenment world-view and the Sheikh's Muslim one? Pretty nearly rubble. The day I looked in a book by the secular humanist thinker A. C. Grayling, I started in recognition at his checklist of Enlightenment values: "pluralism, individual autonomy, democracy, the rule of law, tolerance, science, reason, secularism, equality, humanistic ethics, education, and the promotion and protection of human rights and civil liberties." Most of these values were Akram's—the great exception being secularism. Indeed, he strove to make God central to everything he did. Politics, society, art—all were subsumed to worshipping God. But I was repeatedly amazed at how the Sheikh's faith allowed, even encouraged, critiques that echoed my own. Among other things, the year was a reminder of the possibilities of Akram's particular brand of piety, with its defense of the most basic human rights, its stress on individual conscience over state-mandated laws, and its live-and-let-live ethos.

True, when we talked about women's domestic roles and anything to do with gay rights, I'd bumped up against the limits of the Sheikh's expansiveness. If I really wanted a reading of the Quran whose out-look utterly matched my own, I would need to look to feminist pio-neers like Amina Wadud, Asma Barlas, and Asghar Ali Engineer—or indeed, to the new generation of bloggers, writers, and activists build-ing on their work. Should I want a take on homosexuality more in line with Western legal thinking, I would need to refer to the work of scholars like Scott Siraj al-Haqq Kugle, whose work on Islamic homophobia has included a return and a rereading of the story of Lot, or Lut, in the Quran.

When the Sheikh and I did disagree, our collisions only served to remind me how relatively recently the prevailing Western views had formed. Our lessons coincided with the evolution of what tolerance and human rights meant in Europe and North America. Month by month, it seemed, more states and nations expanded their definitions of the meaning of justice. Of what constituted a family. A couple. Equality. When I was born, gays in England were criminals. Midway through writing this book, they won the right to be brides and grooms. Lessons with the Sheikh underscored not merely the dynamism of contemporary Muslim societies, but also the dynamism of the West.

Not long after his lecture on Yusuf, Akram and I met in the Ash-molean Museum in Oxford for a lesson. We strode past the Greeks and Romans and skirted the Renaissance, heading straight for the Islamic collection. We passed two balding men straining to see a blue-and-white Iznik tile. A lithe young woman in jeans, earbuds firmly in her ears, gazed at the cypress on a frieze from Damascus. As we walked, something caught my eye. "Come," I said to the Sheikh. "You've got to see this!"

On a wall hung a set of Persian tiles decorated to illustrate "Yusuf and Zuleikha," a poem by the Sufi poet Jami that was based on the Quran's story of Yusuf. In lapis and turquoise, with touches of pink to set off the cool blues, some eighteenth-century Iranian artist had painted the women of Memphis, lounging on rugs and looking, amazed, at handsome Yusuf. I was ridiculously pleased to stumble upon this so soon after the Yusuf lecture, and to see it with the Sheikh. The tile hung a short walk from where he worked—what were the chances? To find an image based on the sura of Yusuf in the Ashmolean, that venerable British institution, seemed like some sort of cosmic nod. We stood there for a minute, and it felt urgent that he acknowledge it. For a secularist like me, the coincidence reinforced Akram's lesson on the circle and the line. What prayer gave him, art gave me. Each reassured that no matter what space you find yourself in, even in this fractured world, there was a unity. The sign that you weren't alone, the means of making a connection. I'd grown up trying to bridge my life in St. Louis with my worlds in Kabul or Cairo or Delhi. To make the world seem whole, I'd read Rudyard Kipling in Clayton, Missouri, and tales of Midwestern prairie girls on the road to Kandahar.

Besides, the tiles were gorgeous. Look at Yusuf, I exclaimed, with that halo-disk illuminating his head! How the artist had managed to make him look stoic, but also shocked, with one eyebrow slightly raised? The bowls of fruit, the lounging women?

Akram glanced at the tiles for a second. He nodded politely. He knew the poem they were based on, he said. And that was that. He turned away and made for a nearby bench, sitting down to begin the lesson.

At first I wondered whether I'd upset him. I knew that like many Muslims, he preferred to avoid figurative art. Just now, getting lost looking for the Islamic art, we'd strode past a Michelangelo sketch and a row of Greek busts without slowing our steps; they might have been McDonald's ads for all the attention he gave them. He was simply indifferent: unmoved by the art around him but willing to sit on a bench in the middle of it.

Later, when I asked him whether I'd offended him, he'd assured me I hadn't. It was simply that Muslims didn't hold with images of prophets, he explained. "To depict them limits them," he explained. "Out of respect for the prophets, we don't like to limit them."

That upended my pat ideas of art's power. For Akram, pictures stunted the imagination rather than stretched it. I felt deflated. Out-flanked, somehow. Looking back on it, I wonder whether I'd been hoping, that day at the Ashmolean, for some sort of conversion from the Sheikh. Not a religious conversion, obviously. But I know I hoped he'd see the tile, or perhaps a Titian, and see, for a minute or two, its beauty. There was, I suspect, an element of Show and Tell in me, some need for approval, or if not that, for connection. The year had included endless amounts of hospitality and kindness from him, and boundless generosity with his time and expertise. But I suspect I wanted some mutual curiosity from him. Just for a second, I wanted him to take a step toward my worldview, as I'd done toward his. It wasn't that I wanted him to change his outlook, just to acknowledge the beauty of mine.

In truth, he had already endorsed many of my values simply by showing up at the Ashmolean. By the standards of Uttar Pradeshi Muslim purdah, just agreeing to my solo lessons was a major cultural leap. Born in a household where brothers and sisters didn't talk to one another, he was now meeting a woman—a nonbeliever, no less—in an art museum. Was our conversation not my precious pluralism in action? With exquisite manners, the Sheikh said as much when I asked him whether there were elements of Western culture that might shock his younger self. "For example, I'm sitting here with you now," he said. "If someone sees in Nadwah that I am sitting with you, they cannot imagine it! An *alim* with a woman!"

In the most polite way, he was saying: "I'm here, aren't I?" We were talking. About death. And sex. And marriage. Nature. What it means to be human. That we didn't always agree, or that he didn't fall into raptures over Western civilization on our way to the Islamic gallery— what of it? Surely he had offered me much more than a few shared seconds in front of a pretty bit of art.

When the novelist Salman Rushdie was living under a death threat issued by the Ayatollah Khomeini for alleged blasphemy against Islam, Rushdie wrote of literature as a sacred space, remaining "the one place in any society where . . . we can hear voices talking about every-thing in every possible way." There were no voices in the Quran, just a single, omnipresent one. Nor, despite passages of exquisite power and beauty, was the Quran literature. But for the Sheikh, the Quran was as infinite as a novelist deems literature to be. For me, reading the Quran with Akram allowed us to talk, if not about "everything in every possible way," then at least about far more than I ever thought possible. At the start of these lessons, I'd known of the dazzling possibilities of Islamic culture to embrace points of view like my own. But I'd expected to find them among Muslim progressives, not with a conservative madrasa scholar.

The lesson that followed, as we sat on the wooden museum bench surrounded by fragments of Muslim cultures, reminded me how tricky these boundary crossings could be. We were talking of the widespread practice in many Muslim societies of marrying girls young. Predictably, I'd railed against it. What about education? Personal choice? Hopes for a career? The usual, in short.

The Sheikh listened—and then suggested I take a look at Western civilization. One had to look back only three hundred years or so in Europe's history, back before the Industrial Revolution, to find early marriages. No public schools, or truant authorities, or Rights of the Child manifesto, or underage statutes. My outrage may have burned, but it cooled slightly after Akram reminded me that Western absolutes were made, not born. What I take as Truth is built on a history of revolutions—political, industrial, and personal. A girl's right to school and a childhood weren't fixtures of the landscape, like a boulder or an ocean. They had to be fought for, and then created. It was bracing, this reminder of my own culture as a living tradition, built by framing and reframing the norms of what justice means.

"When we grow up in a certain culture, a certain context, the mind is so fixed that we cannot think in any other," the Sheikh observed, picking up his coat. "It is very hard to see the whole situation."

Having gently pointed out the girders holding up Western morality, he left for evening prayers.

I sat for a moment on the bench in that museum, surrounded by all manner of Islamic objects. A twelfth-century turquoise bowl from Central Asia. An Iznik tile painted in russet and lapis. An Egyptian mosque lamp. When Akram left, I felt oddly bereft. He'd gone to his mosque, and I was left, like my father before me, to admire the beauty of Islamic cultures without enjoying the full expanse of belief. Only nearing the end of our lessons did I recognize the irony of the year's project. Studying the Sheikh's faith had allowed me to practice mine. Our lessons were rites paying tribute to my belief that to be fully human is to try to understand others. Had he been entirely convinced of my worldview, or me of his, we would have risked destroying the fragile ecosystem of our friendship, made richer and stranger by our differences. For if understanding difference is among my own key values, it is also a Quranic one. Only through diversity, says the Quran, can you truly learn the shape and heft of your own humanity:

> O humankind, We created you from a male and a female,
> and We made you races and tribes
> for you to get to know each other. (49:13)

And also to know ourselves. Without a year trying to see the world from Akram's vantage, I wouldn't be able to make out the contours of my own.

AUTHOR'S NOTE

While the events in this book are true, I have occasionally compressed or rearranged them for thematic clarity and narrative flow.

Unless otherwise indicated in the text or notes, the quotations from the Quran used throughout are taken from *The Quran: A New Translation* by Thomas Cleary (Chicago: Starlatch, 2004).

GLOSSARY

adab: The Muslim cultural notion of good manners, morals, and humane behavior.

Alhamdulillah: Arabic for "Thanks and praise to God."

alim (fem. alima): Muslim religious scholar.

amir: Leader.

aya: Literally, a sign or message, evident in God's creation. A verse of the Quran.

biryani: South Asian rice dish.

chador: An enveloping cloak covering the head and body, worn by women in Iran.

dawa: Calling people to Islam.

fatwa: A nonbinding legal opinion issued by a religious scholar.

faqih: An Islamic jurist.

fiqh: The body of laws founded on human reasoning. Man-made, and thus subject to change, it is not to be confused with **sharia**, or the unchanging, divine revelation derived from the Quran.

hadith: Words or deeds of the Prophet Muhammad. After the Quran, the second source of knowledge for Muslims on their faith.

hafiz: Someone who has memorized the entire Quran.

hajj: Pilgrimage to Mecca, required by every Muslim with the physical and financial means to undertake it.

halal: Goods or deeds that are permissible in Islamic law.

hanif: A name for pre-Islamic monotheists in Arabia who, while not embracing Christianity or Judaism, nonetheless rejected pagan idol worship.

haram: Goods or deeds that are forbidden by Islamic law.

hijab: The Muslim term for dressing modestly; also, the scarf used to cover a woman's hair.

hijra: The emigration of Muhammad and his companions in AD 622 from Mecca to Medina, the event that marked the start of the Islamic calendar.

hikma: Wisdom.

ibada: Worship.

ihram: Sacred state of purity the pilgrim adopts during a pilgrimage to Mecca.

ilm: Knowledge.

ijaza: Certificate of learning.

imaan: Belief.

inshallah: God willing, a term employed by Muslims when referring to a future event.

isnad: Chain of narrators used to show the validity of a hadith.

itikaf: A spiritual retreat held in a mosque, usually during the final ten days of the holy month of **Ramadan**.

jahiliyya: Pre-Islamic Arabia; term used by Islamists to connote un-Islamic behavior.

jihad: A struggle, either armed, or for personal improvement.

jilbab: Loose, long garment designed to cover the outline of a woman's body.

jinn: Creatures created from smoke by God; source of the English word "genie."

Kaaba: The black cube located in Mecca, housing idols in pre-Islamic Arabia and the House of God with the advent of Islam.

kafir: Unbeliever.

karakul: A type of sheep wool and pelt, as well as the hats made of it, commonly worn by men in Central and South Asia.

khutbah: Sermon delivered by a mosque imam.

madrasa: Islamic religious seminary.

mahram: A man whom a woman may never marry because of familial bonds, such as a father, brother, uncle, or son. Under the Saudi guardianship system, Saudi women are required to obtain permission from a *mahram* to travel or study; foreign women pilgrims require a *mahram* to accompany them on **hajj** or **umra**.

Maulana: An honorific, particularly prevalent in South Asia, for a Muslim scholar or learned man.

masjid: Mosque.

mehr: Money or goods given to a bride by the groom or his family at the time of marriage.

mufti: A scholar trained in Islamic law, qualified to give fatwas, or nonbinding religious opinions.

mujahidin: Those who undertake **jihad**.

mullah: a learned Muslim, educated in religious studies.

niqab: A veil covering a woman's entire face, showing only the eyes.

qibla: Direction of the **Kaaba**, and thus of a Muslim's prayer.

qiwamah: Protection and maintenance afforded a wife by a husband.

Ramadan: The ninth month of the Islamic calendar, during which the Quran was first revealed to the Prophet Muhammad. Muslims fast from dawn to dusk during this month.

sabr: Patience, endurance.

shahada: Profession of the Islamic faith, in which one testifies that "There is no god but God, and Muhammad is His Prophet."

shalwar kameez: Long tunic and baggy pants worn by women in South and Central Asia.

sharia: Literally, "the Path to the Water"; the divine way, or moral and ethical values, handed down in the Quran and **hadith**.

shehrwani: Long, formal coat worn by South Asian men.

Sheikh: Literally "Elderly Man," the honorific accorded a religious scholar, or a tribal or local leader.

shirk: Associating partners with God; Islam's gravest sin.

sira: Traditional biographies of the Prophet Muhammad.

sunna: The guiding example of the Prophet Muhammad, in his statements, actions, and beliefs.

sura: A Quranic chapter.

tafsir: Commentary, exegesis on the Quran.

taqwa: God-consciousness.

tawaf: The ritual in which **hajj** or **umra** pilgrims walk around the **Kaaba** seven times.

thobe: Long robe worn by men in the Arab Gulf.

ulama: Islamic scholars (plural of **alim**).

umma: The worldwide Muslim community.

umra: The minor pilgrimage to Mecca, with fewer rituals than the **hajj.**

wudu: Ritual ablution before Muslim prayers.

Zamzam: The well near the **Kaaba** in Mecca.

zenankhaneh: Women's quarters of a house.

zina: Adultery.

NOTES

INTRODUCTION: A MAP FOR THE JOURNEY

3   *And when the University of North Carolina*: "The 2002 UNC Summer Reading Program of the Qur'an: A National Controversy," accessed April 28, 2014, www.unc.edu/~cernst/quran.htm.

3   *the planet's fastest-growing religion*: "Muslims" in "The Global Religious Landscape: A Report on the Size and Distribution of the World's Major Religious Groups as of 2010," December 2012, Pew Forum on Religion and Public Life, accessed March 19, 2014, www.pewforum.org/2012/12/18/global-religious-landscape-muslim/.

4   *(Chapter 18: Verse 109)*: Henceforward in this book, Quranic citations longer than two lines will be shown as Chapter Number: Verse Number, within the text.

6   *"You're either with us"*: "Bush Says It Is Time for Action," CNN.com, November 6, 2001, accessed March 20, 2014, http://edition.cnn.com/2001/US/11/06/ret.bush.coalition/index.html.

10   *"On reciting it"*: Mohammad Akram Nadwi, *Madrasah Life: A Student's Day at Nadwat al-Ulama* (London: Turath Publishing, 2007), p. 13.

19   *"as toilsome reading"*: Thomas Carlyle, *On Heroes, Hero Worship and the Heroic in History*, edited by Carl Niemeyer (Lincoln: University of Nebraska Press, 1966), p. 64.

20   *"Nothing but a sense of duty"*: Ibid., p. 65.

1: THE QURAN IN TWENTY-FIVE WORDS

28   *"I've tried to worship Allah in every way"*: Carla Power, "A Secret History," *New York Times Magazine*, February 25, 2007, accessed April 13, 2014, www.nytimes.com/2007/02/25/magazine/25wwinEssay.t.html?_r=0.

29   *"equals two-thirds of religion"*: I. Goldziher, "Adab," *Encyclopaedia of Islam, First Edition (1913–36)*, edited by M. T. Houtsma, T. W. Arnold, R. Basset, and R. Hartmann, Brill Online, 2014, accessed March 27, 2014, http://referenceworks.brillonline.com/entries/encyclopaedia-of-islam-1 /adab-SIM_0300.

30   Some Muslims carve it: Mahmoud M. Ayoub, *The Qur'an and Its Interpreters*, vol. 1 (Albany: SUNY Press, 1984), p. 44.

30   *"a source of healing for every ailment except death"*: Ibid., p. 45

30   *"In the Name of God"*: In Arabic, "Al-Fatiha" has either twenty-five or twenty-nine words, depending on whether one counts the Bismillah, that is, the phrase "In the name of God, the Merciful, the Compassionate," which appears at the beginning of every sura except the ninth. English translations make it considerably longer.

31   *In a God-centered universe*: The Islamic feminist scholar Amina Wadud writes of the flattening of earthly gender hierarchies due to God's wholeness, singularity, and indivisibility. See Amina Wadud, *Inside the Gender Jihad: Women's Reform in Islam* (Oxford: Oneworld Publication, 2006), pp. 24–32.

33   *"some people have said"*: For a brief discussion of those who have commented on the last line of "Al-Fatiha," see, for example, Ayoub, *The Qur'an and Its Interpreters*, vol. 1, p. 49.

33   *"I'm not a Jew"*: "Jonathan Miller" in *The Yale Book of Quotations*, edited by Fred R. Shapiro (New Haven: Yale University Press, 2006), p. 518.

35   *"Those who believe"*: Fazlur Rahman, *Major Themes of the Qur'an* (Chicago: University of Chicago Press, 1980), p. 166.

2: AN AMERICAN IN THE EAST

38   *I daydreamed of a stall*: Carla Power, "An American Childhood in Afghanistan," *Vogue*, December 2001, p. 86.

41   *Château Lafite*: James A. Bill, *The Eagle and the Lion: The Tragedy of American-Iranian Relations* (New Haven: Yale University Press, 1988), pp. 182–83.

41   *diamond-studded collar*: Charlotte Curtis, "Neighbors Go Visiting in Iran's Tents," *New York Times*, October 16, 1971.

41   *"A West-stricken man"*: Jalal Al-e Ahmad, *Plagued by the West (Gharbzadegi)*, translated by Paul Sprachman (Delmor, NY: Columbia University Center for Iranian Studies, 1982), p. 67.

41   *the fifty-thousand-strong force of Americans*: Bill, *Eagle and the Lion*, p. 381.

42   *"If someone runs over a dog"*: Mojtaba Mahdavi, "Ayatollah Khomeini,"

in *The Oxford Handbook of Islam and Politics*, edited by John L. Esposito and Emad El-Din Shahin (New York: Oxford University Press, 2013), p. 183.

43   *The Soviets built Kabul's airport*: Edward Giradet, *Afghanistan: The Soviet War* (New York: Routledge, 2011), p. 94.

44   *"They cannot represent themselves"*: Edward W. Said, *Orientalism: Western Conceptions of the Orient* (Penguin Books, 1978), epigraph.

45   *"An amazing place"*: Carla Power, "City of Secrets," *Newsweek International*, July 13, 1998, p. 14.

45   *"Dear sister"*: Power, "City of Secrets," p. 13.

3: A MUSLIM IN THE WEST

49   *They burned books*: Malise Ruthven, *A Satanic Affair: Salman Rushdie and the Rage of Islam* (London: Chatto and Windus, 1990), p. 2.

50   *"Dr. Akram Nadwi's disastrous mistake!"*: MyBeliefs.co.uk, accessed March 20, 2014, http://mybeliefs.co.uk/2012/04/26/dr-akram-nadwis-disastrous -mistake/.

50   *"Akram Nadwi's Strange Views"*: Akram Nadwi's Strange Views, akram-nadwi.wordpress.com/2012/09/18/akram-nadwis-strange-views-on-seggregation/[sic].

51   *"Don't Fear All Islamists"*: Robin Wright, "Don't Fear All Islamists, Fear Salafis," *New York Times*, August 19, 2012, accessed April 13, 2014, www .nytimes.com/2012/08/20/opinion/don't-fear-all-islamists-fear-salafis .html?_r=0.

51   *No woman, they claimed*: See, for example, "Rejected 'Modernism': Women Speakers Addressing Mixed Gatherings," accessed March 20, 2014, www .central-mosque.com/index.php/Civil/free-mixing.html.

55   *"Never once . . . did I receive a revelation"*: quoted in Karen Armstrong, *Muhammad: A Biography of the Prophet* (San Francisco: HarperSanFrancisco, 1992), p. 89.

56   *all people are "as the teeth on a comb"*: John L. Esposito and Dalia Mogahed, *Who Speaks for Islam? What a Billion Muslims Really Think* (New York: Gallup Press, 2007) p. 11.

57   *"To the Jew who follows us"*: Ibn Ishaq, *The Life of Muhammad*, translated by Alfred Guillaume (Oxford: Oxford University Press, 1955), p. 232.

57   *Shariati, preaching against the Shah's regime*: See, for example, Shariati's lecture "Approaches to the Understanding of Islam" in *On the Sociology of Islam: Lectures by Ali Shariati*, translated by Hamid Algar (Oneonta: Mizan Press, 1979), p. 3.

58   *Non-Muslims have handpicked*: Armstrong, *Muhammad*, pp. 29–38.

58   *George Sale, who produced the first English translation*: Ibid., p. 37.

59   *"The Prophet once prayed a funeral salah"*: Shaykh Mohammad Akram Nadwi, *Rites of Purification, Prayers and Funerals*, vol. 1 of *Al-Fiqh Al-*

Islami According to the Hanafi Madhhab (London: Angelwing Media, 2007), p. 289.

63   *"We sense very little of his own thoughts"*: Jonathan A. C. Brown, *Muhammad: A Very Short Introduction* (Oxford: Oxford University Press, 2011), pp. 99–100.

71   *"food for no thought"*: Fay Weldon, *Sacred Cows* (London: Chatto & Windus, 1989), p. 6.

4: ROAD TRIP TO THE INDIAN MADRASA

78   *bristling with Post-it notes*: Carla Power, "The Muslim Moderator," *Newsweek International*, August 19, 2002, p. 57.

80   *Even not having a* jilbab: Mohammad Akram Nadwi, *al-Muhaddithat: The Women Scholars in Islam* (Oxford: Interface Publications, 2013), p. 40.

82   *"they hate our freedoms"*: "Text: President Bush Addresses the Nation," *Washington Post*, September 20, 2001, accessed March 20, 2014, http://www.washingtonpost.com/wp-srv/nation/specials/attacked/transcripts/bush address_092001.html.

93   *The men who founded Nadwah*: Muhammad Qasim Zaman, *The Ulama in Contemporary Islam: Custodians of Change* (Princeton: Princeton University Press, 2002), p. 69.

94   *Akram and his friends begged*: Nadwi, *Madrasah Life*, p. 95.

5: A MIGRANT'S PRAYER MAT

98   *"To behave differently"*: Muhammad Akram Nadwi, "Manners in Islam," notes from a lecture, unpublished.

106 *the dislocations of the migrant experience*: See, for example, the explanation of radicalization in Olivier Roy's *Globalised Islam: The Search for a New Ummah* (London: Hurst, 2004), pp. 308–19.

6: PIONEER LIFE IN OXFORD

114 *"The best means of destroying"*: Asfaneh Najmabadi, "Feminism in an Islamic Republic: 'Years of Hardship, Years of Growth,'" in *Islam, Gender and Social Change*, edited by Yvonne Yazbeck Haddad and John L. Esposito (New York: Oxford University Press, 1998), p. 60.

115 *Satan only wants to sow hostility*: Thomas Cleary, *The Quran: A New Translation* (Chicago: Starlatch, 2004), 5:91.

115 *"Don't swagger around on earth"*: Cleary, *Quran*, 31:18.

117 *"If there was chicken"*: Virginia Woolf, "Professions for Women," in *The Death of the Moth and Other Essays* (Middlesex: Penguin Books, 1961), p. 202.

121 *"Why did you not treat them equally?"*: Nadwi, *al-Muhaddithat*, p. 37.

7: NINE THOUSAND HIDDEN WOMEN

128 *"For what?"*: Power, "City of Secrets," p. 11.

129 *A couple of historiographers*: Before Akram, at least two Islamic historiographers had written about a few women hadith experts. A century ago,
the famous German orientalist Ignaz Goldziher estimated that about 15
percent of medieval Muslim scholars were women. In 1994, Ruth Roded,
a scholar at the Hebrew University of Jerusalem, published a book on
women in Islamic biography, *Women in Islamic Biographical Collections
From Ibn Sa'd to Who's Who*.

130 *"I do not know of another religious tradition"*: Nadwi, *al-Muhaddithat*, p. 16.

130 *In medieval Mauritania*: Power, "Secret History."

130 *"This is not from you"*: Nadwi, *al-Muhaddithat*, p. 144.

131 *The life of a prominent eleventh-century hadith scholar*: Ibid., pp. 57, 75,
112, 169, 201.

134 *"Our traditions have grown weak"*: Power, "Secret History."

135 *"I tell people, 'God has given girls'"*: Ibid.

137 *"Gray said that the villagers"*: Ibid.

8: "THE LITTLE ROSY ONE"

138 *"He did not marry any other virgin"*: Muhammad Ibn Sa'd, *The Women of
Madina*, translated by Aisha Bewley (London: Ta-Ha Publishers, 1995),
p. 46.

139 *"I like you because of our relationship"*: Armstrong, *Muhammad*, p. 80.

139 *"I insulted her father"*: Ibn Sa'd, *Women*, p. 56.

139 *"Take half your religion from Humayra"*: Ibid., p. 69.

140 *"How many of the world's major living religions"*: Leila Ahmed, *Women in
Gender in Islam: Historical Roots of a Modern Debate* (New Haven: Yale
University Press, 1992), p. 73.

140 *"The Messenger of Allah married me"*: Ibn Sa'd, *Women*, p. 43.

140 *"I was playing on a seesaw"*: Ibid., p. 44.

140 *"Marry her"*: Ibid., p. 46.

140 *"like a firm knot in a rope"*: Asma Afsaruddin, *The First Muslims: History
and Memory* (Oxford: Oneworld Publications, 2008), p. 66.

141 *"a dog, a donkey, and a woman"*: Hadith no. 493 in "Chapter no. 9, Book of
Virtues of the Prayer Hall," last modified March 28, 2014, www.ahadith
.co.uk/chapter.php?cid=33&page=3, accessed March 28, 2014.

141 *"By Allah! I saw the Prophet praying"*: Leila Ahmed, "Women and the Rise
of Islam," in *The New Voices of Islam: Reforming Politics and Modernity: A
Reader*, edited by Mehran Kamrava (London: I. B. Tauris, 2006), p. 183.

145 *"dropping from his body like pearls"*: Nadwi, *al-Muhaddithat*, p. 195.

148 *One Jewish tradition*: Tamar Kadari, "Rebekah: Midrash and Aggadah," in
Jewish Women: A Comprehensive Historical Encyclopedia, edited by Paula

E. Hyman (Jerusalem: Shalvi Publishing, 2006), accessed online March 28, 2014: http://jwa.org/encyclopedia/article/rebekah-midrash-and-aggadah.

148   *scholars estimate Mary gave birth*: "Mary," last modified August 2, 2011, accessed April 1, 2014, http:www.bbc.co.uk/religions.

151   *the memory of Nujood*: Carla Power, "Nujood Ali and Shada Nasser: The Voices for Children," *Glamour*, November 13, 2008, accessed April 26, 2014, www.glamour.com/inspired/women-of-the-year/2008/nujood-ali -and-shada-nasser.

9: VEILING AND UNVEILING

159   *innuendo-laced banter*: Armstrong, *Muhammad*, p. 197.

159   *"one eye or both eyes"*: Muhsin Khan, trans., Quran, chapter 24, "surat l-nur (The Light)," on corpus.quran.com/translation.jsp?chapter=24& verse=31, accessed April 28, 2014.

160   *"veiling, like seclusion"*: Ahmed, "Women and the Rise of Islam," p. 191.

160   *"If you think the difference"*: Wadud, *Inside the Gender Jihad*, p. 219.

162   *"All the problems Muslims have faced"*: Fatima Mernissi, *Beyond the Veil: Male-Female Dynamics in Muslim Society*, rev. ed. (London: Al Saqi Books, 1985), xvii.

162   *"The Arabs elude us"*: Joan Wallach Scott, *The Politics of the Veil* (Princeton: Princeton University Press, 2007), p. 55.

163   *"Baby steps!"*: Carla Power, "Taking Baby Steps, for Safety's Sake," *Newsweek International*, December 28, 1998, p. 16.

165   *"You Westerners make love in public"*: Carla Power, "Indecent Exposure," *Time*, November 8, 2007, accessed April 26, 2014, content.time.com/time/ magazine/article/0,9171,1682277,00.html.

168   *"Your women are a field of yours"*: Cleary, *Quran*, 2:223.

168   *"Your wives are a tilth for you"*: Cleary, *Quran*, 2:223 (Medina: Ministry of Hajj and Endowments, Kingdom of Saudi Arabia, 1989).

168   *"A man's sexual play"*: Scott Siraj al-Haqq Kugle, "Sexuality, Diversity and Ethics," in *Progressive Muslims: On Justice, Gender and Pluralism*, edited by Omid Safi (Oxford: Oneworld Publications, 2003), p. 193.

168   *"In the Christian context"*: Tom Peck, "Timothy Winter: Britain's Most Influential Muslim—And It Was All Down to a Peach," *Independent*, August 20, 2010, accessed April 29, 2014, www.independent.co.uk/news /people/profiles/timothy-winter-britains-most-influential-muslim—and -it-was-all-down-to-a-peach-2057400.html.

169   *When Muhammad was unsure*: Omid Safi, *Memories of Muhammad: Why the Prophet Matters* (HarperCollins e-books, 2009), p. 107.

171   *"I used to scratch the sperm"*: cited in notes to lecture "What Every Muslim Woman Should Know" by Mohammad Akram Nadwi, at Discover Islam UK, Parsons Green, London, March 9, 2013.

172   *"a system for dominating"*: Said, *Orientalism*, rev. ed. (London: Penguin Books, 1995), p. 3.

174   *persecution of Nigeria's* yan daudu: Monica Mark, "Nigeria's Yan Daudu Face Persecution in Religious Revival," *Guardian*, June 11, 2013, p. 21.

10: READING "THE WOMEN"

175   *"DNA of patriarchy"*: "Decoding the 'DNA of Patriarchy' in Muslim Family Laws," Musawah, accessed March 28, 2014, http://www.musawah.org /decoding-dna-patriarchy-muslim-family-laws.

175   *"Men are in charge of women"*: Muhammad Marmaduke Pickthall, trans., *The Meaning of the Glorious Quran* (Dublin: Mentor Books), 4:34.

176   *"turn away from"*: Aslan, *No god but God*, p. 70.

178   *"to go about the business of life"*: Virginia Woolf, *A Room of One's Own* (New York: Harcourt Brace Jovanovich, 1929), p. 112.

181   *"Their very being and legal existence"*: William Blackstone, *Commentaries on the Laws of England*, book 1, chapter 15 (London: 1765), accessed April 29, 2014, www.ebooks.adelaide.edu.au/b/blackstone/william/comment /book1.15.html.

181   *Early Islamic histories report*: Aslan, *No god but God*, p. 62.

181   *"Those who disobey God"*: Cleary, *Quran*, 4:14.

183   *"Now if she had gone into business"*: Woolf, *Room*, p. 21.

183   *"for partridges and wine"*: Ibid, p. 23.

184   *"would necessitate the suppression of families"*: Ibid., p. 22.

186   *"peripheral Jews"*: Rachel Adler, "The Jew Who Wasn't There," in *On Being a Jewish Feminist: A Reader*, edited by Susanne Heschel (New York: Schocken Books, 1983), p. 13.

187   *"They feel trapped in the lives they are leading"*: Nadwi, printed notes for lecture "Jinn—What Is Their Benefit to Humans?" February 23, 2013.

192   *"Among His signs"*: Wadud, *Gender Jihad*, p. 161; also Cleary, *Quran*, 30:21.

193   *"dominion over the vagina"*: Ziba Mir-Hosseini, "Towards Gender Equality: Muslim Family Laws and the Shari'ah," in *Wanted: Equality and Justice in the Muslim Family* (Kuala Lumpur: Sisters in Islam, 2009), p. 29.

193   *"They are a garment for you"*: Cleary, *Quran*, 2:187.

11: A PILGRIM'S PROGRESS

199   *"If someone annoys you"*: Al-Salam Institute Umrah 2013 Course Handbook; unpublished document, al-Salam Institute, 2014.

202   *with a skinful of water*: Malise Ruthven, *Islam in the World* (London: Granta Books, 2006), p. 14.

206   *"Those who lower their voices"*: Cleary, *Quran*, 49:3.

206   *the house of Muhammad's beloved Khadija*: Jerome Taylor, "Mecca for the Rich: Islam's Holiest Site 'Turning into Vegas,'" *Independent*, September

24, 2011, accessed April 12, 2014, www.independent.co.uk/news/world/middle-east/mecca-for-the-rich-islams-holiest-site-turning-into-vegas-2360114.html.

12: JESUS, MARY, AND THE QURAN

215   *probably had a better grounding in Bible stories*: Ingrid Mattson, *The Story of the Quran: Its History and Place in Muslim Life* (Oxford: Blackwell, 2008), pp. 192–93.

215   *Mecca was a multifaith city*: Aslan, *No god but God*, p. 17.

216   *"They don't belong to the same community"*: For a thoughtful exploration of the potential pitfalls and possibilities of discussions between the major faiths, see Amy-Jill Levine, *The Misunderstood Jew: The Church and the Scandal of the Jewish Jesus* (New York: HarperCollins, 2006). Though the book focuses on Christianity's discussions of Judaism, its broad themes are trenchant for discussions on Islam's relationship to earlier monotheisms.

216   *"Abraham was not Jewish or Christian"*: Cleary, *Quran*, 3:67.

219   *"And shake the trunk"*: Cleary, *Quran*, 19:25-6

220   *They did not crucify him*: Cleary, *Quran*, 4:157.

221   *"whose every stride carried it"*: Martin Lings, *Muhammad: His Life Based on the Earliest Sources* (Cambridge: Islamic Texts Society, 1991), p. 101.

221   *"When I told him fifty"*: Ibn Ishaq, *The Life of Muhammad*, p. 252.

224   *"no one group"*: Safi, *Memories of Muhammad*, p. 200.

226   *"spiritual cousins"*: Aslan, *No god but God*, p. 100.

13: BEYOND POLITICS

230   *"In the Quranic worldview"*: Safi, *Memories of Muhammad*, p. 200.

230   *bin Laden's 1996 declaration of jihad*: www.pbs.org/newshour/updates/military-july-dec96-fatwa-1996/, accessed April 12, 2014; also Cleary, *Quran*, 3:102.

233   *"Spread peace, feed the hungry"*: Tariq Ramadan, *In the Footsteps of the Prophet: Lessons from the Life of Muhammad* (Oxford: Oxford University Press, 2007), p. 87.

233   *"He who wrongs a Jew or a Christian"*: Aslan, *No god but God*, p. 94.

234   *"of a proud new Muslim identity"*: Armstrong, *Muhammad*, p. 163.

235   *"the politically incorrect truth"*: "Befriending Christians and Jews," The Religion of Peace, accessed April 12, 2014, www.thereligionofpeace.com/Quran/009-friends-with-christians-jews.htm.

236   *"Allah has forbidden the believers"*: "Islam Question and Answer; General Supervisor: Shaykh Muhammad Saalih al-Munajjid," accessed April 12, 2014, http://islamqa.info/en/59879.

237   *"delinked"*: See Roy, *Globalised Islam*, pp. 148–201.

14: THE PHARAOH AND HIS WIFE

242 *the famous footage of a twelve-year-old*: The footage of Muhammed al-Durrah remains controversial. In 2013, the Israeli government published the findings of an investigation into the footage, declaring, "There is no evidence that the [Israeli Defense Forces] were in any way responsible for causing any of the alleged injuries to Jamal or the boy."

242 *"A just leader"*: cited in "A Collection of Hadith on Non-Violence, Peace and Mercy," accessed April 28, 2014, www.sufism.org/foundations/hadith/peacehadith-2.

245 *shaving one another's heads*: Lings, *Muhammad*, p. 254.

251 *Across the rail tracks*: Lawrence Wright, "The Man Behind Bin Laden," *New Yorker*, September 16, 2002, accessed April 12, 2014, www.newyorker.com/archive/2002/09/16/020916fa_fact2.

252 *For Egyptian Islamists*: Gilles Kepel, *Muslim Extremism in Egypt: The Prophet and Pharaoh* (Berkeley: University of California Press, 1985), p. 50.

252 *"build me a house in Your presence"*: Cleary, *Quran*, 66:11.

253 *"vanguard"*: Kepel, *Prophet and Pharaoh*, p. 12.

253 *Qutb's concept of the vanguard*: Malise Ruthven, *A Fury for God: The Islamist Attack on America* (London: Granta Books, 2002), p. 91.

254 *"beautiful, tall, semi-naked"*: John Calvert, " 'The World Is an Undutiful Boy!': Sayyid Qutb's American Experience," *Islam and Christian-Muslim Relations*, vol. 11, no. 1, pp. 87–103.

256 *"the first written constitution"*: www.constitutionofmadina.com, accessed April 28, 2014.

15: WAR STORIES

261 *The events unfolding after that first coup*: See, for example, Jonathan Steele, *Ghosts of Afghanistan: The Haunted Battleground* (London: Portobello Books, 2011).

262 *"A brilliant strategist"*: Carla Power, "In the Realm of the Angels," *Newsweek International*, February 18, 2001, accessed April 13, 2014, www.newsweek.com/realm-angels-155563.

262 *"Believers fight for the sake of God"*: Cleary, *Quran*, 4:76.

265 *Court scholars during the Muslim Empires*: John L. Esposito, *The Future of Islam* (New York: Oxford University Press, 2010), p. 49.

266 *"shibboleth, the battle cry"*: Bruce Lawrence, *The Qur'an: A Biography* (Atlantic Books, 2006), p. 181.

266 *An influential study*: Marc Sageman, "The Normality of Global Jihadi Terrorism," *Journal of International Security Affairs*, Spring 2005: 8, accessed April 13, 2014, www.securityaffairs.org/issues/2005/08/sageman.php.

267 *"defeated people"*: Sayyid Qutb, *Milestones*, accessed April 12, 2014, majalla.org/books/2005/qutb-nilestone[*sic*].pdf, p. 48.

267   *"today, information is available"*: "Questions & Answers with Shayk Abu
      Hamza," posted March 8, 2002 (7:16 a.m.), www.angelfire.com/bc3/john
      sonuk/eng/abu_hamza.html.

269   *"You want to be a real man"*: Carla Power, Christopher Dickey, et al.,
      "Generation M," *Newsweek* (Atlantic edition), December 1, 2003, accessed
      April 12, 2014, www.highbeam.com/doc/1G1-110537991.html.

270   ilm, *or knowledge*: Akbar S. Ahmed, *Discovering Islam: Making Sense of
      Muslim History and Society* (Routledge and Kegan Paul, 1988), p. 16.

270   *"September 11 put me on a heightened state of alert"*: Carla Power and
      Christopher Dickey, "Muhammad Atta's Neighborhood," *Newsweek*,
      December 16, 2002, p. 45.

16: THE LAST LESSON

277   *"Who would wait for me"*: Allama Muhammad Iqbal, 1914, www.poemhunter
      .com/allama-muhammad-iqbal/biography/, accessed April 11, 2014.

278   *"the wooden ritual of those"*: Muhammad Asad, *The Road to Mecca* (New
      York: Simon and Schuster, 1954), p. 55.

278   *During World War II*: Asad himself told the anecdote to the Islamic
      Information Service in an interview, "God Man Relationship—Part 2,"
      available on YouTube.

279   *son Talal was growing up*: Talal Asad, "Muhammad Asad Between
      Religion and Politics," accessed April 12, 2014, www.interactive.net.in
      /content/muhammad-asad-between-religion-and-politics.

280   *"like the prospect of venturing out onto a bridge"*: Asad, *Road to Mecca*,
      p. 308.

280   *"without any faith in binding truths"*: Ibid., p. 309.

CONCLUSION: EVERLASTING RETURN

290   *Born a Christian*: "Part of an Interview with Abdalhaqq Bewley," accessed
      April 10, 2014, bewley.virtualave.net/interview2.html.

293   *Scientists who have studied the postures*: Shabbir Ahmed Sayeed and Anand
      Prakash, "The Islamic Prayer (Salah/Namaaz) and Yoga Togetherness in
      Mental Health," *Indian Journal of Psychiatry*, January 2013, 55 (Suppl. 2),
      accessed April 10, 2014, www.ncbi.nlm.nih.gov/pmc/articles/PMC3705686/.

294   *"translated men"*: Salman Rushdie, "Imaginary Homelands," in *Imagi-
      nary Homelands: Essays and Criticism 1981–1991* (London: Penguin Books,
      1992), p. 17.

294   *The powerful Ottoman Empire*: Mustafa Akyol, *Islam Without Extremes:
      A Muslim Case for Liberty* (New York: W. W. Norton, 2011), pp. 139–41.

295   *a 2011 Pew survey*: "Muslim Americans: No Signs of Growth in Alienation
      or Support for Extremism" (Pew Research Center, August 2011), accessed

April 28, 2014, www.people-press.org/2011/08/30/muslim-americans-no
-signs-of-growth-in-alienation-or-support-for-extremism/.

295 *"pluralism, individual autonomy"*: A. C. Grayling, *Ideas That Matter: A Personal Guide for the 21st Century* (London: Weidenfeld and Nicolson, 2009), p. 164.

298 *"the one place in any society"*: Salman Rushdie, "Is Nothing Sacred?" in *Imaginary Homelands*, p. 429.

BIBLIOGRAPHY

Abdul Kodir, Faqihuddin. *Hadith and Gender Justice: Understanding the Prophetic Traditions*. Cirebon: Fahmina Institute, 2007.

Adler, Rachel. "The Jew Who Wasn't There: Halakhah and the Jewish Woman." In *On Being a Jewish Feminist: A Reader*. Edited by Susannah Heschel. New York: Schocken Books, 1983.

Afsaruddin, Asma. *The First Muslims: History and Memory*. Oxford: Oneworld, 2008.

Akyol, Mustafa. *Islam Without Extremes: A Muslim Case for Liberty*. New York: W. W. Norton, 2011.

Ahmed, Akbar S. *Discovering Islam: Making Sense of Muslim History and Society*. London: Routledge and Kegan Paul, 1988.

Ahmed, Leila. "Women and the Rise of Islam." In *The New Voices of Islam: Reforming Politics and Modernity—A Reader*. Edited by Mehran Kamrava. London: I. B. Tauris, 2009.

———. *Women and Gender in Islam: Historical Roots of a Modern Debate*. New Haven: Yale University Press, 1992.

Al-e Ahmad, Jalal. *Plagued by the West (Gharbzadegi)*. Translated by Paul Sprachman. Delmor, NY: Columbia University Center for Iranian Studies, 1982.

Armstrong, Karen. *Muhammad: A Biography of the Prophet*. San Francisco: HarperSanFrancisco, 1992.

Asad, Muhammd. *The Road to Mecca*. New York: Simon and Schuster, 1954.

Aslan, Reza. *No god but God: The Origins, Evolution, and Future of Islam*. London: Arrow Books, 2006.

Ayoub, Mahmoud. *The Qur'an and Its Interpreters*. Vol. 1. Albany: SUNY Press, 1984.

Brown, Jonathan A. C. *Muhammad: A Very Short Introduction*. Oxford: Oxford University Press, 2011.

Calvert, John. "'The World Is an Undutiful Boy!': Sayyid Qutb's American Experience." In *Islam and Christian-Muslim Relations*. Vol. 11, Issue 1, 2000.

Carlyle, Thomas. *On Heroes, Hero Worship and the Heroic in History*, ed. by Carl Niemeyer. Lincoln: University of Nebraska Press, 1966.

Cleary, Thomas. *The Quran: A New Translation*. Chicago: Starlatch, 2004.

Cook, Michael. *Muhammad*. Oxford: Oxford University Press, 1983.

Cooke, Miriam, and Bruce B. Lawrence. *Introduction to Muslim Networks from Hajj to Hip Hop*. Chapel Hill: University of North Carolina Press, 2005.

Esack, Farid. *The Qur'an: A User's Guide*. Oxford: Oneworld, 2005.

Esposito, John L. *The Future of Islam*. Oxford: Oxford University Press, 2010.

———, and Dalia Mogahed, *Who Speaks for Islam?: What a Billion Muslims Really Think*. New York: Gallup Press, 2007.

Giradet, Edward. *Afghanistan: The Soviet War*. New York: Routledge, 2011.

Grayling, A. C. *Ideas That Matter: A Personal Guide for the 21st Century*. London: Weidenfeld and Nicolson, 2009.

Haddad, Yvonne Yazbeck, and John L. Esposito, eds. *Islam, Gender and Social Change*. Oxford: Oxford University Press, 1998.

Heschel, Susanne, ed. *On Being a Jewish Feminist: A Reader*. New York: Schocken Books, 1983.

Husein Muhammad, Faqihuddin Abdul Kodir, Lies Marcoes Natsir, and Marzuki Wahid. *Dawrah Fiqh Concerning Women: Manual for a Course on Islam and Gender*. Cirebon: Fahmina Institute, 2007.

Hyman, Paula E., ed. *Jewish Women: A Comprehensive Historical Encyclopedia*. Jerusalem: Shalvi, 2006.

Ibn Ishaq. *The Life of Muhammad*. Translated by Alfred Guillaume. Oxford: Oxford University Press, 1955.

Ibn Sa'd, Muhammad. *The Women of Madina*. Translated by Aisha Bewley. London: Ta-Ha, 1995.

Kamali, Mohammad Hashim. *Freedom, Equality and Justice in Islam*. Kuala Lumpur: Ilmiah, 2002.

Kamrava, Mehran, ed. *The New Voices of Islam: Reforming Politics and Modernity—A Reader*. London: I. B. Tauris, 2009.

Keddie, Nikki R., with a section by Yann Richard. *Roots of Revolution: An Interpretive History of Modern Iran*. New Haven: Yale University Press, 1981.

Kepel, Gilles. *Muslim Extremism in Egypt: The Prophet and Pharaoh*. London: Al Saqi, 1985.

Kugle, Scott Siraj al-Haqq. "Sexuality, Diversity and Ethics in the Agenda of Progressive Muslims." In *Progressive Muslims: On Justice, Gender and Pluralism*. Edited by Omid Safi. Oxford: Oneworld, 2003.

Lawrence, Bruce. *The Qur'an: A Biography*. London: Atlantic Books, 2006.

Levine, Amy-Jill. *The Misunderstood Jew: The Church and the Scandal of the Jewish Jesus*. San Francisco: HarperSanFrancisco, 2007.

Lings, Martin. *Muhammad: His Life Based on the Earliest Sources*. Cambridge: Islamic Texts Society, 1991.

Mattson, Ingrid. *The Story of the Qur'an: Its History and Place in Muslim Life*. Malden: Blackwell, 2008.

Mernissi, Fatima. *Beyond the Veil: Male-Female Dynamics in Muslim Society*. London: Al-Saqi Books, 1985.

Mortimer, Edward. *Faith and Power: The Politics of Islam*. London: Faber and Faber, 1982.

Nadwi, Mohammad Akram. *Al-Fiqh al-Islami According to the Hanafi Madhhab*. Vol 1: *Rites of Purification, Prayers and Funerals*. London: Angelwing Media, 2007.

———. *al-Muhaddithat: The Women Scholars in Islam*. London: Interface, 2007.

———. *Madrasah Life: A Student's Day at Nadwat al-Ulama*. London: Turath, 2007.

———. "Manners in Islam," unpublished.

———. *Shaykh Abu Al-Hasan Ali Nadwi: His Life and Works*. Batley, UK: Nadwi Foundation, 2013.

Najmabadi, Afsaneh. "Feminism in an Islamic Republic: Years of Hardship, Years of Growth." In *Islam, Gender, and Social Change*. Edited by Yvonne Yazbeck Haddad and John L. Esposito. New York: Oxford University Press, 1998.

Qutb, Sayyid. *Milestones*. Edited by A. B. al-Mehri. Birmingham: Maktabah Booksellers and Publishers, 2006.

Rahman, Fazlur. *Major Themes of the Qur'an*. Chicago: University of Chicago Press, 2009.

Ramadan, Tariq. *In the Footsteps of the Prophet: Lessons from the Life of Muhammad*. Oxford: Oxford University Press, 2007.

Roy, Olivier. *Globalised Islam: The Search for a New Ummah*. London: Hurst, 2004.

Rushdie, Salman. *Imaginary Homelands: Essays and Criticism 1981–1991*. London: Penguin Books, 1992.

Russell, Bertrand. *Why I Am Not a Christian and Other Essays on Religion and Related Subjects*. New York: George Allen and Unwin, 1957.

Ruthven, Malise. *A Fury for God: The Islamist Attack on America*. London: Granta Books, 2002.

———. *Islam in the World*. 3rd ed. London: Granta Books, 2006.

———. *A Satanic Affair: Salman Rushdie and the Rage of Islam*. London: Chatto and Windus, 1990.

Safi, Omid. *Memories of Muhammad: Why the Prophet Matters*. HarperCollins e-books, 2009.

———, ed. *Progressive Muslims: On Justice, Gender and Pluralism*. Oxford: Oneworld, 2003.

Said, Edward W. *Covering Islam: How the Media and the Experts Determine How We See the Rest of the World*. New York: Pantheon Books, 1981.

———. *Orientalism: Western Conceptions of the Orient*. London: Penguin Books, 1991.

Sardar, Ziauddin. *Reading the Qur'an*. London: Hurst, 2011.

Schimmel, Annemarie. *And Muhammad Is His Messenger: The Veneration of the Prophet in Islamic Piety*. Chapel Hill: University of North Carolina Press, 1985.

Scott, Joan Wallach. *The Politics of the Veil*. Princeton: Princeton University Press, 2007. ˈ

Shariati, Ali *On the Sociology of Islam: Lectures by Ali Shariati*. Translated by Hamid Algar. Oneonta: Mizan Press, 1979.

Siddiqui, Mona. *How to Read the Quran*. London: Granta Books, 2007.

Sisters in Islam. *Wanted: Equality and Justice in the Muslim Family*. Kuala Lumpur: Sisters in Islam, 2009.

Steele, Jonathan. *Ghosts of Afghanistan: The Haunted Battleground*. London: Portobello Books, 2011.

Wadud, Amina. *Inside the Gender Jihad: Women's Reform in Islam*. Oxford: Oneworld, 2006.

———. *Qur'an and Woman: Rereading the Sacred Text from a Woman's Perspective*. New York: Oxford University Press, 1999.

Weldon, Fay. *Sacred Cows*. London: Chatto and Windus, 1989.

Woolf, Virginia. *The Death of the Moth and Other Stories*. Middlesex: Penguin Books, 1961.

———. *A Room of One's Own*. New York: Harcourt Brace Jovanovich, 1929.

Zakaria, Rafiq. *Muhammad and the Quran*. London: Penguin Books, 1991.

Zaman, Muhammad Qasim. *The Ulama in Contemporary Islam: Custodians of Change*. Princeton: Princeton University Press, 2002.

ACKNOWLEDGMENTS

Sheikh Mohammad Akram Nadwi and his family were unstinting in their time, knowledge, and generosity of spirit. My thanks for the patience and graciousness you showed during the countless hours of interviews, visits, and other intrusions that this project required of you.

Arzoo Ahmed, Tara Bahrampour, Professor Bruce Lawrence, Mehrunisha Suleman, and Justine Thody gave thoughtful critiques on manuscript drafts. The Reverend Jane Eesley provided incisive context on Christianity's discussions of Judaism. Tom Gouttiere provided helpful insight into Kabul in the late 1970s. Selina Mills offered razor-sharp advice on structure. For their support and encouragement over the lifetime of this project, thanks to Nina Berman, Sarita Choudhury, Hanna Clements, Caroline Douglas-Pennant, Amy Dulin, Rana Foroohar, Jill Herzig, and Liz Unna. A special thanks to Anne Treeger for the painting *Jane Eyre in Oceans of Ink* and much besides.

I owe a debt of gratitude to Irene Skolnick for encouraging the ideas that would become this book and for introducing me to my agent, Erin Harris, a writer's fairy godmother.

At Henry Holt, Paul Golob provided wise counsel and eagle-eyed attention to detail, while my editor Emi Ikkanda's skill, sensitivity, and dedication singlehandedly restored my faith in the contemporary publishing process.

Finally, to Antony Seely and Julia and Nic Seely-Power, thanks beyond measure.

INDEX

menstruation, 172–73
Mernissi, Fatima, 162, 165
Mexico, 275–77
Middle Ages, 17, 43, 58, 130, 136, 160
migration, 43–44, 91, 105–8, 237–38,
    294
  of 1980s–90s, 44
Miller, Jonathan, 33
misogyny, 17, 56, 134–35, 141, 177,
    180
modernity, 245–46, 265, 267
monotheism, 31, 33, 140, 221, 227
Morocco, 9, 290
Morsi, Mohamed, 240–41
Moses, 214, 216, 221, 223, 252
mosques, 16, 48, 59, 75, 128, 129, 215,
    280
  first, 57
  itikaf, 210–13
  pilgrimage to Mecca, 197–210
  women praying in, 28–29, 79–80,
    130, 134, 187
Mubarak, Hosni, 241–42
Mughals, 73, 85, 234
Muhammad, Prophet, 3, 5, 16, 19, 49,
    53–61, 65–66, 72, 77, 79, 120,
    133, 206, 242
  biography, 221
  Christianity, Judaism, and, 214–28,
    229–39
  Companions of, 55–57, 59, 60, 61,
    72, 107, 109, 139, 152, 191, 232,
    244, 245, 256
  Danish cartoon controversy, 232
  death of, 57, 141
  dress of, 109
  grave of, 136, 206
  life of, 54–60
  revelations received by, 55–60, 139,
    145
  roles of, 57–60
  sex and, 167–69
  Treaty of Hudaybiyah, 243
  veiling and, 159–60

wives of, 60, 129, 138–55, 159–60,
    168–69, 173, 191–92
Munir, Lily, 168, 169
Mursi, Anhar Sayyad, 270–71
Musawah, 175, 193
Musharraf, Pervez, 262
Muslim Brotherhood, 107, 240–42,
    249
Muslims, 1–21
  anti-Western attitudes of, 26, 41,
    82–83, 92, 231–32, 235, 247–49,
    254–56
  apolitical, 245–47
  Bosnian war, 82
  British, 25, 48–50, 62, 72, 91,
    97–110, 113–27, 142, 161, 187,
    198, 210–13, 232, 235, 250,
    268–69, 294
  Christianity, Judaism, and, 214–28,
    229–39
  Companions, 55–57, 59, 60, 61, 72,
    107, 109, 139, 152, 191, 232, 244,
    245, 256
  death and, 272–89, 290
  discrimination against, 2–3, 25,
    29–30, 161, 231–32, 235–36
  extremism, 8, 13, 26, 29, 48, 67, 77,
    81, 235, 245, 253–57, 259–71
  French, 108, 246
  Indian, 49, 73–96, 181–82, 187
  marital rights, 175–94
  migration, 43–44, 91, 105–8,
    237–38, 294
  moderates, 13, 27
  of 1970s, 37–44
  pilgrimage, 9, 16, 56, 57, 76,
    197–213
  politics and, 240–58, 259–71
  polygamy, 138–55
  population growth, 6, 25–26
  post-9/11 world and, 5–6, 9, 14, 30,
    77, 82, 162, 294
  Satanic Verses controversy, 48–50,
    71, 273, 298

332 INDEX

Muslims (*cont'd*)
sex and, 167–74
stereotypes, 6–7, 44–45, 231
terminology, 230–31
umma, 4, 6, 67, 227
in United States, 45, 106, 294, 295
veil, 156–67
war and, 259–71
women scholars, 5, 8, 28–29, 52, 54,
70, 114, 126–27, 128–37, 138, 184,
198
see also Islam; *specific countries*
Muttaqi, Ali, 168

Nadwat al-Ulama, 5, 13, 17, 75, 91,
92–96, 98, 101–2, 116, 127, 150,
181, 216, 248
Nadwi, Mohammad Akram, 4–21, 28,
32–33, 47–48, 290–300
on Aisha, 141–51
*al-Muhaddithat: The Women
Scholars in Islam,* 114, 129–37
on child marriage, 141–55
children of, 114–27, 156–57, 161,
163, 200, 201, 288
Christianity, Judaism, and, 214–28,
229–39
daily life of, 60–65
on death, 272–89
humor of, 229–30, 238
India and, 73–96, 98
on jihad, 264–71
Madrasah Life, 10
Magnificent Journey lectures,
68–69, 272–73
at Nadwat al-Ulama, 92–96, 98,
101–2, 116, 127, 181, 216, 248
Oxford life, 97–110, 114–27, 294
pilgrimage and, 197–213
politics and, 240–58
on polygamy, 151–55
radicalism of, 245–47
Salafi label, 51–52
on sex, 166–74

on sharia law, 247–50
teaching style of, 68–71, 247–50
on veiling, 156–67
on women and gender roles,
113–27, 128–37, 141–55, 156–74,
175–94, 295–96
on Yusuf sura, 103–8
Nadwi, Muzzammil, 76–79, 83–87
New Mexico, 78
Newsweek, 4, 6, 9, 44, 45, 82, 262, 270
New Testament, 215
New York, 254–55, 259
New York Times, 50, 189
New York Times Magazine, 135
Nigeria, 174
9/11 attacks, 2, 5–6, 9, 14, 30, 78,
254–55, 259, 261, 270, 294
niqab, 52–53, 85, 88–91, 109, 156–67,
200, 206
Noah, 214, 216
Nujood, 151

Obama, Barack, 29
Ottoman Empire, 234, 294
outsiderdom, 79
Oxford Centre for Islamic Studies,
4–5, 13, 48, 64, 97–103, 131, 165
Oxford University, 2, 5, 7, 8, 14, 15,
28, 35, 52, 70, 91, 97–103, 127,
153, 183, 294

pagan Arabs, 215, 226, 233, 236
Pahlavi, Mohammad Reza Shah,
39–42, 57, 162, 243, 252, 253
Pakistan, 9, 77, 79, 81, 107, 131, 193,
205, 237, 246, 250, 259–62, 265,
277, 278, 283–84
creation of, 259
Palestine, 44, 92, 160, 242, 243
-Israel conflict, 228, 238–39
2000 intifada, 242
Persian, 76, 86, 131
Peshawar, 38
Philadelphia, 44

ABOUT THE AUTHOR

CARLA POWER writes for *Time* and was a foreign correspondent for *Newsweek*. Her writing has appeared in *Vogue, Glamour, O, The Oprah Magazine, The New York Times Magazine,* and *Foreign Policy*. Her work has been recognized with an Overseas Press Club award, a Women in Media Award, and the National Women's Political Caucus's EMMA award. She holds a graduate degree in Middle Eastern Studies from Oxford as well as degrees from Yale and Columbia. She lives in England with her family.